The Two-Wheeled COWBOY

A Man, His Bike, and a Land as Big as the Sky

Yahoo!

N. Lebo

Nelson Lebo III

In Memory of Scott Pond

*All in all, my years on the trail were the happiest I ever
lived. There were many hardships and dangers, of course,
that called on all a man had of endurance and bravery; but
when all went well there was no other life so pleasant.
Most of the time we were solitary adventurers in a great
land as fresh and new as a spring morning, and we were
free and full of the zest of darers.*
—Charles Goodnight

Text copyright 2000 by Nelson Lebo

Published by Nelson Lebo and Recycled Paper Printing, Boston, MA

First printing 2000
Printed by Recycled Paper Printing
Boston, MA 02210

Lebo, Nelson
    The Two-Wheeled Cowboy: A Man, His Bike, and a Land as
    Big as the Sky

ISBN: 0-615-11704-X

In writing, fidelity to fact leads eventually to the poetry of truth.
—Edward Abbey

I do my best writing in the morning when I'm jacked up on three or four cups of coffee and the creativity is flowing. The words may not always be right, but the ideas flow into sentences, leading me someplace I don't know where. I just leap in and ride it as long as I can. More often than not, it's a stomach not satisfied by caffeine and sugar that derails the process around noontime. At that point I may leave my journal or computer, but I don't stop writing. Mornings are just the time I get it down in black and white. In fact I'm usually writing all day long, and sometimes in my dreams. I write while I'm eating. I write while I'm reading. I write while I'm riding. If I had my way, that's all I'd do—eat, read, ride and write.

To be honest, I don't know that much about writing. As a kid, the only thing I hated more than writing was reading. I slacked my way through every English course I ever took. I don't know the proper use of colons and semi-colons, and I am notorious for dangling my modifiers. I don't write for the money—this book will never be a commercial success. In the words of Ed Abbey, "I write to make a difference...Distrusting all answers, to raise more questions. To give pleasure and promote esthetic bliss. To honor life and praise the divine beauty of the world. For the joy and exultation of writing itself. To tell my story."

This is my story. It's not just about a four week bike trip "out West," it's about thirty years of observation, conversation and speculation. It's about looking beyond the surface, about questioning beliefs, about finding balance. I've been writing this book for six years and my entire life. It's not finished yet. It never will be. But I think the time has come to share it with others. You may find a typo or two, and I can guarantee—despite the best efforts of my editors—that there are still dangling modifiers lurking in the depths. If they're anything like the ones we've rooted out so far, you're sure to get an added chuckle. Enjoy.

Nelson Lebo

Andover, NH
June, 2000

The Route

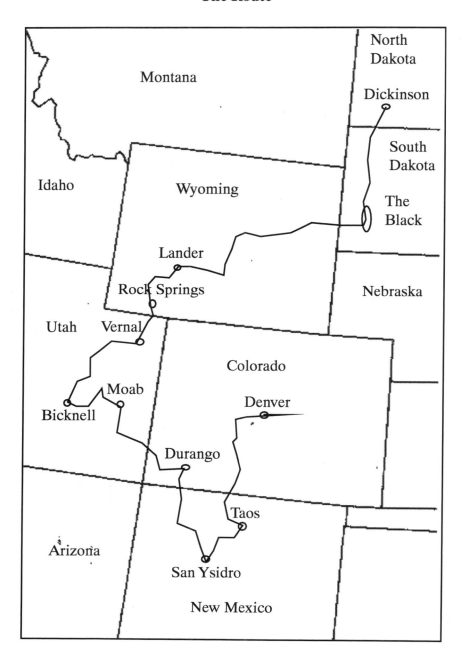

Contents

Part One
The Greenhorn
1

Part Two
Rustlers
38

Part Three
Cowboys
133

Part Four
Indians
201

Part Five
Peacemakers
238

Epilogue
The Upshot
272

Acknowledgments

No matter how solitary the writer or writing process, it cannot be done in a vacuum. I'd like to thank those people who have helped and encouraged along the way. These include the readers: Shauna, Peg, Jan, Judy, Dalene and Za; the writing group: Laurie, Sarah and Tom;the librarians: Judy, Marie and Debra; and whomever I've forgotten. I'd also like to thank my family and closest friends, as well as those kind people I've met on my travels. One final bit of gratitude goes to those who have made the Scott Pond Prize available to adventurers like me. When my energy in this project was low, the Prize allowed for me to return to the West on my bicycle to reconnect with the land and reinvigorate the writing process.

Part 1
The Greenhorn

Chapter 1

In this country, you cannot raise your eyes without looking a hundred miles.
–Wallace Stegner

Between that earth and that sky, I felt erased, blotted out.
–Willa Cather

Five miles south of Dickinson, North Dakota, my eyes were drawn from the pitted shoulder of Route 22 by the high-pitched call of a hawk in flight. The bird sailed effortlessly on an airy ocean of blue—wide, white wings with black shoulder bands. The sun shone through red tail feathers. Golden prairie spread out below. Where the sky had always been the roof of my world, the earth became a floor to the sky.

Each pedal stroke carried me further into a landscape of endless horizons where a new sense of space stretched my perceptions. For the first time I felt the curvature of the Earth, its graceful arc. It's said that prairie doesn't give up anything easily but horizon and sky. Covering more than a million square miles, the Great North American Prairie stretches from central Canada to the Mexican border, and from Indiana to the Rocky Mountains. Deep, porous loam, thick sod, and grass—acres and acres...and acres of grass. The continent's largest continuous ecosystem, the Great Plains, America's heartland.

The smooth feel of a leather saddle suited my backside much better than the molded plastic seats of the bus terminal. Waves of grass under a brilliant blue sky replaced smoke-stained walls and plastic flowers. The smell of unshowered passengers faded into a fresh prairie wind. I rode slowly, easing my legs out of four days of Greyhound paralysis. Each pedal stroke put the sounds of video games and departure announcements further behind and carried me into a landscape of destiny.

I felt a freedom like my first freedom—the freedom only a bicycle could provide a kid in suburban America. The training wheels were off for the first time and dad was running behind me holding the seat. It was a brilliant summer day, maybe even the Fourth of July. I pedaled like mad, making a wavy line for the end of the block when I suddenly realized dad wasn't holding onto the seat anymore. I was free, flying on

1

two wheels. I could go anywhere...like the big kids. No longer would I be left behind while they rode off to the candy store a whole mile away.

Twenty years later the feeling was the same. It held all the magic and mystery one finds at the beginning of a great adventure. My seat was an inch too low, a clicking sound sprang from the rear derailleur, and a layer of stiff whiskers rubbed against my chin strap. But none of that mattered. I was free.

The open air engulfed me, embraced me, and caressed me all at once. Flowing across my bare arms and legs, filling my lungs, fueling my desire. The staleness of the depot shrank in memory, diluted in a vaporous sea. Wind whistled through barbed wire fences and across endless miles of undulating prairie. Horizon grew in abundance in a land as big as the sky.

For the Kiowa people who once migrated throughout the Great Plains, stature was judged by the distance one could see. By those standards, I was suddenly a man of great distinction. But nothing could be further from my mind. This trip was not about fame or fortune. No sponsors. No fund raising. No destination. Free to roam and explore as the spirit moved me, I'd be a tumbleweed blowing through the heart of the West.

Grand and gritty like the land itself, the legends of the American West promote the same candor. A simple code: strength, independence, honesty. A young man could find his fortune with nothing more than sheer guts, the family Bible, and a Winchester rifle. The basic truths of frontier justice captured the country's imagination. America came of age on the cattle drive.

Davey Crockett, Daniel Boone, Annie Oakley and Buffalo Bill Cody— our greatest heroes proved their mettle beyond the ninety-eighth meridian. On the outer fringe of civilization, anything is possible, or at least believable.

But lately I'd been hearing otherwise. Controversies over land and water rights, government subsidies and something called the "Wise Use Movement" became feature articles of *Sierra, Audubon,* and *Outside* magazines. I wanted to see for myself.

Chapter 2

Every sunset I witness inspires me with the desire to go to a West as distant and as fair as that into which the sun goes down.
–Henry David Thoreau

Prairies let us out...They aid to grow a roomy life.
–William Quayle

Finally on the road, the test of my preparations could begin. "Travel light," advise cycle touring books. "Set out all of the gear you plan to take...and then discard half." A century earlier, the advice was pretty much the same. "Dump excess baggage" was a popular saying among pioneers, especially those without draft animals who walked from Missouri to Utah pushing handcarts. In the *Hand-Book to Kansas Territory*, James Redpath and Richard Hinton advise: "Let your trunk...be of moderate size and of the strongest make. Test it by throwing it from the top of a three-storied house; if you pick it up uninjured, it will doo...Not otherwise." I had packed with due care.

Stowed in two rear panniers were all my clothes for the next month: two pairs of shorts, two t-shirts, polypropylene tops and bottoms, an extra pair of socks, rain gear, gloves, hat, fleece jacket. A pair of bungee cords held my sleeping bag, Crazy Creek folding chair (also to be used as a sleeping pad), and a small plastic tarp in place atop the rear rack. Serving double duty as an aerobar, a U-shaped Kryptonite lock was lashed secularly between my shift levers. A pair of Nike running shoes dangled from it by their strings.

Clinging to the underside of the seat, my repair kit consisted of a set of metric Allen keys, a small adjustable wrench, three tire irons and a spare inner tube. A small hand pump was suspended beneath the top tube of the bike's frame, while a pair of water bottles set securely in their aluminum cages.

A set of maps and a small journal fit neatly in the side pocket of one pannier, while my shaving kit filled that of the other. I wore a pair of Diadora cycling shoes, padded shorts, a short-sleeved acrylic jersey, and a Gyro "Hammerhead" helmet. I caught my first glimpse of the Dakota plains through a pair of Vuarnet sunglasses.

With child's eyes, I looked out over the mysterious landscape. Everything was fresh and new—sights, smells, sounds, and feelings. I had returned to a sense of wonder.

Rising in the southeast, Camel and Black Buttes catch the attention of a traveler locked in horizontality. The twin monoliths growing at the edge of the world offer relief to the linear severity of the landscape—a

3

strange and wonderful sight for one used to the tree-covered hillsides of New England. Except for glacially scoured summits and a handful of avalanche scars, the geology of Maine, Vermont and New Hampshire remains hidden under a vast blanket of green. Down the Atlantic seaboard and inland to the Mississippi River, forests offer residents a familiar security. But to those accustomed to eastern woodlands, the prairie comes as a shock to the system. Square pegs are suddenly forced into round holes. Perceptions are challenged.

The sons and daughters of our founding fathers stalled for nearly half a century at the western edge of the forests because they didn't trust the grasslands. "The first experience of the plains..." wrote Richard Irving Dodge over a century ago, "is apt to be sickening. This once overcome, the nerves stiffen, the senses expand, and man begins to realize the magnificence of being."

Raw boned and sinuous, the grace of a butte lay in its starkness. Solid, straight-forward, honest—it has nothing to hide.

"Welcome to New England," the sign said, but the dusty little town looked no more Yankee than suburban Connecticut. Without a leafy town square or even a hint of white clapboard, the origin of its name remained a mystery as I pedaled through without stopping to ask.

Crossing the Cannonball River, I turned west onto Route 21 and into a setting sun. For sixteen miles I struggled against the glare. Ultraviolet rays bombarded me from 93 million miles away, but my eyes remained safe behind a coating of "full-spectrum UV protection."

When I reached Scenic Route 85 and turned south, I had the expectation that it would be...well, scenic. I was wrong, but only by New England standards. As I passed through Amidon and entered the Little Missouri National Grassland, it occurred to me that I needed to develop a new definition of scenic. To one accustomed to the lush hillsides of the East, the high plains seem stricken, monotonous. The ability to appreciate their beauty does not come easily. It requires patience, stamina, endurance. In the buttes, grasses, and even the brief spring flowers, there is an unfamiliar austerity.

The prairie is a gift in a plain brown wrapper. It is a bag lunch, cold cereal, burger and fries. Nothing about it shouts "Look at me!" People don't climb the prairie, they don't paddle it, and contrary to a bumper sticker popular in Nebraska, they don't surf it either. To most who encounter it, the prairie is merely something to cross. Early settlers could walk for twelve hours and feel they had taken only a few steps.

People may prefer to live in the mountains or near the coast, but the human species owes its existence to grasslands. Several million years ago on the East African Savannah, we stood up because of tall grasses. We are bipedal because of the African prairie.

Maybe because I was no longer riding into the sun, or maybe because I was within an *officially designated* grassland, but the landscape suddenly demanded more attention. It's said that desert air contains more dust than air in humid regions. Higher concentrations of particles mean more light is refracted, and thus, more colors visible. Dust and light. Light and dust. One need only see a western sunset to believe.

Inch by inch, the luminous orb lay down its sweet head along the distant horizon. Glowing in the last rays of a setting sun, White Butte faded into deeper shades of evening. Purple shadows crept across the monolith leaving coyotes to mourn the passing of another day. At 3,506 feet, White Butte is the highest point in North Dakota. On that evening I would argue, it was also the most stunning.

"Every sunset that I witness," wrote Henry David Thoreau, "inspires me with the desire to go to a West as distant and as fair as that into which the sun goes down. Eastward I go only by force; but westward I go free."

Evoking in me that same spirit of Manifest Destiny, I was drawn from a comfortable yet mundane life teaching high school science in central New Hampshire to a land where anything was possible. Forty acres and a bicycle! Westward the course of a Nelson!

Lengthening shadows made the landscape look even larger and more ominous. Small hills grew into mountains and narrow washes became deep valleys. A blanket of night had unfurled over the Little Missouri National Grassland by the time I reached Butte View State Campground. A sign hung ominously in the window of the entry booth: FULL.

While peeking through a dusty pane of glass, I drew the attention of a gray-haired couple walking a humorously small dog. It offered a half-hearted bark and then set about sniffing my ankles. I felt its small tongue lapping salt off my Achilles as the pair offered directions to the campground hosts.

"Their trailer is just up the road."

"It's the green one off to the right."

I leaned my bike against the aluminum siding and rapped on the hollow wooden door. The hinges creaked and a woman appeared. She wrung her hands on a gingham apron. Her tired eyes sized me up through a pair of drug store bifocals. Blue light from a black and white television streamed over her shoulders and through her thin, gray hair. "Can I help you?"

I could see a man sitting in front of the TV behind her. "Just looking for a place to camp."

"We're full," he shouted over the ticking sounds of Wheel of Fortune.

The woman frowned. "There's another campground over in Marmarth. It's only twenty-five miles."

"Well, I'm on my bicycle, and..."

"Why didn't you say so to begin with? We've got a big field right behind the trailer here. You go right ahead and find a comfortable spot. Feel free to clean up at the shower house too."

A series of low, grumbling sounds came from behind her.

"Don't mind him. He's just..."

"Watch it, Carol!" called the man from his Lazy Boy.

There was an awkward silence.

"Thank you," I said, turning toward my bike.

"You're welcome," she said as her smile disappeared behind the creaking door.

Chapter 3

It is not the most beautiful lands, nor those where life is most agreeable,
that seize the heart more, but those where the terrain is the plainest,
most humble, the nearest to man, and speaks to him in a language both
intimate and familiar.
—Romain Rolland

Soapy fingernails dug into my scalp. Rich lather oozed over my clenched eyelids. Warm water soothed the back of my neck. Salt, dirt and tension swirled clockwise down the drain beneath my feet. I felt renewed, fully alive.

The slender crescent of a new moon offered just enough light to follow the path back to the field. A chorus of cicadas droned in the distance. A cool breeze tickled my damp skin. A million stars sparkled and winked above. I winked back.

Slipping into my nylon sleeping bag, I gazed up at the wide, western sky. A host of summer constellations vied for my attention, but my eyes were drawn to Arcturus, the brightest star of the kite-shaped Bootes, the herdsman.

It was during the 1530's that the Spanish conquistador Francisco Vazquez de Coronado first brought cattle to the New World. The original Andalusian beasts were later crossbred with Hereford and Durham cattle from Europe to produce a uniquely American breed—the longhorn. Well-suited to the harsh western environment, it was proven that this hearty subspecies could over-winter on the plains with little care. This being the case, it was then just a matter of time before agriculture in the region was completely transformed. By the 1890's, there were over 26 million cattle on the western range.

Out of this abundance grew the American cowboy—a lone rider bent to the wind against fields of blue and green. And out of his experience came a simple code, the code of the West. Honesty, strength, independence—the frontier virtues embodied by Owen Wister's hero in *The Virginian*, the first of many cowboy novels to entrance a nation searching for identity. Strong, self-confident, solitary, alone—the image of the cowboy has shaped our national mythology and captured the imagination of the world. The mythology of America is rooted in the western experience.

It had been two nights earlier that the very embodiment of that myth began to tear it down.

After forty-eight hours on a Greyhound, Southern Comfort was the only comfort I could find. Raising the bottle to my lips, I drank

7

generously. The new moon offered little competition to a million stars twinkling above the dimly lit avenue.

A raspy voice split the stillness of the North Dakota night. "Drownin' your sorrows only irrigates 'em."

It came from the shadows of a narrow alley beside the station. My eyes struggled against the gloom, making out only the silhouette of a man in a long coat and wide-brimmed hat. As he stepped into the street lights, his features became clear. He was old, very old, with a long, white beard and a deeply etched brow. He was built of sun-scorched leather and wind-blown sand. His clothes were as wrinkled and faded as his face, and the sound of his boots echoed through the empty street. He stepped out of *High Noon*, and into midnight. He hobbled, bow legged, up the steps and stood before me. "You ain't from around here."

"No...I'm not."

"Back East I reckon."

"Is it that obvious?"

He grinned and shook his head. "What're you doing here?"

"Waiting for my bike."

He stared blankly.

"They said it would be on the next bus."

His stare remained.

"You see, I was gonna spend the summer riding through the West. I put together a special bicycle for the trip, but it seems that Greyhound has gone ahead and lost it."

"Lost it?"

"Yes. Lost it." The words cut deeply as my thoughts drifted back to the process of assembling the right set of wheels. Designed specifically for this trip, the bike represented not only an investment of money but also of time. Evenings and weekends had been dedicated to building it piece by piece. The process had been slow and expensive, but with every hour and every dollar, my commitment was deepened. As the bike took shape, the trip grew from a random idea hatched on a cold January night into reality. It became a symbol of the future—a promise, a passion, a need.

"The last time I saw it was when I transferred in Chicago. When I got off here in Dickinson, the bike was no longer on the bus."

He shook his head slowly. "Why Dickinson?"

"No reason."

Another blank stare.

"It didn't have to be Dickinson. It could just as well have been...Quartzite, Arizona."

His stare remained.

"Let me start from the beginning."

He nodded his approval.

"Like most kids, I grew up with this image of the 'Wild West.' The Lone Ranger was on TV and Louis L'Amour was on the bookshelf. My brother and I knew every line from 'Butch Cassidy and the Sundance Kid.' John Wayne, Clint Eastwood, Redford and Newman—they were our heroes. We'd stay up and watch the late night movies on channel fifty."

He grinned and shook his head.

"Of course I've learned that Hollywood hasn't always been exactly accurate in its portrayal of the West. 'Dances with Wolves' was an eye-opener. It challenged those old 'spaghetti westerns.' About the same time, I started reading about land use issues and conflict over the 400 million acres of public land. National Forests I'd heard of, but what the hell was BLM?

"I grew anxious. Questions. Questions. Questions about the West. Questions about myself. Who am I? Teacher? Twenty-something? Gen X poster boy? Saturday morning cartoons and Indiana Jones movies were fine when I was a kid, but my need for adventure has grown. Sure, I've got the Travel Channel, but how many train trips through India can you watch? The Internet did nothing for me. Cyberspace is not the kind of space I need."

"You lost me, kid."

"Sorry, I got a little carried away. What I'm trying to say is that I'm looking for something more than a trip—an exploration, not just of a place, but of myself.

I spent sixteen years of my life staring at a blackboard and another six standing at one. I need to get away from lesson plans, syllabi, and fifty-minute blocks of time. I need to just take things as they come.

"So Dickinson is my jumping-off place. It has the special distinction of being the farthest West I could travel from Concord, New Hampshire, on a fifteen day advance purchase one-way bus ticket for under $200."

The old man chuckled softly and shook his head.

"What?"

"So you're gonna see the West?"

"That's right."

"Well, you better watch yourself. Things are different this side of the Missouri River."

"What do you mean?"

"There's a way of life that's developed here based on what folks learned on the range. It's a way of looking at the land, treating people and taking care of business. This is a hard land, unforgiving. Philosophers call it a 'school of humility,' farmers call it 'the next year country.' Maybe next year the rains will come at the right time. Maybe next year a hail storm won't ruin the crops a week before harvest. Maybe next year I'll get a fair price.

"Within twenty years of settling, eighty percent of the original homesteaders abandoned their land, their homes and their dreams. But those who made it work, those who endured the hardships developed a respect for the land and a cautious outlook on life that is unique to this region. It's pure American—not imported from anywheres. Just growed up out of experience."

"How does it differ from any other?"

"Let's take your problem for example. How'd you react?"

"Well, I was pretty mad. I've been planning this trip for months and to get here without the bike..."

"So you went and got yourself a bottle?"

"It's just to help me relax. I'm a little stressed out right now."

"'Stressed out?' What the hell's that supposed to mean?"

" Oh," I said sarcastically, "it must be an *Eastern* term. It means I'm worried about getting my bike back."

He was silent.

"So tell me, how would you handle this situation? How would a cowboy handle it?"

"First of all, a cowboy wouldn't never lose his horse. And if he did, he sure wouldn't be sitting on the steps of a Greyhound station drinking whiskey."

"Why not? I thought cowboys were big drinkers."

"Sometimes they are, but a real cowboy knows that drinking won't fix him permanent."

"Of course not, but you don't need to be a cowboy to know that."

"No, but something about living out here affects the way folks think. It's something that came along during a hundred years of riding, roping, living and loving in big country. But now-a-days it's a changing world: interstate freeways and fast food restaurants. Nobody seems to care much about the past. Most are moving too fast to take the time to learn the real lessons of the land."

"Not me, I'm taking it slow this summer. Maybe even slower without my bike."

"It'll get here."

"How do you know?"

"Even the longest winter is followed by spring."

"More cowboy philosophy?"

"That's right," he smiled. "Now pass me that bottle of tangleleg."

"What about that 'drowning your sorrows' business?"

"I ain't the one that's sorry."

I handed him the bottle.

"And besides, when a man's too old to set a good example, he hands out bad advice."

We spent the next hour passing the bottle back and forth, talking about the West he remembered, a West considerably less glamorous than Louis L'Amour had led me to believe. He described a place where loneliness and hardship were far more common than heroism and high adventure.

"Life on the frontier was a might bit duller than most folks want to remember. More people died of smallpox and cholera than a gut full of lead. But the ones to survive the hardships, those were the real Westerners. You want to talk about self-reliance, the motto of the North Dakota Workers Union is 'Every man for himself.'"

He drained me of my wild notions as thoroughly as he did the whiskey. The bottle was soon as dry as his sense of humor.

"The land was once so plastered with mortgages that farmers had to bore holes through 'em before they could do any plantin'. But I s'pose they did serve a useful purpose at that. Sometimes the winds were so strong that puttin' a mortgage on a farm was the only thing that kept it from blowin' away.

"Oh, the weather," he lamented. "Only in the Bible can you find lands that endure such floods, droughts, storms and plagues. You might say North Dakota is a kind of scriptural kingdom. It's hard to take at times, but it tends to keep the riffraff out."

Chapter 4

When you get the feeling that the whole world can see you but no one is watching, you have come to the grasslands of North America.
–Dan O'Brien

My horse fights with me and fasts with me, because if he is to carry me in battle he must know my heart, and I must know his or we shall never become brothers.
–Plenty-Coups, Crow, 1880

A chorus of bird song told me that I was far from the Dickinson bus station long before the morning light allowed my eyes the same discovery. I lay silently for half an hour listening to the calls of killdeers, buntings and meadow larks. With the slightest hint of predawn, I was out of my bag and walking through damp grass to the shower house. Cool morning air hung above silent tents and sleeping RVs. Thinking the world was mine, I was startled by a man at the shower house door. His long, white beard stopped me in my tracks. Was it him? Was it the man from Dickinson who had vanished two mornings earlier when I stepped into the bus station to wash up?

"Mornin'," he said, "you're up early."

"And you."

"Always. Life's too short to let the sun catch ya nappin'."

"Yeah, I guess you're right," I said mostly to his back as he shot past me through the steel framed doorway and down the gravel path. I watched him disappear around a bend. No, it couldn't be.

After a quick wash, brush and gargle, I walked back to my gear and began to pack. A matted bed of grass gave testimony to my first good night's sleep in three days. As I stuffed my sleeping bag, a glowing sliver of sunlight appeared on the horizon, awakening the colors of dawn. Pausing, I watched as a Robert Frost poem unfolded before my eyes. "Nature's first green is gold, her hardest hue to hold..."

A ring-necked pheasant scurried through the golden grass as a mourning dove cooed softly from a low branch. In the tender moments between night and day, nature held its hardest hue. Eden unfolded before me. The flame hues of a prairie dawn made it easy to see why North Dakota is called, "The Peace Garden State." Elysian fields ran to every horizon. Beauty took its purest form, but soon slipped away as subtly as it had come. As Frost concludes, "nothing gold can stay."

I returned to the work at hand, nibbling on an assortment of dried fruit while I finished packing. Five pounds of dehydrated apples, pears and bananas would serve as ballast as well as sustenance. Within minutes, my gear was loaded and I was lightly spinning south on Route

85. Here and there, massive snow fences stood guard along the highway, their wooden beams bleached gray by summer sun. Viewed on a July morning, it was impossible to imagine the ten foot drifts they face each winter. They appeared surrealistically out of place, but locals know better. Plains weather breeds caution.

At the heart of a continent, temperatures have been known to drop twenty degrees in an hour, hail stones reach the size of baseballs, and children grow up thinking that snow is *supposed* to fall sideways. Stories abound of sod houses so buried with drifted snow that inhabitants were forced to choose between tunneling out through the roof or waiting for a thaw.

The western Dakotas have been identified as the windiest place in the lower forty-eight states. This American mistral literally drove pioneers crazy with its relentlessness. "The Great Dismal" they called the plains. "If it wasn't for bad weather," hardened Dakotans are apt to claim, "we wouldn't have no weather at all."

On a sun-dappled July morning, I found myself without complaint. The traffic was light, the road surface smooth, and a slight tail wind nudged me along. Again, it seemed the morning belonged to me, but again I was wrong. Unable to identify the dark figure on the shoulder ahead when I caught the first glimpse, the horse and rider took form as I approached. Drawing nearer, a matching set of ponytails came into focus—one on the stunning black stallion, the other on its equally attractive rider. She wore dirty blue jeans, a clean white t-shirt, and faded leather boots.

Steering wide left so as not to spook the horse, I came along side halfway down a short hill. Applying pressure to my brake levers, I slowed to their speed. The woman drew the reins in response.

"Morning," I said. "Didn't want to spook your friend."

"That's all right. He's a good boy."

"Gorgeous. How old is he?"

"Three years next month. I've raised him from a colt."

"What's his name?"

"Night. How about yours?"

"Nelson."

"I meant your bike."

"My bike?"

Reaching the bottom of the hill, I released my grip and applied pressure to the pedals. She gave Night a slight nudge with her stirruped boots.

"Sure. Every good ride needs a good name."

"I hadn't really thought about it."

As the grade increased, I rose out of my saddle to keep pace with the trotting horse. I could feel the weight of my panniers swaying back and forth. Her saddle bags bounced to the same rhythm. Conversation lagged for the rest of the climb as I contemplated her statement. Saddle, bags, stirrups, reins—the similarities were obvious, but did the relationship run deeper?

The bike had already proven its adventurous nature by leaving me to wait for two days in the Dickinson bus station while it traveled ahead to Salt Lake City, San Francisco and back via Denver. What could capture that spirit and serve as a reminder of the sense of spontaneity this trip was meant to be about? It would need to be a name with the get-up-and-go quality of a woman riding her horse along a lonely stretch of North Dakota highway at 6:30 in the morning. I turned to my companion. "What's yours?"

Betsy carried me the first sixteen miles to the South Dakota state line in under an hour. Riding a tail wind across the lightly rolling landscape, I became a square rigger on a sea of grass.

Falling near the heart of the Great North American Prairie, the grasses of the Dakotas were once a rich mixture of taller species from the wetter eastern meadows (bluestem, Indian grass and switch grass) and shorter ones from the dryer western fringe (western wheat grass, blue gramma and buffalo grass). Early journals describe cordgrass so tall it could hide a horse. Sorghum, gayfeather, pasqueflower, prairie smoke and big bluestem—a celebration of wildflowers once spread far and wide across the rolling terrain—as many as 150 species in a single square mile.

Where were they now? Where had they gone? The prairie around me had been transformed into a relative monoculture dominated by bromegrass—a weedy invader from Europe.

Only the tree-covered slopes of the Cave Hills offered any indication that the topography of South Dakota would be any different from it's northern neighbor. Hardly enough, it seemed, to admit what was originally called the "Dakota Territory" into the union as two states instead of one. The real difference, I should have guessed, was purely political.

In 1889, President Grover Cleveland signed the Omnibus Bill providing for the admission of Washington, Montana, and two Dakota states into the Union. When Democrats had come into power five years earlier, they saw no advantage in admitting any more states because the territories of the Northwest were mainly Republican. But with the election of Benjamin Harrison in November of 1888, Democrats faced an incoming Republican administration. They scrambled to put together the first edition of the Omnibus Bill which included Democratic New Mexico along with Washington and Montana but only one Dakota. The Democratic House was confident it could beat the deadline, but the plans were foiled by a Republican Senate which revised the bill to exclude

New Mexico, and divide the Dakota Territory into northern and southern sections.

Crossing into the southern section, I was greeted by the gentle geologic rhythm of the Cave Hills. For the first time that morning, I shifted into an easier sprocket to meet the grade.

The rolling terrain gave me a chance to test the range of Betsy's gears. The rear derailleur worked fine. From the thirteen-toothed sprocket to the twenty-six, it shifted smoothly. A test of the front derailleur was not as successful. Negotiating between the forty-eight and thirty-six-toothed chainrings went smoothly, but no matter how I forced my thumb against the shift lever, the chain would not jump into the twenty-six. With no steep climbs in sight, it would not be called into service any time soon. I put the repair off until later.

While my fresh legs met the challenge unequivocally, it was my stomach that threw in the towel. Unsatisfied with a handful of dried fruit, it longed for a tall stack of buttermilk pancakes smothered in maple syrup.

Plum brush and willow thickets grew along the banks of the Bull River just south of Ludlow. A pair of mule deer drank from the coffee-colored water while fork-tailed swallows patrolled its surface for insects. A green highway sign said, "Buffalo - 16," but I saw not a single shaggy-haired beast.

It wasn't until I reached the outskirts of town an hour later that I understood. "Welcome to Buffalo." Fifty miles down.

From a distance, and without my glasses, I thought the next sign said "Prayer Cafe." But as I approached the diner at the edge of town, the last letters came into focus—Prairie. Regardless of name, my digestive tract was prepared for a religious experience.

Little more than a greasy spoon with a western motif, the Prairie Cafe offered sanctuary to those in need. I found a seat among other worshipers at the linoleum lunch counter and prepared for the Eucharist.

The drowning crackle of a deep fryer emerged from the kitchen. The smell of coffee and grease hung heavy in the air. Take away the swinging doors, the horse print menu, the boot-shaped salt and pepper shakers, and you'd have my own Blackwater Diner back home. All the Prairie lacked was real maple syrup. (How *do* you tap a corn stalk, anyway?) Shunning the artificially flavored substitute set before me, I ate the pancakes undamped—as dry as communion wafers.

Coffee filled my cup of salvation, and I gave thanks to Saint Juan (Valdez). I drank generously and stretched my breakfast through numerous refills, an extra donut and a conversation with a waitress named Debra. She abandoned her copy of *A Sand County Almanac* at the end of the counter and joined me for a lesson in plains ecology. Debra was all I dreamed of in a waitress; witty, intelligent, and she even called me "Honey." I wouldn't know until later that she held a degree in resource management from the University of South Dakota.

"Three things," she told me, "shaped the Great Plains: weather, fire and bison."

"Bison?"

"*Bison bison* to be specific. 'Buffalo' is just the common name. There's no direct relation to the African or Asian buffalo.

"Another misnomer."

"You could say that. Can you imagine 75 million darkening the hills from horizon to horizon? That's how the prairie looked 150 years ago—the greatest concentration of large mammals the modern world has known. Hundreds of thousands could be seen at a time. No other animal represents the power and beauty of the Great Plains so well."

Her image was awe-inspiring, but impossible to truly appreciate. "How could they possibly kill that many?"

"Wholesale destruction. During the late 1800's they were killed en masse for hides, meat and sometimes just their tongues. "

"Tongues?"

"That's right. At twenty-five cents each, the tongues were cut out, pickled in brine and sent to eastern markets. The rest was left to rot."

"What a waste. Why would they do it?"

"For profit, for sport, but also as part of a greater plan."

"Greater plan?"

"General William Tecumseh Sherman saw the bison's extinction as part of a greater plan. Get rid of the bison and you get rid of the Plains tribes. The Pawnee, for instance, relied heavily on the bison for their survival. They believed that it had been given to them by the Great Creator. The animal was as critical to their spirituality as it was to their day to day lives. But as numbers dwindled, there weren't even enough to include in their most sacred of ceremonies. Defeated and demoralized, they were forced to use cattle instead."

"Talk about adding insult to injury."

"It was. The plains tribes relied so heavily on the bison that Sherman's genocidal plans nearly worked. Over three centuries of contact with the whites, native populations dropped from over 20 million to under half a million."

"I imagine the buffalo...I mean bison population was even lower than that."

"That's right. By 1883 they had been almost entirely exterminated. It was a Dakota rancher named Dupris—with help from the Sioux—who fought to save them from extinction. From five captured calves, he began a rebound that was continued by others after his death. Nearly all of today's domesticated herds trace their roots to that handful of animals."

"So at one point the population was down to five?"

"Not exactly. Because of their remote location in Yellowstone National Park, a herd of wild bison managed to escape the slaughter. They were so geographically isolated that they had actually evolved into an entirely different breed—one more suitably adapted to the higher elevations at which they lived. Along with those of Dupris, these became important breeding stock for the comeback.

"Ironically, even into the 1990's members of the Yellowstone herd were shot by ranchers if they happened to wander outside the park and onto Forest Service lands leased for grazing. They must not have seen the boundary signs. When it comes to munching grass on one type of public land or another, bison don't discriminate."

"What are the numbers like today?"

"Nationwide, there are over 200,000 bison being managed either by government agencies or private ranchers. About 10,000 are slaughtered each year to satisfy a growing demand for the specialty meat. It sells in supermarkets and restaurants for twice the price of beef.

"Although South Dakota currently has one of the largest populations in the country, they will never blanket the northern plains as they once did. Hybrid cattle and high-tech combines have taken their place. The great herds are gone forever. Only their spirits remain."

Chapter 5

What is life? It is the flash of a firefly in the night. It is the breath of a buffalo in the winter time. It is the little shadow which runs across the grass and loses itself in the Sunset.
—Crowfoot, 1890

We can try to kill all that is native, string it up by its hind legs for all to see, but spirit howls and wildness endures.
—Terry Tempest Williams

Twenty-two miles without a curve would take some getting used to. As flat as the prairie dogs along the roadside, Route 85 offered no opportunity to leave the saddle. Firmly rooted to my thin, leather perch, I was glad to have spent the extra time picking it out.

Although not having had personal experience with penile numbness—a condition reported to contribute to impotence among men—the horror stories that occur regularly in Bicycling Magazine were enough to convince me to take adequate precautions. Foregoing the meager selection at my local bike shop, I had driven over an hour to find the perfect seat. The trip would surely be worth hours of comfort on the bike, not to mention the possibility (no matter how unlikely) of a romantic interlude along the way. Like choosing the perfect melon, I had squeezed, fondled and thumped—finally deciding on a saddle with the right combination of shape and cushioning to provide me with many hours of pain-free pedaling. Seventy dollars was no too much to pay for the priceless benefits.

While I remained seated, herds of cattle stood motionless in the fields. They observed my passing with little interest from behind miles of barbed wire that now cuts the once unbroken prairie into thousands upon thousands of rectangular units of private land. I tried feebly to imagine the landscape so vast and unbroken that Zebulon Pike had felt compelled to compare it to an ocean.

Throughout the 1800's, thousands of settlers, whose European parents or grandparents had immigrated across the wide Atlantic, faced a different type of sea in the middle of the continent, a sea of grass. In "prairie schooners," they sailed west through amber waves of grain while millions of Eskimo curlews—known to the pioneers as "dough birds"—migrated northward. Flocks that could cover fifty acres—that could block out the sun like a dark cloud—passed overhead with the sound of wind through a ship's rigging. In numbers too great to count, curlew populations must have seemed as endless, as vast and indestructible, as the prairie itself.

Within a hundred years the Eskimo curlew was nearly extinct. Like the vast grasslands on which it once thrived, only token examples remain. The life-giving soil had once been so admired it was called "prairyerth," a term no longer used. The Great Plains were once a song of freedom. What have they become?

As I approached the Sand Creek Fork of the Moreau River, I noticed a lifeless form hanging from a fence post across the road. Curious, I crossed the dashed yellow line and braked to a stop on the loose gravel shoulder of the northbound lane. I laid Betsy down and slowly approached.

Mostly brown, with flecks of gray and black, the carcass was the size of my parent's small shepherd. Hanging from the top wire by a twisted cord, the black tip of its tawny tail dangled inches from the ground. Flies crawled in and out the empty eye sockets. The stench of death hung heavy on the air.

"I saw a dog hanging from a fence back on the highway." I told the man behind the counter at the Redig Mercantile.

He shook his head as he rang up my Gatorade. "That'd be a coyote."

"A coyote," I repeated. "Why was it strung up like that?"

"That's what's done around here."

"Why?"

"They're a threat to stock. They take calves, lambs, chickens. The way most folks see it, the only good coyote is a dead coyote. A man won't hesitate to stop his truck on the highway to take a shot at one if it's within distance. Between individuals and the ADC, we manage to keep 'em in check."

"ADC?"

"Animal Damage Control. It's about the only good thing the 'Feds' do for us around here."

"I don't understand."

He explained how, under the authorization of the Animal Damage Control Act of 1931, the Animal and Plant Health Inspection Service (APHIS)—a subsidiary of the United States Department of Agriculture (USDA)—to "control" animals that pose a threat to "regional agriculture." Three-quarters of the program's $36 million budget is used to protect livestock.

In 1990, for example, Uncle Sam funded the extermination of over 800,000 animals in seventeen western states. The official list includes 91,158 coyotes, 9,363 beavers, 8,144 skunks, 7,065 foxes, 5,933 raccoons, 3,463 opossums, 1,083 porcupines, 1,028 bobcats, 265 muskrats, 250 mountain lions, 236 black bears, 25 river otters, and over 500,000 birds. The tally for the year also includes 5,759 "non-target animals."

As the temperature hovered around 100, the concept of siesta finally

19

made sense to one born and raised in a cooler climate. Like the Spanish explorers who knew the value of conserving energy during the hottest part of the day, I would take equal opportunity to enjoy la siesta.

I bought a copy of the Belle Fourche paper and headed out onto the covered porch where rectangular wooden signs dripped from the eaves: GROCERIES... HARDWARE... BEER... SODA... ICE... FIRE WOOD. The Slim Buttes shimmered through waves of heat rising from the highway.

Turning around, my eyes were drawn to the community bulletin board hanging to the right of the door. Layer upon layer, the collage told a story of Redig's most recent history. Only as deep as a few sheets of paper and as far back as weeks or months, it provided a unique sense of the place. Without judgment, the cork board accepts all in a process as dynamic as weather, yet as stable as climate. A free-form work of art, it records the pulse of the town.

Notices. Announcements. Rewards. Larry Johnson has a pickup truck to sell. Max Irwin will rent his cement mixer at a daily rate. The Riley's lost their dog. A garage sale was held at 47 Butte View Road last weekend. Summer Sunday services at Saint Vincent's will be at 9:30 instead of 10:00.

Alcoholics Anonymous will be held on Tuesday nights instead of Mondays. Someone is selling German Shepherd puppies. A kitten needs a home. Project Graduation held a carwash on May 25th.

Still more notices lay below, all but forgotten. Only their curled corners reached out to wave like tiny hands saying, "Remember me?" But the pace of life—even in a small town in rural South Dakota—does not allow an answer.

I took a seat on a plank bench and opened the paper. The upcoming Black Hills Motor Classic dominated the news. Held in nearby Sturgis, the annual rally is attended by over 300,000 motorcycle enthusiasts from across the nation. Some years they increase the state's population by as much as a third. Bikers from all fifty states and Canada come to watch the races, drink beer, and go a little crazy. Familiarity with a similar event in New Hampshire drew me to the conclusion that such events gravitate toward those states without helmet laws.

After reading a plea from the State Highway Patrol about safety, I skimmed through the calendar of events and went on to the classifieds. "Dog for sale," read one add. "Eats anything and is fond of children."

The heat of mid-day kept me in Redig until late afternoon. But as the mercury dipped below ninety, I saddled up Ol' Betsy and headed out. With no doubt why South Dakota is called the "Sunshine State," I donned my Vuarnets and pedaled south, reflecting on the hospitality I'd received since leaving Dickinson. "Dakotah," in the Sioux language, means ally or friend. I understood why.

Twenty miles south of Redig I passed the Geographical Center of the United States. A Ford Explorer had stopped for the photo opportunity. Like a troupe of circus clowns, the occupants piled out, lined up in front of the sign for the shot, and piled back in before driving off.

Passing up the opportunity to stand at the cross-hairs of America, I pushed on as the coolness of evening settled on the prairie. A flock of meadow larks banked and swerved in unison over the waving grass. Dancing on the wind, the aerial ballet spread across the glowing western stage. As a unit they crossed the road before me and disappeared over a low hill to the east. But before I could return my gaze to the route ahead, it was captured by a sudden movement lower to the ground.

The ghostly figure traveled south at a lope, paralleling my direction and matching my progress. The long, slim figure moved effortlessly— its head and tail low to the ground. Every fifty yards or so, it would stop, raise its long, sharp face and cast a furtive eye my way. Mark Twain described this creature as, "a living, breathing allegory of want. He is always hungry. He is always poor, out of luck and friendless. The meanest creatures despise him and even the fleas would desert him for a velocipede. He is so spiritless and cowardly that even while his exposed teeth are pretending a threat, the rest of his face is apologizing for it. And he is homely—so scrawny, and ribby, and coarse-haired and pitiful."

Tawny fur blended neatly into the dry grasses, but a pair of bright eyes reflected the setting sun. They glowed with cautious curiosity. How long had the coyote been watching me?

A mile or two south of the center point of the country, I turned onto a side road and followed it over a small rise. Out of view of Route 85, I laid the bike down and released the bungee cords on the rear rack, pausing to watch a swallowtail butterfly pollinate a prairie forb. It's long, thin legs embraced the violet blossom while its upper wings fluttered lightly to keep the balance. Extending from the lower wings, its namesake appendages hung like a pair of epigloti shimmering in the breeze.

After a short stretch, I slid into my sleeping bag and reached for the dried fruit. Stars appeared one by one as I lay on my back chewing on the familiar mix.

The West, it's been said, is all geology by day and astronomy by night. From the warmth of my bag, I gazed up into the clear night sky. Beside the familiar figure of Bootes hung the six-starred arc of Corona Borealis, the Northern Crown. Next to that was mighty Hercules—a keystone-shaped asterism surrounded by four trailing limbs. But imagining the physique of a legendary Greek hero proved too challenging for my weary mind. I sought a more representative cluster of stars.

It found it to the south in Scorpius. From a curled stinger low on the horizon, through the bright red Antares at the heart of the giant beast, and on to the outstretched claws, the constellation is one of only a few that truly resembles its namesake. As my eyes grew heavy with sleep, I took comfort knowing that the he lay at a safe distance millions of miles away, and not at the foot of my bag.

As a waxing crescent moon appeared over the eastern horizon, the howl of a coyote filled the cool night air. "I'm here!" he called. "Shoot me, trap me, poison me, but I'll still be here. I am a survivor. Call me a thief, call me a tramp, call me a rogue, but I'll still be here, singing to the night."

Chapter 6

Red and yellow, black and white
They're all sacred in His sight.
—Baptist Hymn

The daily routine of a cowboy on a cattle drive began before sunrise. Out of his bedroll, drinking coffee from a tin cup, eating anything from fresh warm biscuits to cold beans. While the cook loaded the chuck wagon, the cowboys would "jingle" (round up) the horses and take their places along the herd. Two point men would lead out, followed by two on the swing, two on the flank, and worst of all, two on the drags. Looking after calves and laggards while sucking up dust, many a buckaroo used his turn on the drags to reexamine his lot in life. "Lookin' at the south end of northbound cattle," a cowboy tune laments, "what am I doin' here?"

With an out of tune guitar and a struggling campfire, a bard in buckskins could lament about how hard, how cold, how lonely a life on the range could be. "Mamas don't let your babies grow up to be cowboys."

Living close to nature, bodily functions become part of the job, and contribute to many of the unique similes and metaphors that abound in cowboy storytelling, poetry and song writing. When it's what his life consists of, can you blame a fellow for writing about a blistered rear end, falling in love with his horse, or eating leftover beans for breakfast?

Even day-old beans would have been a welcome break for me. Although my stomach grumbled in need, it turned at the prospect of more dried fruit. As reluctantly as a dog taking heartworm pills, I forced down a handful of banana chips while packing.

Like saddle bags and a bed roll, I lashed the panniers and sleeping bag to Betsy's rear rack. Better than a canteen or water skin, my plastic bottles slid cleanly into their cages. Cycling shoes and shorts served as boots and chaps, but my helmet was an admittedly poor substitute for a wide-brimmed hat. Remington's engravings never looked like this. What kind of a buckaroo shaves his legs anyway?

Securing the last few items to my trusty steed, I got a message from my equally faithful stomach. It would not be satisfied with banana chips no matter how many I sent its way. According to the map, Belle Fourche and breakfast lay twenty-eight miles to the south. Thus, I left the Geographical Center of the United States stomach first.

Somewhere between Indian and Owl Creeks, I first noticed the Black Hills in the distance. Rising from the tall-grass prairie to elevations of 7,000 feet, these smaller cousins of the Rocky Mountains formed an island of green that grew larger with every passing mile. Rocky needles towered above an emerald blanket of ponderosa pine.

So fixed was my gaze upon the site, I didn't notice the Mud Buttes until I was beside them. Looming above the road, they offered a spectacle of their own. Lit by the low eastern sun, the buttes were without shadow, their beige faces appeared as flawless as giant drive-in movie screens. It was impossible to make out the irregular surfaces that would only be exposed by the shadows of a noonday sun.

A sign for the Belle Fourche Reservoir let me know that I was getting close, while a growl from my stomach let me know it was getting impatient. Wildlife biologists claim a coyote's diet can range from grasshoppers to dead cows. They say its favorite food is anything it can chew. And as Twain points out, "He does not mind going a hundred miles for breakfast..." By the time I reached the outskirts of town, I felt a special kinship with *Canis latrans*.

Minutes later I was sitting on a vinyl stool at the lunch counter of Del's. I'd chosen it over the diner across the street because of the police cruiser parked out front. Reaching out like the long arm of the law, the smell of baking bread drew me inside, where I found the officer in question seated at the counter with a cup of coffee and the obligatory donut—a credit to the force.

As I placed my order with a waitress who neglected to call me "Honey," an African-American man walked out of the bathroom and sat down at the last stool along the counter. He wore black slacks and a white collared shirt with blue stripes. His thin arms hardly filled the sleeves. As I passed him on my way to wash up, I noticed a flaking gold-plated watch on his wrist and a hounds tooth hat on the counter. A suitcase lay on the floor beside him. With tightly curled hair and dark brown skin, he looked as out of place as...a black man in South Dakota.

While frothing a rich lather between my hands, I tried to think of a strategy for striking up a conversation. The placid white suds turned gray as my fingers worked the lather. I dug beneath each nail and then washed the sullied slurry down the drain.

When I reentered the dining room, the waitress had already placed my "Cowboy's Breakfast" two seats away from man. I would soon learn that we were separated by far more than simply an empty stool. I salted my eggs as he peppered his. I poured cream into my coffee while he drank his black.

"Howdy," I said in my best western drawl.

He turned slightly and nodded his head.

"What brings you to these parts?"

"I live here," he said. "How about you?"

With more egg on my face than on my plate, I stumbled over an apology. "I...I'm sorry. It's just that..."

"Save your breath. I hear it all the time."

"Yes, but I really am sorry. With that suitcase..."

"Forget it."

"Yes, but the suitcase..."

"Forget it. I'm just waiting for a bus. The Greyhound station is down the block."

"So you're headed out?"

"Gonna visit my grandchildren."

"Where do they live?"

"Kansas City."

"How old are they?"

"Daniel is eight and Aaron is six. They're at the age when they're just discovering guns and toy soldiers. All they ever want to know is if I killed anybody when I was in the army."

"How long were you in?"

"Thirty years. Joined up in 1954. Saw a sign that said, 'Join the Army and See the World.' So I dropped outta high school and six months later I was in Korea."

"So you fought in the war?"

"Conflict."

"Sorry, 'conflict'?"

"Yes sir, Korea *and* Vietnam. Worst years of my life."

"If they were that bad, why did you stay in?"

He took a deep breath and paused to a moment. I was wholly unprepared for what was about to come, but over the next three weeks I would see the phenomenon repeated over and over again. Recognized by psychologists for years, but entirely new to me, most people are more apt to open up to complete strangers than to their own families or closest friends. The stories they tell are often of the troubles in their lives, the troubles otherwise unspeakable. It is a way to make sense, to work toward recognition, understanding, truth. The telling keeps one sane in a crazy world, and when you've got to get something off your chest, it's safer to lay it on someone you'll probably never see again.

"After Korea," he began. "I come home to Mobile where I grew up. Got a job and figgered I'd find a nice woman and settle down. Well, I married a girl I'd known for years, but didn't exactly settle down. I was home about eight months when a buddy o' mine from the war—a white fella—he was passin' through. So we decide to get a lunch at a diner in town. Well, we went in and sat down at the counter—kinda like you and I are right here—and this ol' boy comes stormin' outta the kitchen and tells me I ain't s'posed to be sittin' with a white fella at the counter. I'm s'posed to sittin' with the other coloreds.

"Well, my buddy—he was from up north and didn't understand these things—he says I ain't goin' nowhere. And that ol' boy from the kitchen says yes I am. Well, they got to scuffling and a couple other fellas joined in. My buddy was gettin' whipped, so I grabbed a steel napkin holder from the counter and started in. It did the trick and we were able to get out the door and back to my place.

"Pretty soon we heard them boys was lookin' for us and they had a half dozen others. We high-tailed it out of there, and headed north to his home in Ohio. But my money was runnin' out and I couldn't find a job. So I went back to the Army. Stayed in another twenty-eight years. All because a lunch counter."

"But that was Mobile, Alabama. You could have moved somewhere else. You could have found a job somewhere else up North, or out here."

"There's racism everywhere. It just ain't as obvious."

"What do you mean?"

"Let me ask you a question. In the old Westerns, what color hat did the hero where?"

"White."

"And the villain?"

"Black."

As we continued to talk, I learned that this man wasn't so out of place after all. He told me of all-black frontier towns in Oklahoma, Kansas, Colorado and California. Half of the original settlers of Los Angeles were African-American, and there was even a time when one out of three cowboys in Texas was dark-skinned. At the peak number of working cowboys in the West—around 10,000—up to a quarter of them were black or Mexican. But in popular American legend, their role has been largely untold.

He talked about the buffalo soldiers—so called by the Indians for their dark skin and tightly-curled hair—of the 9th and 10th Calvary, and 24th and 25th Infantry. He told me about African-American cowboys like Bill "Bulldogger" Pickett and Nat Love, aka "Deadwood Dick." Pickett had earned his name as a steer wrestler by using a technique involving biting the animal's tender upper lip to subdue it before taking it to the ground. "And Love," he explained, "earned his nickname just down the road here in Deadwood. It was during a centennial celebration— July fourth, 1876—that he won an open competition of marksmanship. From then on he was known throughout the West as 'Deadwood Dick.'"

I listened intently until the time came for him to catch his bus. "Nice talkin' to ya," he said, standing up to go.

"You too," I replied, shaking his hand. "By the way, *did* you ever shoot anybody?"

He stopped, leaned forward and lowered his voice. "Don't tell my grand kids."

Chapter 7

The lover of nature could here find his soul's delight; the invalid regain his health; the old, be rejuvenated; the weary find sweet repose and invigoration; and all who could come and spend the heated season here would find it the pleasantest summer home in America.
—A.B. Donaldson, 1878

Too full to ride, I unlocked Betsy and wheeled her down the sidewalk. Near the center of town I found a bench in a prime people-watching location, and took a seat. Little did I realize that I was already in the spot light. The odd man was upon me like a whirlwind as soon as my backside hit the wooden slats.

"How many even numbers are there between one and a hundred?"

"Excuse me?"

"How many even numbers are there between one and a hundred? Quick. Quick."

"Fifty," I said, more to humor him than anything else.

"No, there's forty-nine. You can't include a hundred. I said 'between'." He grinned broadly at my incorrect response.

"What's this mean?" he said holding up his index and forefingers in a V.

"Isn't that a peace sign?"

"No," he replied rotating his hand 180 degrees. "This is a peace sign." He turned them back. "This means victory. Victory"

"Oh right. Like in that movie."

"Not from a movie, World War Two. World War Two."

Before I had a chance to explain that I meant a movie about World War II, he had another riddle. "How far can you run into a forest?"

"Half-way—then you're running out."

"Not fair," he complained. "Not fair. You already knew." For the first time since his exam began, the elfish man paused, giving me a chance to look him over. Short and bald, with only wisps of gray hair on either side of his round head, his nose was so flat, it was more like a slight swelling between two beady eyes. His nostrils were defined less by the holes themselves than the hair which they exuded. A narrow, partially obstructed nasal passage may have been an advantage, however, for the man carried with him the pungent smell of days without a shower. Undisturbed by his own cargo of mephitis, I was left to suffer alone for the remainder our encounter.

Out of brain teasers, he held out his right hand. "G'head and squeeze hard as you can. G'head."

I was reluctant. Who was this guy?

"G'head," he insisted. "G'head."

His hand was wide with fingers as thick as sausages. But it remained limp as I took hold, suddenly understanding what it would be like to shake hands with the Pillsbury Dough Boy. I began to squeeze and just as I thought I was getting to him, he started to apply the vice. Within seconds he had broken my grip, my will, and, from the sound of grating bones, my hand.

"Squeeze harder," he said. "Squeeze harder." He sounded as repetitive as Dustin Hoffman in *Rain Man*.

"I...can't."

"Give up? Give up?"

"Yes."

"Say uncle." He enjoyed prolonging the agony. "Say uncle."

"Uncle! Uncle!" He had me repeating myself.

"I won! I won!" He smiled and sat down on the bench. "Wanna go left?"

"Maybe later," I replied, massaging the blood back into my crippled right hand. "How did you get so strong?"

"Always been strong, always. Even stronger before the accident."

"Accident?"

"Motorcycle accident. Wasn't wearing a helmet. No helmet."

"When did it happen?"

"1985. 1985. Was in a coma for sixty days. State record. South Dakota record."

"What do you do now?"

"Can't work no more. Can't ride motorcycles neither. Can't even ride a bike like yours. That your bike?" He reached out and touched the handlebars as gently as a curious child.

"Yeah. I'm taking a trip."

"Goin' to Mount Rushmore? Gotta go to Mount Rushmore."

"I wasn't exactly planning on it."

"No, no. Gotta go to Mount Rushmore."

"How far is it?"

"Not far. Not far. Hour drive. Just an hour"

"Is that all?"

"That's all. That's all. Down this road. This road here." He pointed to the intersection.

I took out my map. He hovered over my shoulder as I tallied the mileage: Two plus ten, plus seven, plus fourteen, plus ten. Where Dustin Hoffman would have cried out, "Forty-three!," my new friend remained silent.

"By the way," I asked, "what's you name?"

"Billy Weirs," he said with pride. "Billy Weirs."

South of Belle Fourche, camper's replaced pickup trucks as the dominant species on the road: *Vehiculus recreationae*. Darwin himself would have marveled at the richness and diversity of subspecies. Winnebagos, Prowlers, Bounders and Coachmen were most common, but specialization and niche marketing had left room for Sun Sports, Jaycos, and Laytons. Vogues and Dynasties flaunted their pedigrees, while Komforts struggled to hang on in the quaint world of misspellings. Dolphins, Montereys and an Allegro Bay had come inland from the coast, but by far the longest migration route was that of a pair of Dutchmen.

Billboards along the roadside urged them toward Spearfish and its wholesome family attractions: D.C. Booth Historic Fish Hatchery; Matthews Opera House; Black Hills Passion Play; and the Classic Auto Museum. "10 Miles ahead!"

Nine miles, eight miles, seven. With its profusion of billboard advertisements, Route 85 is the West's answer to Madison Avenue. Signs of every type and description promised: "Fun for the whole family;" "Kids eat free;" and "Don't miss it."

As I approached Interstate 90, I could hear the roar of motorcycles bound for Sturgis twenty miles to the east. A whole new crop of billboards suggested I follow.

Instead, I remained true to Spearfish, not because of its tourist appeal, but because it offered the most direct route into the Black Hills. Viewed from a distance, the evergreen-covered slopes, rising above the golden prairie, retained a shadowy hue. Beneath a gathering layer of late afternoon clouds, they lived up to the Lakota name, *Paha Sapa*—"Hills that are black."

As the sun disappeared behind Crow Peak to the west, I turned onto Route 14 A and entered Spearfish Canyon. Ponderosa pine and Engleman spruce reached heavenward while I remained Earthbound—dwarfed among the giants. Kings of the forest, their crowns bathed in an aura of mist.

Wide-eyed, I climbed through narrow gulches and spun across open meadows. Wildflowers grew in abundance: purple asters, blue lupine, yellow columbine. Swallowtail butterflies fluttered among them. Mule deer grazed along the edges. A canyon wren's song filled the gorge with a cascading melody.

Downshifting came as much in response to the heart-stopping beauty as to the steepening slope. By the time I reached Bridal Veil Falls, I had to stop all together. Cascading water sparkled in the last direct rays of evening. The scene was one of almost spiritual beauty. It consumed my being. At once I was both experiencing and being experienced by the forest around me. Watching and being watched. Hearing and being heard. Smelling and being smelled. All my senses merged into a synaesthesia of experience, drawn together by the stunning landscape.

Back on the road, my sense of rapture was reigned in by a bit of technical difficulty. With the front derailleur out of whack, I was stuck in the middle chain ring and forced to stand on the steeper sections. I berated myself with each pedal stroke for not having fixed it earlier. Why not? An entire afternoon in Belle Fourche and I hadn't done a thing. Yet I refused to stop and make the simple adjustment. Road rule #237: never stop on an uphill climb. I forced the left-hand shift lever as far forward as I could. Nothing. It wasn't until I came huffing into Savoy that I conceded.

A pair of heavyset men watched from the front porch of the General Store as I veered into the gravel parking lot. They sat on a wooden bench with a six pack of Budweiser between them. One raised his bottle in greeting. "How'd ya like the hill?"

"Just fine thank you."

"You'd never catch me doin' that."

I leaned Betsy against the building and dug into the tool pouch which hung beneath the seat. Withdrawing a patch kit, wrench and chain tool, I finally found what I needed—the metric hex wrench set. Finding the right sized hex for the job took longer than the actual adjustment. Finishing in under a minute, I felt foolish for having put it off. I vowed then and there to take care of Betsy as a top priority.

Walking across the wide porch, I entered the General Store to quench my thirst, but ended up drinking in the decor. Surrounded by yesterday, my pace slowed to a simpler time. A beautiful wood and glass refrigerator housed six packs of beer while an early Coca-Cola cooler held individual sodas. I slid back the lid and reached for a Mountain Dew. Paying at a classic oak cash register, I commented on the nostalgia.

"Plenty more upstairs," said the woman behind the counter. "Go ahead and have yourself a look."

There were five rooms on the second floor, each brimming with antique tools, gold pans, and leg-hold traps. Rusted picks and shovels, and even an old mining car occupied one room, while an assortment of quilts, clocks and ladies hats filled another. Had it not been for the arrival of a tour bus and its cargo of AARPers, I would have stayed longer. As the second floor filled, I squeezed my way through the mass of gray hair and dentures and back onto the porch.

The boys-on-the-bench were into their second six pack and wished me luck as I walked past. "You'll need it."

Ignoring the comment was easier than ignoring the hills ahead. Why, I thought as my quadriceps began to burn, had I taken advice from the gnome-like Billy Weirs? I should have known better than listening to a man whose Warholian "fifteen minutes of fame" came as a result of an extended period of unconsciousness.

Fifteen hundred pounds of steel, 300 pounds of aluminum, 231 pounds of plastic, 128 pounds of rubber, seventy pounds of glass—yet the Ford Taurus passed me like I was standing still. Weighing in around thirty pounds total, Betsy was lean by comparison. But climbing with an extra twenty-five pounds of gear on the rear rack is like running a marathon with a brick in your shorts.

At Cheyenne Crossing, a last set of plywood promises urged me northward to Deadwood and Lead. But I had little interest in the Black Hills Mining Museum, the Broken Boot Gold Mine or even the Ghosts of Deadwood Gulch Wax Museum.

I stopped at gas station for advice on the shortest route to Mount Rushmore. "All right now," said the woman making sure I was going to get this. "You want to go south on Forest Service road number 196. It's the second right down the street from here. Not the first right—that's 85—but the second. It's a dirt road. Not a paved road—that's 85—but dirt.

"Now pretty soon you're gonna come to a fork. You could go either way, but the right is more direct. So you follow that for about five miles or so and come to another fork. It's not really a fork, just a road coming in from the left. But right after that there *is* a fork, and that's where you wanna go left.

I followed as closely as I could, but all I could here was, "You can't get there from Here." A Down East Mainer would never have wasted that much breath.

"Would it help if I drew a map?"

I nodded approval as she tore a paper towel off the roll and laid it on the counter between us. With full oral accompaniment, she produced what was to become the best paper towel map West of the Mississippi. Not only did she draw the winding roads with what appeared to be precise detail, but she also included important landmarks along the way: a big boulder before one fork; a steep hill before another; and Deerfield Lake. "Oh it's beautiful," she told me. "You should camp there tonight." She finished by drawing a smiley face at Mount Rushmore, and handed it across the counter. Thanking her, I stepped outside and checked my watch—7:30.

Although the grade was more forgiving, the Forest Service road offered a different kind of challenge. While my legs enjoyed a break from the steady climb, my arms and shoulders took up the slack. Miles of rugged washboard rattled every joint from wrist to rotator cuff. All the while I was keenly aware of the fading light.

The first stars appeared. A half moon. I looked up not only in wonder, but also out of necessity. Towering spruce created a near-cathedral effect along the road. Only by looking up was I able to follow the unseen twists and turns ahead. Like one of the Magi, I let the heavens guide me. A narrow pathway of stars—defined by the treetops along the roadsides—showed me the way.

Chapter 8

*Of all our domain we loved, perhaps, the Black Hills the most. The
Lakota had named these hills...on account of their color. The slopes and
peaks were so heavily wooded with dark pines that from a distance the
mountains actually looked black. In wooded recesses were numberless
springs of pure water and numerous lakes. There were wood and game
in abundance and shelter from the storms of the plains. It was the
favorite winter haunt of the buffalo and the Lakota as well. According to
a tribal legend these hills were a reclining female figure from whose
breasts flowed life-giving forces, and to them the Lakota went as a child
to its mother's arms.*
—Standing Bear

*They will not dig the gold or let others do it. They are too lazy and too
much like mere animals to cultivate the fertile soil, mine the coal,
develop the salt mines and wash the gold. What shall be done with these
Indian dogs in our manger?*
–Editorial, Yankton Press and Dakotan

The cool, blue water of Deerfield Lake seemed bottomless by the light
of a half moon. Offering relief from the long ride, it beckoned me to
dissolve within. Hardly taking the time to remove my shoes, I plunged
in, rinsing away the dried salt from my body and the worry from my
mind. A slow underwater somersault sent blood rushing to my head.
Tiny bubbles slid over me, caressing my body on their way to the surface.
A feeling of light-headed euphoria filled my spirit.

I emerged disoriented in space and time, facing an eternal scene: a
still mountain lake at sunset; the flickering flames of a campfire dancing
across the water, inviting a lone traveler to warm himself by its gentle
glow.

After drying off and changing, I grabbed a quick bite and walked
along the beach to the far shore. Four men sat around the fire. A halo of
light hung around them. One man carefully tended the fire while the
others spoke in low voices. It was a language I'd never heard before,
one of -iya's, -ila's and -ota's. Their golden faces turned as I approached.

"*Hau kola.*" I was greeted as a friend. "You wanna sweat?"

"Sweat?"

"*Inipi*—sweat bath. To cleanse your body and soul."

I hesitated.

"Come on. Your grandmother says you're a man." They all chuckled.

Not knowing what to expect, I accepted the invitation and observed
intently as the meaning of *inipi* began to unfold. I entered a world where
life itself is sacred: the sound of birds singing is a choir, the forests are

33

cathedrals and every breath a prayer. Quiet men one and all, their actions taught me as much as their words.

"The *inipi*," said John Highfeather, "is one of our oldest ceremonies. It can be used alone or with others like a vision quest or sun dance. But the *Inipi* always comes first."

He explained that while often serving as part of a larger ceremony, a sweat lodge can also stand alone. This one had been called to deal with a drinking problem in the family. Alvin, John's brother, had a son who suffered from alcoholism. His condition had become so bad that Alvin felt the need to ask *Wakan Tanka*—the Great Spirit—for assistance.

The introduction of alcohol to Native Americans has been blamed for ruining more lives than all the Indian Wars combined. Because of denial, it's impossible to get an accurate assessment on rates of alcoholism among Native Americans except through autopsies performed on victims of automobile accidents. Then, of course, it's too late.

"The rocks are almost ready," said Leonard Thompson. It had been his job to prepare the site.

First he had to find the right kinds of rocks—not those that sparkle and shine, but the dull, solid stones that come from deep in the Earth. They must be hard and strong enough to withstand the heat of the fire without bursting. He called them *sintkala waksu*—bird stones—because of the fine, greenish designs on their surfaces. He said the patterns had been put there by birds, and that in them, legend has it, one can see the future.

I gazed deeply into the fire. The bird stones glowed mysteriously.

Along with the stones, Leonard collected wood. Cottonwood is used for the fire because it is the most sacred tree to the Lakota. Its spiritual flames heat the bird stones for the ceremony. Building the fire is a spiritual act. Four logs are placed on the ground running east-west with four north-south logs laid on top. These honor the sacred directions. Upon this structure is built a small tipi of sticks that represent the Lakota people. It shows that they are a part of the world, and that it is a part of them.

Listening intently to his explanation, I felt more and more honored to have been asked to join. I could not understand why they had asked a total stranger, a *wasichu* no less, to join them in this sacred ritual.

"We are all brothers," said John, his smile growing in the firelight.

By now, the stones were ready. John stood and walked toward the lodge. Its entrance faced west—the direction of the setting sun.

While small, the sweat lodge represents the entire universe to those inside. The spirit of every living being is believed to be present. In the center of the structure a circular hole had been excavated into which the heated stones were placed. During the ceremony, this pit became the center of our universe, hosting the power of *Wakan Tanka*.

The soil displaced by the hole had been used to form a small ridge that led about ten feet from the structure. It served as a path for the spirits to follow. At the end of the ridge was a small mound. John called it *unci*—grandmother.

A few feet from the entrance two forked sticks rose from the ground. A third—covered with small bows of colored yarn—served as a crossbar. Against it leaned a long pipe and a black and white stick.

John entered the lodge and covered the ground with sage. Sitting naked at the right side of the entrance, he lit a strand of braided *wacanga*—sweet grass. As it burned, he pushed the fragrant smoke throughout the lodge. In this way, he explained, bad thoughts were driven out and the space was made sacred.

Stripping off our clothes, Alvin, Gordon (another of John's brothers), and I joined him inside. We entered slowly, pausing in the doorway to bow and say, *mitakuye oyasin*—all my relatives. Two simple words, they acknowledge more than simple kin, but the connection of all things on earth.

We expressed that connection further by crawling clockwise around the pit like the four-legged animals, whose spirits were present. Leonard remained outside, bringing in the heated stones one by one. A forked stick, the traditional tool for this process, had been replaced by an Army surplus trenching tool.

As the first glowing rock settled into the pit, John sprinkled it with sweet grass. "*Pilamaye*," he said, "thank you. We give thanks to grandmother earth."

It occupied the center of the hole representing *wakicagapi*—dead relatives who had returned to earth. "We remember them as the stones are placed."

The next four stones were placed in order of the sacred directions: west, north, east and south. John blessed each with a pinch of sage which crackled orange upon contact. A sweet smell filled the lodge.

A sixth stone was placed on top of the first. "This is for grandfather sky."

A seventh was added for Alvin's son. For his spirit we would pray.

With the stones in place, Leonard entered the lodge and closed the entrance. The smooth, round rocks in the pit glowed a pale ocher, while brighter orange sparks twinkled across them in the silent darkness.

John lit the pipe and passed it clockwise. The smell of *canshasha*—red willow bark tobacco—filled the lodge. "Hold onto the smoke." he told me, "Rub it over your body. It will link us as brothers."

Raising the pipe to my mouth, I inhaled generously. Smoke filled my cheeks, scratched my throat, and burned my lungs. Tears leaked from my squinting eyes as I fought back a retching cough.

After each man had taken smoke, a prayer was offered to the Great Spirit and to the rocks. As John sprinkled water over the roasted stones, a crackling wave of steam heat filled the lodge.

"*Wopila tunkashila*—thank you grandfather. Thank you for this gift."

Breathing became short as the union of clear water and red stones unified earth and sky. Grandmother and grandfather came together in a great surge of power. Sitting quietly, I listened to the screaming stones go silent. I longed to feel the earth-power penetrate my body—healing scars, replenishing my spirit.

The second ladle of water brought on a wave of steam more potent than the first. My throat burned, my lungs boiled. I pushed myself away from the stones. My back pressed against one of the peeled willow saplings that had been lashed together to form the framework of the lodge. Sensing my distress, John whispered "*mitakuye oyasin*," and Leonard threw back the canvas door.

Cool air flooded the lodge. Although revived, I was also embarrassed. But my hosts found my inexperience nothing more than amusing. "Relax," said John. "Its no big thing—just five naked men crouching around some heated stones under a surplus Army tarp. All is pure...except maybe the tarp."

Before the ceremony continued, I switched places with Leonard by the door which offered the coolest spot.

As the rocks were doused, their sacred heat again filled the lodge. The small *tipi* shook as the men began to sing. "*Tunkashila hi-yay hi-yay.*" The sound filled the space around me and its rhythm penetrated my soul. I found myself singing along even though I didn't know the words, let alone the language. I only know that I was moved to sing.

After each of the four rounds, the flap was opened and fresh air and moonlight allowed to enter the lodge. During each round, water was poured over the rocks, the pipe was passed, and singing resumed. After my initial trauma, I felt good throughout the first round. The second round, however, left me dripping with sweat and struggling for breath. I had my doubts about going another. But John explained that the later rounds usually got shorter, and that the third was the round of prayer when one could have the personal attention of the Great Spirit. He urged me to stay and offer a prayer of my own.

After the flap was closed and the rocks were doused, each man spoke in turn, imploring *Wakan Tanka* for help in the family's battle against alcoholism. Gordon, an alcoholic himself, thanked the Great Spirit for another day of sobriety. Alvin prayed for his son.

When it came to be my turn, I offered my voice to their cause, but also prayed for an uncle of mine who had lost himself inside a bottle. I prayed for his wife. I prayed for his children. "*Hau*," the men said when I finished.

Feeling good about my contribution, I stayed for the final round—the round of thanksgiving. The stones were splashed and the pipe was passed a final time. Although the heat was nearly as intense as before and sweat drained from every pore in my body, I felt strangely at ease. My breathing was slow and my mind found peace.

After the final song, we said our last "*mitakuye oyasin*," and the flap was thrown open. Leonard carefully took the pipe apart and cleaned it as the rest of us left the lodge. Emerging from the warm, moist interior of the *tipi* was like emerging from the womb—its dome shaped like the belly of a woman where life is created and nurtured until birth. With a common mother, these men became my brothers.

We drank cold water and wiped ourselves with sage leaves. Refreshed. Purified. Ready to face another day, week, month. Ready to continue with the sacred ceremony of life, of living. Ready to start anew.

Part 2
Rustlers

Chapter 9

The Indian's been living in heaven for a thousand years and we took it away from 'em for forty dollars a month.
—Charlie Russell

The whole emigration is wild and frantic with a desire to be pressing forward... Whenever a wagon unluckily gets stuck in the muck crossing some little rut, the other trains behind make a universal rush to try to pass...Amid the yelling, popping of whips and cursing, perhaps a wagon wheel is broken, two or three men knocked down in a fight, and twenty guns drawn...All of this occasioned by a delay of perhaps two minutes and a half.
—James Evans, 1849

A frenzy seized my soul...Piles of gold rose up before me...castles of marble...myriads of fair virgins contending with each other for my love—were among the fancies of my fevered imagination...in short, I had a very violent attack of the gold fever.
—Hubert Howe Bancroft

When I think of these times and recall back to my mind the beauty and grandeur of those almost uninhabited shores. When I picture to myself the dense and lofty summits of the forests unmolested by the axe of the settler. When I see that the vast herds of elk, deer and buffalo which once pastured on these hills and in these valleys have ceased to exist, I remember that these extraordinary changes have all taken place in less than twenty years, I pause and wonder, and although I know all to be a fact, I scarcely believe it's reality.
—John James Audubon

I opened my eyes but saw nothing. The darkness enveloped me like a net falling from above. Nothing escaped.

It may be cliche to say it's always darkest before the dawn, but the blackness of this predawn redefined the notion. The dense forest sucked in the blackness and held it in a sacred way. Thick cloud cover denied even starlight and moon glow into the Cimmeranian world. The forest eternal, gripped by stillness—not a breath of wind, not a chirping bird. Silence reigned, all-consuming. The Black Hills.

At the first sign of aurora, ponderosa pines emerged out of obscurity. Found in every state west of the great plains, they can grow in soil conditions ranging from glacial till to desert sand. They can survive on less than twelve inches of rainfall a year. Fire scars and beetle borings attest to their resilience. They are the spirit of the West.

I sprung joyously from my blue cocoon and into the cold morning air. Within minutes, the panniers were loaded and lashed in place. Refreshed, renewed, nothing could stop me.

Nothing, that is, but an intersection. I stepped off the bike and gazed down each wooded right of way looking for direction, looking for a sign. Where would they take me? What could I expect?

Four days in the western Dakotas had already confounded the dime novel in my mind. The sharp-edged landscape has a way of popping dreams. Like a politician nearing election day, the West has a history of promising more than it can deliver. With the bison herds decimated, the Indians subdued, and the complexion of the American cowboy considerably darker than popular mythology suggests, my preconceptions had been gunned down without so much as a fight— shot in the back without warning.

I stood at a crossroads—the unmarked junction of two Forest Service roads in the heart of the Black Hills. The paper towel map was of little help. A single line connected Deerfield Lake to the smiley face at Mount Rushmore. No intersection. No fork. One of these roads held my future, the other would be lost to memory.

The roar of a truck covering washboard at a high rate of speed arose behind me. The rust-colored Chevy flew through the intersection in a cloud of dust, but came to a sudden halt fifty yards ahead. A single white backing light announced it's reversal before the vehicle had begun to move. Moments later, I was staring into the cab at a trio of unshaven men in baseball caps. They looked to be in their early twenties.

"Where you headed?" asked the driver.

"Rushmore, if I can find my way through these roads."

"Good luck, it's a maze out here. The Forest Service maintains close to 400,000 miles—eight times the size of the Interstate Highway System. Of course only a fraction of that is in the Black Hills, but it's enough to get you lost."

"No kidding. Why do they have so many?"

"Some are fire roads, but most are for logging—subsidized by your tax dollars."

"Subsidized?"

"Below-cost timber sales—a government give-away."

"Give-away?"

"Five billion dollars over the last ten years."

"What?"

"The Forest Service sells wood at a price below what it costs to prepare the sale—pennies on the dollar. Using much of its budget to build roads, pay engineers, and conduct environmental assessments, the Forest Service operates at an annual deficit of $400 million. After all these free services, the industry pays only for the value of the logs *at the mill*, minus a profit. This means that for every two to three tax dollars spent, the Forest Service sees a return of one. It ends up costing the average American tax payer about twenty-seven dollars a year."

"It sounds like Smoky Bear needs to balance his checkbook."

"If the Forest Service were a corporation, it'd be bankrupt."

"That ain't all," came a voice from the far side of the cab. "There are environmental problems—soil erosion, water pollution, disrupted wildlife habitats, and lower productivity. When they replant after a clearcut, they favor valuable softwood species and use herbicides to kill off hardwood seedlings. Once the desired species are in place, they have to use pesticides because the monocrop is more prone to disease and insect infestation. Being in the Department of Agriculture, the 'Forest Circus' tries to grow trees like they were corn."

"How do you guys know so much about this stuff?"

"We work for a forest advocacy group," said the driver. "We're on our way to the Heart of the Hills Logging Show to set up an information booth."

"A logging show?"

"We're not expecting a warm reception."

"I wouldn't guess."

"We'll take you as far as Hill City if you want to ride in back."

"Thanks." I hoisted Betsy into the bed and climbed in.

As we rattled over washboard, I gazed backward through a dual haze of dust and clouds. Between a low ceiling and a rising storm, my vision narrowed. For the first time in days I was not awed by the vastness of the West. Observations became limited to those of my immediate experience: the dented pickup bed on which I sat; the faint sound of music coming from inside the cab; a hand-painted sign leaning against a mail box: "This family supported by timber dollars."

County Road 17 runs into U.S. 385 at the north end of Hill City. Bisecting the 1.2 million acres of the National Forest from Wind Cave in the south to Deadwood in the north, it is known as the Black Hills Parkway. Judging from the clip of the morning rush, it may as well have been the Black Hills Speedway.

I waved the truck off as soon as I had Betsy on the ground. The driver gave a nod before accelerating from the gravel shoulder and joining the race.

I climbed aboard and headed off at my own pace. Although headed nearly due east, I was not challenged by the rising sun. From the looks of things, it would be in short supply all day long. A steady stream of out of state license plates along 385 provided challenge enough. After four miles, I turned onto Route 16 where the camper to camper traffic was joined by an equally thick string of billboards eerily reminiscent to those outside of Gatlinberg, Tennessee, Lake George Village, New York, and an increasing portion of my own White Mountains.

The merits of Rapid City's "Family-Approved" attractions were extolled with exclamations including, "Must See!" "Unforgettable!" and "Best Museum in America!" Bear Country U.S.A. promises a diversity of mammals including wolves, cougars deer, elk, antelope, buffalo, and numerous specimens of it's name sake—both live and stuffed. If you prefer scales to fur, Reptile Gardens has your answer with alligator wrestling and America's largest reptile collection. Any lover of the cold-blooded would find this a must.

If neither of these phyla strike your fancy, one last place might just do the trick. Over a thousand miles from the nearest ocean, Marine Life hosts a population of trained dolphins, sea lions and seals performing "action packed" shows throughout the day. While local wildlife suffers from loss of habitat, competition with livestock, and the extermination efforts of ranchers, exotics are trucked in from around the world and set behind plexiglass.

If animals—either foreign or domestic—aren't your cup of tea, no need to lose heart. Still more signs touted the Rushmore Water Slide, Sitting Bull Crystal Caves, and the Flying T Chuckwagon Supper and Show, where you can enjoy a cowboy-style meal on a tin plate followed by the Flying T Wranglers' performance of western music and comedy. A week-long family vacation could be had along just an eighteen mile stretch of road!

Fortunately, it was not my stretch of road. I turned south onto 16 A and headed into Keystone with breakfast on my mind. But before the first sip of coffee had passed my lips, I received my first taste of Rushmania—Rushmore Helicopters, the Rushmore Aerial Tramway, Rushmore Chalets, Rushmore KOA, Rushmore White House Resort, Rushmore view Inn, Rushmore Grill and Bar, Rushmore T-Shirts & Co., Rushmore Gift Shop, and the Rushmore-Borglum Museum. With its origin as a small mining town in the 1890's, Keystone owes its modern existence to the massive granite upthrust looming 2,000 feet above. Gift shops, restaurants, motels and even a local plumbing supply store are named after the Memorial. Touted as "America's Shrine to Democracy," it makes good sense to name your business accordingly. The only problem lay in that potential customers may confuse your Rushmore with all the others. How does one decide when nearly half the local businesses are listed under R in the White Pages?

The managers of the Railhead Family Restaurant clearly understand the industry's three principles for success—location, location and location. Alphabetically ahead of the numerous "Rushmores," geographically on a corner at the leading edge of town, and psychologically with a large sign touting it as the "Home of the 5 cent cup of coffee." It was not until I opened the menu that I discovered the fine print which had eluded me outside—"with dessert." No problem. I ordered the "Breakfast Special" and a slice of apple pie.

Heather, the waitress, looked up from her scribbling for a moment to see that I was serious before taking my order to the kitchen. Apparently satisfied, she turned and left me alone at the corner table to occupy myself with "The Original I.Q. Tester." Despite failing test after test, I felt a strange kinship with the triangular piece of wood and it's collection of plastic pegs. Like me, it was "Made in USA," and even more specifically, it promised "Each Game a Solitary Adventure." Think of the money I could have saved by sending away for one and spending the summer in my apartment back home.

As my breakfast was taking some time to assemble itself, I took the opportunity to admire the unique decorating job of the dining room. Maroon carpet not only covered the floor, but worked its way two feet up most of the walls before a transition to wood paneling stretched the rest of the way to the ceiling. A high shelf above the lace-curtained windows held a dusty collection of old frying pans, Dutch ovens, coffee pots, and decorator tins. Plastic ivy spilled out of brass pots hanging from the ceiling. A quartet of stuffed wildlife marked the cardinal directions—a coyote to the north, a pheasant to the south, a pronghorn to the east and a jackalope to the west.

A sunburned family helped itself at the "Buffalo Buffet - All You Can Eat," while a table of eight golden girls talked about what they had seen in the gift shops and what time the tour bus was scheduled to leave. Through it all, a steady stream of oldies was piped in through to complete the illusion that I had indeed returned to the 1950's. Somewhere between "Chapel of Love" and "Boppin' at the High School Hop," Heather returned with my breakfast.

"Sorry the eggs took so long. Some times that chicken just doesn't want to lay."

"At least I know they're fresh."

"Do you want the pie now or later?"

"Do you have to pick the apples?"

She smiled. "No, they come from a can."

Before I had a chance to comment, there arose such a clatter from the wall to my left that my attention deficit went on auto-pilot and I turned to the source of the sound.

Chugga, chugga, chugga, chugga. Choo! Choo! Choo!

I wrinkled my face and turned to Heather. "What the...?"

Choo! Choo! Choo!

"It's a train clock. Took me a week of working here before I figured out what was going on."

Choo! Choo! Choo! Choo!

I lingered at the table eating pie, writing postcards and seeing how long I could string out a five cent cup of coffee. By the time the train came around again I decided to pay my fare and deboard.

Well fed and thoroughly caffeinated, I pedaled through downtown Keystone where brightly painted storefronts claimed "1/2 Off Everything," "Daily Specials," and "Almost Nothing Over $2.99." The spirit of competition thrived as grandiose claims were hurled back and forth across the wide main street, directed as much toward the competition as tourists. Like the escalation of the arms race or the "cola wars," there were no holds barred. "We Gladly Accept All Coupons."

Reaching the center of town, I encountered the ultimate standoff. To my right, reaching two stories high, wearing a coat of red paint with bright white lettering stood, "The World's Greatest Bargains." And to my left, also two stories tall, wearing yellow paint with black lettering was..."The World's Greatest Bargains." How could this be? It's like having two Muhammad Ali's when we know that only one can truly float like a butterfly and sting like a bee. Was there some controversy? An asterisk in the record books?

It may come as a surprise, but I had bigger things on my mind—like the climb up Route 244 and the light rain that had begun to fall. Passing the Parade of Presidents Wax Museum at the edge of town I joined a parade of tour buses and recreational vehicles on their way to the Memorial. Like the children inside them, tired from a long drive, their engines whined against the grade—struggling to pull the massive bulk of a house-on-wheels up the slope. Complete with kitchen, bathroom and color TV, who says you can't take it with you? What could be better than traveling with all the comforts of home? Nothing to worry about, right?

The answer lay half mile ahead where much of the right lane and all of the narrow shoulder were blocked by an aluminum behemoth as big as my apartment. Steam spewed from under its open hood as an aggravated man in plaid shorts and golf shirt fanned the violent emissions with a newspaper. He swore under his breath. I smiled and gave a nod as I passed.

With Betsy in a low gear, progress was slow but I knew I'd get there sooner or later. A cross between the legends of David and Goliath, and

The Tortoise and the Hare, I reached the summit while the Winnebago waited for a tow.

The massive parking structure was as much a monument to human achievement as the carved stone portraits behind it. Three broad tiers cut precariously into the upper slope were filled with cars, R.V.s and motorcycles from across the nation. Washington to Florida, Maine to California, patriotic citizens came from the four corners of America.

I locked Betsy to a sign for handicapped parking near the entrance, and proceeded toward the faces visible only through a veil of pine boughs and mist. Despite the spitting rain, the wide walkway leading to the viewing area was thick with visitors both coming and going. The promenade was lined with flags of the fifty states, Puerto Rico, Guam and a few territories of which I'd never heard and promptly forgot. I paused briefly to honor New Hampshire's blue and gold banner. It lay limp and damp against its pole.

Feeling the chill myself, I pulled on my rain jacket and continued past the alphabetically disadvantaged state flags to the designated viewing area. Washington, Jefferson, Lincoln and Roosevelt (Teddy) loomed above me. Their faces were ashen, their expressions blank. Aloof. Detached. Granite eyes stared into slate gray skies. They were tired eyes, eyes of experience, eyes of challenge, eyes of struggle.

Chosen to symbolize the birth and growing pains of a young nation, each represents a different era in America's development. Washington acted as midwife to a newborn republic while Jefferson—the primary author of the Constitution and Declaration of Independence—set the rules of conduct for what would become a curious toddler. Lincoln stepped in when sibling rivalry threatened to break up the family, and Roosevelt guided us into adolescence by encouraging a more mature role in the world which included leadership and a conservation ethic.

As one would expect, conversations throughout the Memorial were equally diverse. Ranging from historical to political, opinions were shared freely between friends and strangers alike. My quest for a rest room was interrupted by one such exchange. I stood within earshot, pretending to read a plaque while I listened.

"If only those God-damned tree huggers would get out of the way and let a working man work," said a tall man in a blaze orange raincoat. In profile, only his nose and moustache emerged from beneath the hood. "They've got us so bound up with regulations that you can't even take it shit in the woods without an environmental impact statement."

"I know what you mean," replied another man wearing a bluejean jacket. He held a lit cigarette at waist level in his left hand while making abrupt gestures with his right. "America was running along just fine till those eco-freaks came along. What the hell are they tryin' to prove. If they had their way we'd all be out of work. My brother out in California, he's a logger. You should hear what he's got to say. Those idiots are blockin' roads, and some of the crazy bastards are chaining themselves to trees."

"They're not the kind of people who ever had to work for a living, or worry about feeding their kids. They throw on their lycra and head out on their thousand dollar mountain bikes paid for with trust funds."

"Some of 'em even put spikes in trees. Imagine what happens when a chain saw hits a quarter inch steel spike."

"They're tryin' to kill people."

"They think animals are more important. Like that owl up in Oregon. What's the deal? Men are losing jobs because of that thing. If animals are so important, if animals are so smart, show me the owl that can program a computer. Show me the dolphin that invented the television. Show me the wolf that wrote the Declaration of Independence."

"Exactly! If those extremists think that humans are so bad, why don't they do us all a favor and off themselves. That's my kind of population control."

"They don't even have their facts straight. You know who's the number one creator of of greenhouse gases? Mother Nature."

"I was listening to Rush Limbaugh yesterday and he said that volcano in the Philippines spewed out more than a thousand times more chemicals to destroy the ozone than all the man-made stuff in history."

"They're running around like Chicken Little saying the sky is falling. They're going to ruin the American economy, and why? Because they are scared to death of imagined threats."

"And they're letting those imagined threats effect real people."

"Yeah, Rush said most carbon dioxide is caused by nature—rotting trees and termites. Stuff like that. He said America's forests are healthier today than a hundred years ago. The tree huggers got more to hug than ever."

They both laughed. "And they're still bitchin' and moanin'. What are they trying to prove?"

"They're just scared. They have no faith in America."

"Ditto."

Chapter 10

Whose voice was first sounded on this land? The voice of the red people who had but bows and arrows...What has been done in my country I did not want, did not ask for it; white people going through my country...When the white man comes to my country he leaves a trail of blood behind him...I have two mountains in that country—the Black Hills and the Big Horn Mountains. I want the Great Father to make no roads through them. I have told these things three times; now I have come here to tell them the fourth time.
—Red Cloud, Oglala Sioux

He who has learned to love the land has loved eternity.
—Stefan Zeromski

About a mile off the back side of the Memorial on Route 244, an unmarked dirt road lead me to a primitive Forest Service campground. Rutted and bumpy, the double track took me past a red Toyota pickup truck and a "NO HUNTING" sign peppered with buckshot. Lichen-covered granite pierced the thin, sandy soil. Ponderosa pine cones—about the size and shape of large goose eggs—covered much of the ground.

Further along, I encountered a light green Volkswagen van. Badly rusted and missing the large V.W. monogram from its front end, I couldn't tell whether it belonged to someone or had been abandoned. If the latter were true, it would make a good roof should the skies decide to open up again. I laid Betsy against a nearby pine and walked behind some bushes to take a leak.

When I returned, a man was crouched beside her. He stood upon my approach. Broad-shouldered and husky, he was a bear in red flannel. A long, gray beard hid most of his face, and he peered through wire-rimmed glasses. His hair—what was left of it—was greasy and matted—as though he hadn't showered in a week. I could tell right away we'd get along marvelously.

"You got the right idea." He said smiling.

"That's what I keep telling myself, but sometimes I don't know."

"Sure ya do." He extended his right hand. "Name's Tom Kemp." We shook. "Traveling is what it's all about. New places. New people. New experiences. I've been at it all my life. It's in my blood."

"I've been feeling that itch lately myself. That's what brings me out here."

He nodded his agreement and approval. "Nothin' like the Black Hills on a rainy afternoon. Brings out the true colors—the meaning of the name. I just had to come back."

"So, you've been here before?"

"Many times. It's got a hold on me like it's had one many people for many years. Kiowa, Arapaho, Cheyenne, and Sioux all came—and some still come—to seek visions. Black Elk, the Oglala holy man, received his great vision in these hills. He heard the voices from the Powers of the World. The power of the West, where the Thunder Beings live. The power of the North, where the Great White Giant lives. The power of the East , where the sun always shines. The power of the South, where you always face. The power of the Sky, the oldest of them all. And finally the power of the Earth—the power that created these Black Hills."

"No wonder the Native Americans consider them sacred."

"More than sacred—if there's such a thing. For the plains tribes, this was the center of their world. Summer was traditionally the time for communing with the Great Spirit, and they would come to the sacred places of the Black Hills to beseech his pity and seek visions.

"That's why it was so hard to give them up. The Fort Laramie Treaty established the Black Hills as part of the 'Great Sioux Reservation' in 1868, but within a few years it began to unravel. That treaty was the *only* recognition of unconditional defeat ever signed by a U.S. president. It was stone in the road of Manifest Destiny and Washington couldn't stand it. Eight years later, Red Cloud was forced to sign another document effectively nullifying the Fort Laramie Treaty and turning the Black Hills over to the U.S. government in exchange for subsistence rations. The white man stole the Black Hills for green and gold."

"But this is still a sacred place."

"*All* land is sacred. All land has a story to tell."

"A story?"

"Sure, only most of the old stories are gone. With the destruction of the indigenous cultures of the West, many of the stories of this land simply disappeared. Without them, the pioneers saw the wilderness as dark, dangerous, evil. They tried to make the West extension of the East— tried to explain away the spiritual value of the land with scientific explanations.

"Take Devils Tower over the line here in Wyoming. The plains tribes called it *Mateo Tepee*, "Bear Lodge." It was a place of wonderful stories and magical events. Legend has it that a great bear scratched the deep grooves into the rock while trying to get at a young maiden who had taken shelter on the summit. For countless generations, the rock itself came alive in the stories it told. The history of a people cannot be separated from the history of their land. It's the stories that give the relationship deeper meaning.

"It wasn't until the Tower was 'discovered' by white men that it was renamed Devil's Tower. But more than just the name changed. The story changed too. Now it's all about an ancient volcanic event, plutonic magma and an exposed igneous core. I like the bear story better.

"What's most ironic is that the plains tribes had no concept of the devil. He played no part in their mythology. John Lame Deer said, 'You people invented the devil, you can keep him.'"

I smiled.

"You look cold. How 'bout a cup of tea?"

I grabbed the bag of dried fruit and followed Tom into the classic Volkswagen to discover an interior as weathered as exterior. Scratched wooden paneling lined the walls and a worn-out brown carpet covered the floor. A small table made out of plywood and two by fours was tucked in behind the driver's seat. Tom lit a backpacking stove on top of it, filled a blackened pot from a five gallon jug, and set it on to boil. Within minutes steam filled the van. Tom handed me a mug and a tea bag.

"Hope you like Pekoe."

With both hands wrapped around the mug, I sank my nose into the warm vapors, inhaling the moist aroma into my lungs. My fingers tingled with pleasure as I took the first sip. Soothing liquid tumbled down my throat. I let out a long sigh. Satisfaction.

Tom smiled, raised his mug in a silent toast and took a drink. Returning the mug to his lap, he leaned forward until elbows were on knees. His eyes grew wide and his smile broad as he whisked me into a world of keen words and clever allusion.

"We are story-telling beings," he explained. "It's the way we structure our lives—the way we think, relate, communicate. When we're not telling stories, we're making them, living them. These are the stories of our lives, and we tell them to try to make sense of it all. Old stories are great, but like road maps, they only take us so far. Sooner or later we need a new one to continue our journey.

I sat back and listened as, pot after pot, Tom recounted his adventures across decades, states and what he liked to called "Turtle Island"—the North American continent. His narrative held the collected knowledge of a lifetime of adventure.

Fueled by the elixir of flavorful leaves, Tom went on for hours. Nibbling on the last of my dried fruit, he told stories of exotic people in far away places as well as ordinary folks in Memphis, Pittsburgh and Portland, Maine.

"I met this fella in Madison, Indiana," he said with a smile. "That son-of-a-gun never gave me a single straight answer. You see, Madison is right on the border with Kentucky and I was driving through at night.

It's all winding, hilly roads in that area and I didn't know if I'd crossed the state line. So I stop in at this little gas station to fill up and find out. 'What state is this?' I ask this skinny fella workin' the pump. Well, he looks at me kinda funny, spits and says, 'That's a good question mister. We seem to be right on the border here and folks in this town are havin' what you might call an identity crisis. We're havin' trouble alignin' ourselves, and since the town is split on each state, we decided to compromise. Only problem now is whether to call it Kentuckiana or Indiucky.'"

His keen ear for dialect and passionate mimicry were so shrewd, so utterly merciless, laughter became painful. My cheeks ached from smiling.

"I talked with that fella for nearly an hour and it was one riddle after another. Same thing happens all time up in Maine," Tom lamented. "That's one state you never stop to ask for directions. 'You can't get they-ah from he-ah.' It oughta be the state motto. Speaking of state mottoes, you ever been to New Hampshire?"

"Careful Tom, that's where I live."

"Don't you think 'Live Free or Die' is a little harsh?"

"Yeah, but sometimes in the winter we prefer to say 'Live, *Freeze* or Die.'"

"I'll have to remember that one. How about Pennsylvania..." Until late that night, Tom spun his stories, weaving the brilliant tapestry of his life. He wrapped me in a quilt of words and images, and I dozed within their warmth.

Like the oral traditions of most native cultures, the importance of place remained central to his tales. He took great care to identify the precise geographical locations at which specific events unfolded. Never treated as passive or inert, the settings themselves were as alive as their inhabitants. Sometimes more so.

Tom was no blushing violet when it came to relating his extraordinary exploits.

From northern Canada to the Florida Keys, Baja California to Cape Fear, his tales were stitched together by colorful people, embroidered with wonderful places and knit from a pure sense of adventure.

Chapter 11

But I don't think he [Wakinyan Tanka, the Great Thunderbird,] lives there anymore since the wasichu have made these hills into a vast Disneyland. No, I think the thunder beings have retreated to the farthest end of the earth...where there are no tourists and hot-dog stands.
—John (Fire) Lame Deer

A great thunderclap woke me, but Tom's snoring kept me there. Like echoes of crosscut saws that once rang throughout the hills, his rhythmic breathing was as synchronous as a pair of lumberjack's push and pull. The stertorous wheezing lasted hours.

Unwilling to face the rain, and uncomfortable with waking Tom in his own van, I endured. Despite attempts at plugging my ears with rolled up pieces of paper, fuzz balls from the carpet, and even the last pieces of dried fruit, I could not escape.

At last the gloom was broken. Along with an aura of light, the morning brought a break in the rain and an end to Tom's snoring. Taking advantage of both, I stepped into the still morning air to relieve myself and returned for some long awaited silence.

I next awoke at 8:30. Tom was nowhere to be seen, but a note stuck in the door said he'd gone for a walk and would be back soon. Not wanting to leave without saying goodbye, I wrote in my journal until he returned a half hour later.

"Saw a doe with her fawn."

My grin mirrored his. "What do you think of this weather?"

He looked skyward. "Gonna be with us another day."

"I was afraid of that."

"Where ya off to?"

"Custer first, then maybe Wyoming."

"Once you get outta the hills, it oughta dry up."

"Hope so."

"Et yet?"

"Just did," I lied, not wanting Tom to feel badly about finishing off the dried fruit. To tell the truth, I was thankful he had. I'd have a proper breakfast in Custer just twenty miles away.

With a strong handshake and a slap on the back, Tom sent me on my way. "You writin' down that stuff from last night?" he asked sheepishly as I threw a leg over Betsy.

"Some."

"Told ya lot o' lies."

The rain resumed its vigil over the Black Hills as I reached Route 244 at the end of the gravel road. A thin, cold drizzle fell from a low, gray sky. Fog filled the spaces between trees. No need to fill my water bottles—I could simply lick the air.

I paused briefly to wipe the dirt from Betsy's tires before rolling onto the glistening blacktop. Clouds reflected in its sheen wetted me from below as Betsy's tires threw up a fine spray.

The Black Elk Wilderness Area lay hidden in the mist. Harney Peak—at 7,242 feet, the highest point east of the Rocky Mountains and west of the Pyrennes in Europe—was a lost castle in the clouds. Like the spire atop Disney's Magic Kingdom, an immense lookout tower rises from the summit. On a clear day, visitors can view four states but not a single thunder being.

With chin tucked and fingers clenched, I built up speed on the long descent leading to the junction of 244 and U.S. 385. I flew through the intersection like a thunderbird in a full dive.

"NATURAL CROSS," a sign proclaimed, welcoming me to the Black Hills Holy Land. "SCULPTED BY GOD! Approved Family Attraction." Curious, I turned onto the shoulder for a look. Gazing at the forested base of the Santa Cruz Peaks, I failed to discern the religious symbol in question. No amount of searching could make out the feature "Carved From Stone in Nature's Wonderland."

"There it is," came a voice from behind me. "Down by the left side of the cliffs. That clearing in the trees."

A slight turn revealed a bearded man standing on the gravel beside me. Looking remarkably like Tom Kemp, it was only after he began to speak that I realized John Birch was a better fit. Within minutes his speech became eerily reminiscent of the Big Lie and Hitler's final solution. He wore a dark green Army coat with a swastika embroidered below the name patch which read Walker. "You see it?"

Before I had time to answer, he turned and motioned to a rusty pickup truck parked on the opposite shoulder. A plastic tarp lashed down with nylon cord covered the bulging cargo in back. I could hear the passenger door creak open, but saw no one until two small children and a woman holding a baby appeared in front of the truck. *Kirche, Kuche, Kinder.* They paused momentarily at the roadside and then crossed with caution, joining the man in the green coat.

"There it is," he said, putting his arm around the woman. "If that ain't a sign from Yahweh, I don't know what is."

"You mean God?" I asked.

"It's Yahweh," he responded sharply. "God is a derogatory term promoted by the Judahs. It's nothin' more than dog spelled backward."

"I'm sorry. I wasn't aware."

"Of course you weren't. You're just another product of this Zionist Occupied Government. They're trying to destroy our Christian identity.

Can't you see it's all controlled by the Jews and their sympathizers." He paused, "You ain't a Jew, are you?"

With dark hair and a name like Lebo, I had been mistaken as Jewish before and never thought anything of it. In this instance, however, I felt it best to make things perfectly clear. "No, I'm not."

"That's a good thing," he said as a cavity-filled grin spread across his face. "Cuz Jews are just one step above niggers, and niggers are nothin' but animals without souls. It's the Jews that are controlling all the money in this country—just like they did in Germany.

"Hitler wasn't after the Jews at first. He was just trying to make Germany stronger. He only targeted the Jews because they were ruining the economy. You ever hear the expression, 'I'm going to Jew you?' Where you think that came from?"

He paused for a moment to let it sink in. I said nothing.

"The whole Holocaust is overblown. The German's got credit for killing way more Jews than there even were at that time. Sure some people got killed, but they deserved it. Now-a-days all you hear is those Jews cry-babying about the Holocaust. They've been so good at it they got the niggers and the Indians trying it too. They all claim to be put upon and expect something for it. This whole country's goin' to hell."

Unable to respond, I stared in disbelief as his wife and children stood nodding their heads. With their consent, he continued, "You got to realize that white America is under siege. The Jews are the real liars and bloodhounds. It's not the Jews and coloreds that are in danger of losing their identity, it's us. We are headed for oblivion unless we rise and turn the tide. The downfall of the democratic system is coming. Our Constitution is hanging by a thread.

"The federal government has become our worst enemy. It wants to do away with the Constitution and Bill of Rights. America is being merged into a One World Government under the United Nations. When the New World Order is in place, we will no longer have the rights of Americans. We'll be forced to bow in submission before people who make the rules who aren't Americans."

"Wait a minute," I said. "You think the United States government is trying to destroy the United States?"

"It's no secret," he snorted. "The President signed an order to give control of the U.S. Armed Forces to that camel jockey from Egypt, Butros-Butros. America as we know it is being threatened. A New World Order is forming and we have to be prepared."

Wasn't this blasphemy in the shadow of our "Shrine to Democracy?"

"How are you going to prepare?"

"If America is to be saved, it will be by the Christian Scriptures. It tells us in Matthew: 24, 'When you see the abomination of desolation, which was spoken of by Daniel the prophet, stand in the holy place, then let them which be Judee's flee into the mountains.' *We* are the true Israelites. *We* are the persecuted, and I'm taking my family to the promised land."

"The promised land?" It sounded more like Lebensraum.

"Almost Heaven. We're on our way to join the Aryan Nations in Idaho. Bought five acres in the panhandle. I've got to get my children away from all of these Jews, niggers, communists and faggots. They're in it together—trying to drag us down. But I ain't gonna let it happen. If any one of them steps foot on my land, they'll be sorry. When the end comes down here, they better not come running up my mountain. I'll blow their fuckin' heads off."

I stood dumbfounded, trying to make sense of his words. I could not. The only thing of which I was certain was that I had had enough of his jingoist blather. There is only so much Neo-Nazi rhetoric one can take before breakfast.

Gazing at the children, I shook my head and rolled Betsy onto the road. Throwing my left leg over the bike, I turned back to the family standing in the drizzle by the side of the road. The words came out in a whisper as light as the mist that fell around us. "I pity you."

Two miles down 385, Crazy Horse Mountain came into view. From the road it appeared little more than a horses head painted on a rock face with a hole carved out above it. A massive pile of scree suggested a work in progress, but only with imagination could one picture the great warrior on horseback pointing into the distance.

It is only with imagination that one can picture Crazy Horse at all. Afraid of losing his soul to the whites, he refused to be photographed. No chromographic image exists of the legendary brave whose fearlessness led him to ride into battle naked, believing from a vision he received at age thirteen, that he would never die in combat. Without so much as a snapshot to reveal his flesh and bones, his image has become larger than life.

Initiated on June 3, 1948 by sculptor Korczak Ziolkowski, only the face—an artists rendition—is scheduled for completion by the year 2000. The Crazy Horse Mountain brochure claims, "weather and financing uncertainties make it impossible to project when the entire carving might be completed." In the meantime, the Ziolkowski family goes on collecting five dollars from each visitor who enters the complex which includes an Indian Museum, theater, gift shop, restaurant and marble Crazy Horse 1/300th scale of the mountain carving. Wondering what the great warrior himself would think, I rode on.

Further down the parkway lay The Fort. "Best View of Crazy Horse. Free Parking." Again I passed. The absence of breakfast had my stomach grumbling, and I pushed on to Custer City. A man on a mission, not even the PeeWee Van Family, Hillbilly-Style, Mountain Music Show ("Lots of music and clean family fun!") could stop me. Custer or bust!

"Why, sometimes," the White Queen said to Alice beyond the looking glass, "I've seen as many as six impossible things before breakfast." I felt I could say the same.

Drizzle became shower as I hit the outskirts of town, but my spirits refused to be dampened. With a wide main street and plenty of "All-U-Can-Eat" restaurants, it's the ideal place for a long distance cyclist. The bonanza had not run out of Custer with the last of the gold. Having to stake a claim on just one establishment was a daunting task, but one I had to make quickly. My stomach growled in protest as I mulled it over.

With a lack of patrol cars to make the decision easy, the choice would have to be based on character. In this category, one restaurant stood alone. Above the swinging saloon-style doors of Ju-Dee's Cafe hung a plaque: "Site of the saloon where James Fowler alias Fly Speck Billy murdered Abe Barnes in Feb. 1881." As the story goes, Billy was hanged by an angry mob, shot twice—setting him on a 'fast freight to Hell—left swinging overnight, and dumped the next morning in a mine shaft near French Creek. I hitched Ol' Betsy to a post and swaggered in.

A row of vinyl-topped stools paralleled the long counter to the right of the swinging doors. A gray-haired man wearing blue coveralls sat at the far end, sipping coffee and reading the paper. Another man—younger and sporting a beard—sat closer to the center. The sight of a stack of pancakes on his plate made my mouth water. And their smell...carbohydrate heaven.

Taking a seat between the two men, but not too close to either (I would need plenty of elbow room), I picked up the menu and looked it over. "Buttermilk pancakes: 3 for $2, 5 for $3, All-You-Can-Eat for $4." For a budget minded traveler, the choice was clear.

A friendly waitress with dyed hair and long, red fingernails took my order. Her name tag said Verlie. She smiled and called me "Honey" (Yes!).

"It'll be a few minutes. The grill is broke so we gotta fry 'em up in a pan two at a time."

"No problem," I lied. Maybe this wasn't the right place after all.

Waiting impatiently, I gazed into the long mirror hanging on the wall behind the counter. Was it the same that had seen the likes of Abe Barnes and James Fowler? Had Fly Speck Billy gazed at his own dirty, unshaven mug as I did. Before earning myself an equally sordid nickname, I headed for the bathroom. A quick scrub in the sink helped, but only marginally.

The first pair of buttermilk pancakes awaited my return. Spreading a pat of butter and drowning them in syrup, I dug in, so driven by hunger that I didn't even mind the doctored-up corn syrup laced with artificial maple flavor I would normally avoid. Once you've been to the top, it's hard to settle for less.

A syrup connoisseur, yes. A syrup snob, never. I laid my discriminating taste aside and devoured stack after stack of light, fluffy pancakes. Coming slowly in installments of two, it was an hour before I began to feel their presence. I'd lost count, but Verlie apparently hadn't. "Hoowee," she exclaimed. "You sure can eat a lot for such a small feller. That's a dozen right there. How do you stay so slim?"

"I guess riding does it."

"Just ridin' your bike and you can eat like that? I gain weight just looking at the food. Put on half a pound just *watching* you eat."

"It's just a matter of burning off more calories than you take in."

"Believe me honey, I've heard it all before, and there ain't nothin' that's worked. I tried Weight Watchers, Slimfast, Nutri-System...you name it. Just ain't fair."

"Have you tried an exercise program?"

"Get real, darlin'. I work a ten hour day and when I get home it's time for a nice warm bath and a drink. I ain't got time for that."

I nodded, pretending to understand. "Now I suppose," she asked looking at my empty plate, "you're ready for more?"

"Yes Ma'am...And give my compliments to the chef."

Moments later, a man appeared in the doorway at the end of the counter. He stepped out of the kitchen and walked slowly toward me with another pair of flapjacks. Grease stains covered his white apron, and beads of sweat clung to his brow. "This is it," he said, punctuating the statement by dropping the plate on the counter.

"But the menu said, 'All-U-Can-Eat."

"Son, that *is* all *you* can eat."

With a full belly and an empty agenda, I had time to see what Custer had to offer. The County Courthouse Museum would make a good start. Standing at the west end of Main Street, it's Italianate architecture sets it apart from other buildings in town. Made of local brick, the museum was built as a courthouse in 1881—eight years before South Dakota became a state. For ninety-two years it held trials for crimes ranging from cattle rustling and horse thieving, to drunk driving and grand theft auto. In 1973, a new courthouse was built and the museum began to take shape.

At the top of a dozen wide granite stairs, a faded sign hung from one of a pair of heavy, oak doors: "Museum Hours: 10 -5." No other information was given regarding days, months, seasons or years. As open-ended as history itself, the museum was appropriately unabridged.

A tiny woman seated in a folding chair beside a card table greeted me. Her wrinkled face held a history of its own. Etched across her forehead and around her dimming eyes, deep lines attested to the years they had seen. Using her cane, she pulled herself to a standing position. She spoke slowly and deliberately. "Welcome to the Custer County Courthouse Museum and Bookstore." She paused to take a piece of paper from the card table. Her hand trembled slightly as she handed it to me.

"This is our brochure. In the room across the hall, you'll find displays of native birds and animals as well as a collection of rocks and minerals. There is also a replica of a mine shaft to explore. The next room contains antique tools used in local industry. It also has photographs taken during the Custer Expedition. Upstairs you'll find the old court room, Judges Chambers and Jury Room. Also upstairs are the Ranch Room, Forestry Room and the old Schoolroom. The basement houses the Custer County Jail as it has for over one hundred years. Although no vicious criminal was ever held here, the steel bars have detained a number of lesser offenders. Do you have any questions?"

"No," I responded, amazed at her recitation. "Thank you."

"Enjoy the museum and please sign our guest book before you leave."

"I will."

As promised, the first room contained the flora, fauna and geology of Custer County. Stuffed birds perched eternally on wooden stands, while a bobcat held an endless, silent growl. Rows of rocks were neatly arranged on wide shelves inside glass cases, their once carefully affixed labels yellowed and peeling. The bottom of the case was littered with those that had already given in to time.

The next room, "Local Industry," held tools of the logging, mining and farming trades: two man saws, a grist mill, corn planters, gold pans, an ox yoke, drills, hammers and square nails. Wood clamps, planes, lathes, mallets, buck saws, sharpening stones and a handmade wooden water pipe; the tools that built Custer. Hundreds of men spent thousands of hours carving it out of the wilderness while the man whose name it bears never came closer than three miles away.

Upstairs in the Forestry Room, among long crosscut saws and double-bladed axes, a crosscut from a 326 year old tree covered most of one wall. It's growth rings were used as a concentric time line, giving a history of significant events which occurred between it's germination in 1596 and its untimely death at the hands of lumberjacks in 1920: 1620 - Pilgrims; 1706 - B. Franklin born; 1732 - G. Washington born; 1776 - Declaration of Independence; 1809 - A. Lincoln born; 1843 - First Telegraph; 1861 - Civil War; 1897 - Black Hills Nat'l Forest.

"Don't grow 'em like that no more," came a voice from behind me.

I turned from the massive tree cookie to face an elderly gentleman in blue jeans and a red flannel. A spry seventy-four year-old, Walter Duncan did not appear a day over sixty. Only a slight limp gave any indication that he had suffered the ravages of time.

"We'll never see trees like that again in these hills."

"Why not?"

"You'll get a different answer from almost anyone you ask, but I suppose it boils down to quotas."

"Quotas?"

"Gettin' the cut out."

"I don't understand."

"Each year Congress mandates the sale of a certain amount of timber from public lands. It's measured in board feet. You heard of that?"

I nodded.

"Well, each National Forest has to produce a certain number of board feet to meet it's quota. Forests are managed so that trees are harvested in cycles. They're only allowed to grow for fifty or sixty years, not 300. You can get an idea from these old photos how different these hills used to be."

"And I thought some of the trees I've been seeing are big. To think how much denser the forest used to be."

"Not denser. There are actually more trees in the Black Hills now than when Custer arrived. Years of fire suppression have lead to a forest that many think is unhealthy—small, even-aged stands. They see a need cutting and clearing sections with controlled burns. Meanwhile, you got people who don't want to see any cutting at all. It's a sore subject for loggers and mill workers who feel their jobs are threatened."

"Do a lot of people make a living those ways?"

"Not as many as in the old days. But to be honest, more of that has to do with mechanization than anything else. Despite an increase in timber production on federal lands over the last twenty years, employment in the industry has declined. Automation and the export of raw logs have caused the loss of more jobs than limiting access to public lands. Mechanized feller-bunchers can can cut a tree, limb it, clip it to length and load it onto a truck, displacing sixteen loggers in the process. Volume is up at the mills, but jobs are down due to computerization. Very little of the profits go into hiring or wages."

"Where does the money go?"

"Stockholders. Most of 'em never set foot in the woods. They don't know the first thing about forest ecology let alone logging: hefting a thirty pound chainsaw up a twenty percent grade; breathing the fumes as it cranks uncooperatively to life; drinking cheap coffee from a battered thermos. If you're lucky you lose a few fingers. If you're unlucky you lose your job."

"It's a hard life."

"You bet. Contrary to popular opinion, loggers are not necessarily the bad guys. Sure there are those who couldn't give a damn about much of anything, but they are far outnumbered by those simply suffering from misinformation.

"Loggers don't wake up before dawn and spend their days outdoors in all types of weather because it'll make them rich. They don't expose themselves to the rigor and danger of the job because of a benefit package with stock options. It's long hours of back-breaking work day in and day out. A logger has got to love the woods, love his place in them. There is a certain sense of accomplishment and pride that comes from being a part of a process that turns living trees into houses, furniture, newspapers. It's a kind of magic."

"So if loggers and environmentalists both love the woods, why can't they agree on how to treat it?"

"All most loggers know is what the industry tells them. A drowning man will grab any rope he's thrown and ask questions later about who's pulling him in. Most are convinced that the enemy is not automation, but soft-bellied environmentalists and laws like the Endangered Species Act. Timber jobs were disappearing long before the northern spotted owl was protected, yet it's become a symbol of the controversy."

"I heard that protecting the spotted owl has cost thousands of jobs."

"Maybe so, but that still pales in comparison to the number of layoffs caused by automation. A simple ban on the export of raw logs would create more jobs than those lost due to protecting endangered species."

"But what if logging in spotted owl habitat is all the economy a town has?"

"Everyone knows you shouldn't put all your eggs in one basket. Look here at Custer. When gold was discovered down at French Creek in 1874 it didn't take long for the news to travel. Before you knew it, the rush was on. Custer was settled the following summer and by '76 the population was over 5,000.

"But it was a matter of time before the pans were comin' up empty, and a big strike up north later in '76 sent folks running. The population of Custer fell to fourteen almost overnight. That's what a narrow economy can do."

"How did Custer rebound?"

"Slowly. Logging at first, and then tourism. The population is up to about 2,000 year-round residents now, but we only approach the days of '76 at the peak of tourist season.

"There's plenty of employment during the summer, but most of it dries up after Labor Day. The Chamber of Commerce will spend hundreds of dollars on glossy brochures, but those don't do much for a young couple on food stamps in the middle of January. I don't know whether I'd call it resentment, but I'd say there's a healthy skepticism about the tourist industry. Folks around here don't much trust outsiders, the federal government and especially environmentalists."

After visiting the museum store and writing a brief message in the guest book, I walked back down toward Ju-Dee's. A sign hanging in the window of a hardware store caught my eye. The "Heart of the Hills Logging Show" promised events ranging from axe and pole throwing to choker setting and even a Jack and Jill crosscut. At the bottom, in bold letters, it announced a new attraction, "Spotted Owl Trap Shoot."

Chapter 12

Whoopee ti yi yo, git along little dogies
It's your misfortune, and none of my own
Whoopee ti yi yo, git along little dogies
For you know Wyoming will be your new home.
—Cowboy Song

By late afternoon, my digestive tract was still working overtime, but I was tired of wandering aimlessly through souvenir shops. The Black Hills Trading Post, Custer Gift Shop, and Dakota Dan's became a blur of t-shirts, ashtrays, shot glasses and coasters all saying, "Custer, South Dakota." As John Highfeather had told me, "The only Sioux left in the Black Hills are Souvenirs."

A steady rain fell from a slate gray sky, but I had to get back on the road. Before leaving, I put in a quick call to a friend in Lander, Wyoming. A familiar voice greeted me on the other end.

"Where are you?" asked Michelle.

"Custer, South Dakota. I came down from Mount Rushmore this morning."

"Custer? Did you go to the Black Hills Holy Land?"

"No, but I stopped along the road and met an interesting family. I'll tell you about it later. Listen, I'm headed your way. Can I crash at your place?"

"Of course, but I'm going away this weekend. If you can get here by Friday night, I'll cook dinner. Any requests?"

We both knew the answer—her famous bean burritos.

"Friday night, huh? That gives me two and a half days. Do you think I can make it?"

"It's about 250 miles."

Despite what I had promised myself, I set a goal. If you've ever had Michelle's burritos you'd understand why.

On the outskirts of Custer, I passed the last of the great Rushmore area attractions, but the National Museum of Woodcarving and Flintstone's Bedrock City garnered little more than side wards glances. I was far more concerned with the large orange sign ahead. "Construction - Bumpy Road Next twenty miles." Yabba Dabba Doo!

The road surface alone may have been tolerable, but in conjunction with the hills and a steady rain, it began to effect my mood. My jersey was soon drenched, and by the time I reached Jewel Cave National Monument, my shoes and socks had joined it. My feet felt as cold and damp as the extensive limestone caverns underlying this section of the hills. My toes squished with every pedal stoke. It was all of the miserable rides I'd ever done rolled into one. Like flies on a windshield, unpleasant memories pelted my thoughts. It took a state line to change my state of mind.

All at once the rain ceased, the construction ended, and level grasslands spread out before me. "Wyoming—Like Nowhere Else on Earth."

It's been said that Wyoming is just one big small town with very long streets. So long, in fact, that it leads the nation in motor vehicles per capita (there are actually more of them than there are state residents), as well as miles driven per person. A special driver's license is issued to fourteen and fifteen year-olds for the sole purpose of traveling to and from school. With a human population of 465,000 (roughly equal to the number of pronghorn antelope) spread over 97,800 square miles, Wyoming is not only the least densely populated state in the nation, its the least populated. Fifty miles to the southwest, Lost Springs (Population 4)—the smallest incorporated town in America—gives new meaning to what most consider rural living.

With the clouds gone, my spirit returned. Large, purple coneflowers grew along the side of the road. The indigo flash of a male bluebird caught my eye. A pair of industrious nuthatches flitting about the base of a tree. A feisty blackbilled magpie—refusing to be ignored—called loudly from its perch on a naked branch.

Wherever the mountains meet the plains, an extensive variety of birds can be found. More than ninety species have been recorded along the western edge of the Black Hills, including two kinds of hawks, bald and golden eagles, prairie falcons, turkey vultures, and American kestrels. Ground dwellers include prairie chickens, pheasants and grouse.

Drivers along this stretch of road, however, seemed to have their minds less on Audubon and more on *Autobahn*. An abundance of roadkill indicated a large population of prairie dogs flourished (and perished) at the edge of the hills. Underground colonies of the tan-colored rodents stretched across much of the borderland I crossed that afternoon. Their high-pitched "barks" announced my coming to those further west. Although most retreated into their burrows when I got near, one brave soul stood his ground alongside a fallen comrade on the opposite shoulder. His black-tipped tail wagged up and down and he let out a series of chirps as I passed—as if crying out in anger and sorrow. Looking for someone to blame.

Beyond a series of signs claiming I must see the "Famous Hand-Dug Oil Well," I passed through the intersection of Routes 16 and 85 and into Newcastle (Population 3003 - Elevation 4334). A coyote's whisker before five o'clock, I pulled into the Chamber of Commerce which doubled as a Visitor Center. A wide banner announced the crowning of a local girl as Miss Rodeo Wyoming. Beside it, another read simply, "Welcome Bikers."

With the clip-clop of a hackney, I scrambled up the rickety steps in my cleated cycling shoes. Bowlegged and saddle sore, I moseyed through the door feeling more like a cowboy than ever. An elderly woman stood up from behind a desk and welcomed me while glancing at the clock on the wall. I told her I wouldn't be long.

Apart from the racks of colorful brochures vying for my attention, a small bulletin board carried news of local services and events. Along with a calendar of events and a handful of business cards, a hand-written sheet of notebook paper instructed prairie dog hunters to report to the USDA regional office next door.

"What's this about prairie dog hunters?" I asked.

She gave me a skeptical look. "You don't want to know about that."

"I do. Honestly, I do."

"Well, if you really want to know, you should go next door to the USDA. They can tell you more than I can. Of course they're closed by now, so I'll do the best I can."

"Thanks."

"I can't remember exactly when it was, but the government stopped distributing strychnine and cyanide. They were having trouble with eagles and ferrets eating the poisoned prairie dogs. The black-footed ferret was thought to be extinct until a handful were found on a rancher's land. A group of biologists collected them up and tried to boost the numbers a little before setting them back on the range. From what I understand, the project has had mixed success. But I'm getting off the topic. You wanted to know about Prairie dogs."

"No, this is fine. It's all connected."

"Yes it is, and isn't it. Anyway, without using poisoned bait, there need to be other ways to control the population."

"Why?"

"Why what?"

"Why do they need to control the population?"

"Because those dogs are a threat to cattle. You get a heifer stepping in one of those holes and she can break an ankle. Besides that, they compete for forage."

"Those tiny critters compete with cattle for food?"

"Sure they do. They did a study on it down at the University."

I nodded.

"Now where was I?"

"Since they don't use poisons anymore..."

"That's right. Since they don't use poisons anymore, a couple of different things are done. Now If you go down around Boulder, Colorado, they've got these giant vacuums that suck the little fellas out of their holes and into a padded cage for relocation. But this is Wyoming. Some folks use traps, but most just shoot them. It's become quite a popular sport. Families will go out for an entire afternoon. Out-of-staters will pay good money. Some folks like to use those bullets that explode on impact, but I think that might be a little much." She glanced back at the clock with its minute hand dangling precariously close to the ten. I was keeping her past quitting time.

I thanked her and apologized in the same breath and headed out the door. It was not until I reached Betsy that I realized I had failed to fill my water bottles and use the rest room. The 4-Way Gas-N-Go across the street handled the liquid exchange, and I was soon headed west on State Route 450.

Anyone looking for a blank spot on the map would find one here. It's been said that Wyoming is where you're a hundred miles from the nearest Post Office, fifty miles from water, twenty-five miles from wood, and six inches from Hell. On this particular evening, I'd say it was even closer to heaven.

With the hills and weather behind me, the sky became half my world. On a distant horizon, the lips of Heaven and Earth met in a passionate embrace. How far away? Twenty miles? Fifty miles? One hundred? No way to tell. Like the future itself, the horizon revealed new and unexpected vistas as I pedaled toward it. Yet all the while, it maintained a mysterious distance, unwilling to reveal too much of what lay ahead.

Despite the name, nary a cumulonimbus billowed over the Thunder Basin National Grassland. The only clouds in sight were those that clung to the cordillera behind me—dissolving into the horizon of my past.

Under clear skies, the low, western sun set the prairie aglow. Yucca, prairie cactus and a dozen species of wildflowers grew among the earth-gray sage. Gooseberry, buffalo berry and chokecherry clung to the shelter of scattered coulees. Lonely junipers dotted the low hills. With the fading light, the prairie's nocturnal residents began to stir—kangaroo rats, coyotes, burrowing owls, night hawks. A light wind held hundreds of square miles of sedges, forbes and grasses in constant motion. Rippling like waves on an open ocean, the Lakota call it "greasy grass."

In just a week, my perspective had matured immensely. No longer did the vast expanses seem dull and monotonous. My eyes found beauty in the subtle nuances of shade and texture. My ears tuned in to the uniquely placid sounds. My nose explored the soft smells of the desert. I inhaled deeply.

The omnipresence of air has always held an uncommonly sacred power among Native Americans. Although invisible, its virtue is felt everywhere, giving life to the land and all its inhabitants. In Lakota tradition, the wind is called *Tate*, and is believed to have been given to the world by *Taku Skanskan*, the Enveloping Sky. A later union between *Tate* and *Ite*, a beautiful Buffalo woman, resulted in the births of the North Wind, the South Wind, the East Wind and the West Wind. These four sacred winds offer direction, personality and meaning to the Lakota people.

Darkness found me somewhere between New Castle and Wright—in the heart of what had once been Crow Country. "Good country," Chief Arapooish had called it in the 1800's, "The Great Spirit has put it in exactly the right place. It is good for horses—and what is a country without horses?...To the north...it is too cold and to the south it is too hot. The Crow country is just right. The water is clear and sweet. There a plenty of buffalo, elk deer, antelope, and mountain sheep. It is the best wintering place in the world..." On this prairie between the Black Hills and the Bighorn Mountains, the great tribe flourished, and on this prairie it nearly perished.

In the summer of 1865, U.S. General Patrick E. Conner began organizing columns of soldiers for an invasion of this region. All Indians north of the Platte River, he claimed, "must be hunted like wolves." His edict was simple. "Attack and kill every male Indian over twelve years of age." In the wake of such policies, and coupled with famine and disease, the population of Native Americans declined from 20 million to 360,000 during the first 350 years of European occupation of the continent.

A luminous quarter moon turned the golden grasses silver, but my thoughts were black.

Chapter 13

*The progress of two years more, if not of another summer, on the
Northern Pacific Railroad will of itself completely solve the great Sioux
problem, and leave the ninety thousand Indians ranging between the
two transcontinental lines as incapable of resisting the Government as
are the Indians of New York or Massachusetts.*
—Francis Walker, Commissioner of Indian Affairs, 1872

*Hear ye, Dakotas! When the Great Father at Washington sent us his
chief soldier to ask for a path through our hunting grounds, a way for
his iron road to the mountains and the western sea, we were told that
they wished merely to pass through our country, not to tarry among us,
but to seek gold in the far west. Our old chiefs thought to show their
friendship and good will, when they allowed this dangerous snake in our
midst...*
*Yet before the ashes of the council fire are cold the Great Father is
building his forts among us. You have heard the sound of the white
soldier's axe upon the Little Piney. His presence here is an insult and a
threat. It is an insult to the spirit of our ancestors. Are we then to give
up their sacred graves to be plowed for corn? Dakotas, I am for war!*
—Red Cloud

*The buffalo hunters have done more to settle the vexed Indian question
than the entire regular army has done, because they are destroying the
Indian's commissary. Indeed, for the sake of lasting peace, let them kill,
skin and sell until the buffaloes are exterminated. Yes, then your prairies
will be covered with your speckled cattle and the festive cowboy.*
—General Philip Sheridan

A long, low roar echoed across the prairie. Thunder Basin, I thought,
was living up to its name. Although the sky was clear, the sound hung
in the air, persisting until a train whistle revealed the secret. A little over
a century ago it was widely held that the iron of the rails and the metal
in telegraph wires altered the natural electrical cycles of arid regions,
bringing increased rainfall. Like many beliefs of the time, it was based
on false hope and crumbled in the face of the Great American Desert.

A mile down Route 450—where steel rails run alongside asphalt—I
got my first look at the train. Like a millipede passing a mite, it seemed
to go on forever. I stopped counting after 100 cars. Rumbling toward
power plants in the Midwest, the locomotive labored across the Wyoming
plains pulling a cargo from the largest open pit mine in the western
hemisphere—Black Thunder.

The massive energy potential underlying eastern Wyoming, and the labor required to realize it, led the Atlantic Richfield Company (ARCO) to build the town of Wright in the late 1970's. With a population of 1,236, the '70s middle-income housing development looked just that. The Mini Mart at the junction of 450 and State Route 59, however, was appropriately up to date. Gatorade and Power Bars would serve as my fuel source for the rest of the morning. I commented on the length of the train to the young woman working the register.

"Shoot, they fill eight or nine of those every day—each a mile long."

"Eight or nine?"

"That's right. They pull a ton of coal per second outta that mine."

Natural gas wellheads and pipeline stations replaced coal silos west of town. Old King Coal wasn't the only royalty around. A sign for Teapot Dome stirred a deeply buried memory from American History class, but it melted under a torturous sun. Road signs and naked buttes shimmered in waves of heat. The landscape swayed.

Hot. Dry. Still. The torrid air hung over me like a quilt on a summer night. My eyes throbbed. My brain baked. Sweat evaporated instantly in the open-air sauna, leaving deposits of salt on my darkening skin.

Early homesteaders claimed summers were so dry that cows gave condensed milk and chickens laid powdered eggs. "The only crop you can raise out here," they claimed, "is taxes." Trees were so rare that a broken man had to walk a hundred miles to hang himself.

Beyond the boundaries of Thunder Basin National Grassland, the land grew drier as I approached the rain shadow of the Continental Divide. It is rugged, honest country, where rainfall averages less than ten inches a year, and the grasses—blue grama and buffalo—turn brown and lay dormant during the driest summer months. It gives what it takes in a precarious balance unfamiliar to one from the humid East.

Between grassland and desert in terms of rainfall, climate and vegetation, the western shortgrass prairie exists in a delicate balance that supports a variety of well adapted animals. Birds, reptiles and small mammals have evolved to coexist in this unforgiving ecosystem without exhausting the resources. Their continued existence has been assured through a series of natural checks and balances such as competition, disease and predators.

Somewhat less adapted to these conditions were the pioneers. It was along these arid stretches of the Oregon Trail where the alkaline water caused many of them to suffer bouts of diarrhea they called the "Relax." Not the definition I had in mind, I pushed on through Pine Tree Junction and Linch toward a proper siesta in Sussex.

Further west, stunted sage replaced the grasses. Ruminants, wild or domestic, would be hard pressed to find even a withered stem. Prairie dogs grew scarce. Green faded to brown and gray. It would take a real guts-and-leather cowboy to raise a steer in these parts. But not long ago his grandfather did—on a grand scale. The abundance of tiny yellow flowers along the roadside told the tale. Broom snakeweed.

Economically useless, the bushy opportunist has moved into overgrazed rangeland throughout the West. Unpalatable, and even somewhat poisonous to livestock, the narrow stalk of the resinous invader is ineffective at retarding erosion. Bare soil around its base is exposed to the full force of wind and rain. The history of recent land use is written in gullies and punctuated by a loss of productivity.

Marginally productive land avoided by the native bison was forced into the service for longhorns the the late 1800's. Stocked at rates far exceeding carrying capacity, the hungry beasts nibbled vegetative cover to the roots, killing the grasses and changing the ecology of the plains.

When cattle are allowed to overgraze perennial native grasses, annual weeds and shrubs begin to disappear. Along with snakeweed, rabbit brush, thistle poppy, sage, and cheatgrass fill the void. With the perennial grasses no longer serving as tinder, fires that once controlled the spread of shrubs no longer occur with the same regularity. The result is degraded range in which the diversity of both flora and fauna is diminished as quality forage becomes scarce for all animals, including cattle. Further overgrazing results in compacted soil over which rainwater runs instead of soaking in, leaving behind a barren landscape etched by gullies. A cycle of flood and drought occurs where a small creek once flowed.

The massive erosion that follows further reduces fertility, while further trampling and tearing by hooves and incisors open the door for weeds to colonize the broken land. With the loss of productivity, previously described "semi-deserts" also lose the prefix. After the turn of the century, fewer and fewer acres were able to support livestock. Historian Vernon L. Parrington referred to the carefree period of exploitation as "The Great Barbecue." The were few leftovers.

A 1992 report estimates that fully one half of rangeland in the U.S. is severely degraded—its carrying capacity reduced by over fifty percent. Semiarid regions of the southwest can generally support a single cow on 100 acres. By contrast, in Georgia it takes one acre.

Many of the hands that once roped cattle in Wyoming have been forced to turn to its vast energy deposits to make a living. Oiljacks have replaced cattle along many roadsides—their mechanical appendages pumping in synchrony. Like giant, steel grasshoppers, their conquest of the Wyoming range rivals the legendary infestation of flesh and blood arthropods the Mormons faced at Salt Lake.

As suddenly as a pop quiz, the sign for Johnson County had me back in American History class. (This one I remembered.) In the early 1890's, powerful cattlemen convinced themselves that small ranchers were building their herds by rustling. Although they had no proof, the cattlemen drew up a list of seventy suspects—including sheriffs and county commissioners—who would feel their wrath. Hiring twenty-five gunmen from Texas, and calling themselves the Invaders, the cattlemen raided the KC Ranch, killing one alleged rustler along with his companion. When the word spread forty miles to Buffalo, another set of men armed themselves and set out to stop the Invaders, but were cut off by federal troops, thus ending Johnson County War with a minimum of casualties. The Invaders stood trial in Cheyenne but were released when key witnesses failed to appear. (It should also be noted that the court could find only eleven men in all of Wyoming it deemed sufficiently free of bias to serve as jurors.)

The town of Sussex baked in the sun below the confluence of Salt Creek and the South Fork of the Powder River. Slightly larger than Wright, its dining options were similarly limited. A man at the gas station where I filled my water bottles told me of a diner in "Casey." It wasn't until I got there—seventeen miles later—that I realized it was actually Kaycee, and I was wrong in thinking he had put the emphasis on the wrong syllable.

The lunch rush at The Roundup was winding down when I arrived. Sunburned families in t-shirts and shorts piled into cars with out of state plates, while men in greasy coveralls stepped into tall pickups. An optimist might describe the seating area as half full, but I saw it more like the western shortgrass prairie I'd ridden through—half empty. I took a stool at the counter and opened the menu.

In the heart of cattle country, beef ruled the menu like a jealous monarch. Token allotments were offered to the Earl of Chicken and the Duke of Pork—confined to the principalities of appetizers and side dishes. King Cow alone reigned in the land of entrees: beef stew, barbecued ribs, t-bone steak, burgers, pot roast, and veal (a young prince). The menu even offered Rocky Mountain oysters which have absolutely nothing to do with seafood. Ordering this "delicacy," is like deciding to have children. The less you know, the more likely you are to try it.

Men, women and children munched happily on the flesh of former Wyoming residents. Desperately hungry, I settled for a grilled cheese sandwich from the "Kiddie Menu," fries, and a glass of iced tea.

The waitress looked at me skeptically. "You're not one o' them vegetarians, are ya?"

"When you call me that, smile."

She gave me a sidelong glance and headed to the kitchen.

Waiting for my meal, I noticed a pair of well-dressed men enter and adopt a booth near the front window. The handsome duo had fallen from the pages of GQ and landed in the middle of Wyoming. Their wool suits and silk ties were as out of place as shit-caked boots on Wall Street.

Curiosity forced me into an empty booth next to theirs. Like joining a regularly scheduled program already in progress, it took a few minutes to catch up with the characters and plot. As the conversation continued, it became apparent that they were a pair of lawyers from Denver on their way to Billings, Montana to meet with a group of angry ranchers about the "wolf issue," as they put it.

"It's not right to force these men to accept the very menace their forefathers worked so hard to remove."

"Absolutely. They've lost their right to protect their property. Under the current law, they can't kill a wolf even if it's going after their cattle. There's not a damn thing they can do about it."

"Yet."

"Yet."

Their job, as I understood it, was to develop a legal case proving wolves were a menace to society. The goal—to rid the region of wolves for a second time.

Government-sponsored extermination campaigns began in the late nineteenth century and continued until the 1930's when the wolf had essentially been eliminated from the lower forty-eight states. With insidious precision, wolves were shot, poisoned, burned alive, and even dragged behind horses. Their carcasses adorned fenceposts from Brownsville, Texas to Bonners Ferry, Idaho. Until recently, federal bounties were offered on their heads.

But with an about-face not untypical of Washington, the gray wolf was listed as endangered in 1974. A team of biologists began considering their reintroduction that same year. Backed by overwhelming popular support and millions of federal dollars, in January of 1995 the U.S. Fish and Wildlife Service released twenty-nine Canadian wolves into Yellowstone National Park and a wilderness area in north central Idaho. Similar releases were planned over the next four years, but not if these legal eagles had anything to do with it.

Their view is not one of an ecosystem restored after years of nonfulfillment, but a life or death struggle between good and evil. Ignoring the fact that in Alberta, Canada—where wolves roam freely— the predatory rate of cattle is close to .001 percent, the law school graduates in the next booth saw removal as the only option. Having passed the bar, their next step was to raise it.

"We'll take this to the Supreme Court if we have to. There's plenty of precedent."

"Do you think so?"

"Of course. Keep in mind that Wyoming's House has already passed legislation that puts a bounty on wolves, and creates a defense fund for anyone caught killing one. And Montana has approved a provision requiring federal agents to seek written permission from county sheriffs before investigating crimes within their jurisdiction."

"That's right. And Idaho, Utah and Arizona have established 'Constitutional Defense Councils' to challenge federal laws that conflict with state interests."

"I'd say Little Red Riding Hood is about to kick some ass."

By the time they left, I was the lone customer at the Roundup. I had nibbled away at most of the fries, but my grilled cheese sandwich had grown cold. I ordered another iced tea and opened my journal.

A sprinkling of customers came and went throughout the afternoon, but when the early dinner crowd began filtering in, I took it as a signal to leave. I pointed Betsy west and rode a short mile to the I-25 overpass. Although I had planned on taking State Route 190—which was mostly a dirt road—to Waltman, and then U.S. 26 to Lander, an alternative presented itself as I looked down at the smooth, wide shoulder of the Interstate. Although a river of traffic flowed beneath me, the right bank offered plenty of space. Even if the cars ran as thick as spawning salmon, I would be well away from the frenzy.

Although a sign on the entrance ramp stated clearly that bicycles were prohibited, I was willing to take the chance. The short cut would put me that much closer to Michelle's burritos. With the confidence of an experienced river guide, I pedaled down the entrance ramp. It would be a cinch—like going over the falls in a barrel.

The ticketing officer pulled me over five miles south of the on ramp. The lights of his cruiser remained flashing as the trooper stepped out and walked back to where I stood with Betsy between my legs. Tall and well-built, the struggling buttons on the front of his uniform gave only the slightest hint that the donuts were taking their toll. He wore sunglasses despite an overcast sky. His boots did the talking as he approached.

Stopping at my side, he spoke through a solemn face. "License and registration."

What? Was this guy kidding? Despite my better judgment, I let my natural tendency toward sarcasm take over. "I'm sorry officer, this is an unregistered vehicle."

"So we got a joker here?" He removed the sunglasses and furrowed his brow. "Are you aware that it is illegal to operate a non-motorized vehicle on the Interstate Highway System?"

"No sir," I lied.

"Did you see the sign explaining this where you got on?"

"No sir," I lied again.

"Do you know the fine for non-compliance?"

"No sir." Finally the truth.

"Seventy...five...dollars," he said in a tone as rigid as the stick up his ass.

I swallowed hard. Kiss up time.

"Gee, I'm really sorry officer, but I got a late start this morning and had some catching up to do. I was just going to get off at this next exit anyway. I tell you what, I'll get off here and promise not to ride on the interstate any more. How's that?"

I could tell he was enjoying this. A cheek muscle twitched, and he almost broke a smile. Almost. Keeping his composure, Stone Face brought the uncooperative nerve under control with clinical precision. He answered with cold pleasure, "I'm sorry but I'm bound by the badge I wear to issue you a citation. Identification, please."

"What if I don't have any?"

"Then I'll impound your bike, and take both of you down to the station."

"Just wondering," I quipped, fishing my wallet out of a side pocket of a pannier.

He carried my New Hampshire license back to his patrol car, and returned it to me minutes later along with a ticket for seventy...five...dollars.

"I'll escort you to the exit," he said, turning away once more.

His flashing lights led me the final half mile along I-25 and up the ramp of exit 249—anything but the police escort I believed I'd receive one day.

Chapter 14

At night in this waterless air the stars come down just out of reach of your fingers. In such a place lived the hermits of the early church piercing to infinity with uninhibited minds. The great concept of oneness and of majestic order seems always to be born in the desert.
—John Steinbeck

Plan B.

According to the map, a "Graded or Earth Road" led south and west for twenty miles to Waltman and U.S. 26. I've ridden lousy roads, but this one took the biscuit. Ruts, washboard, rocks and loose sand—the silk ribbon of the exit ramp deteriorated into a tattered corduroy rag. Flash floods had torn the road in places, requiring me to dismount and wheel Betsy across. Although "Earth" was an accurate description for this track, in terms of a grade I'd give it a generous D-.

The sun fell rapidly over the Bighorn Mountains. Cool shadows swept down from the ridge. A nighthawk patrolled for its supper.

Within a half-hour darkness settled over central Wyoming like a cloak of twill. Navigating the road was as difficult as double-stitching in the dark. I pulled off and called it a day.

Still too warm to get inside my sleeping bag, I spread it over the dry ground and laid on top, looking up at the sky. Star light, star bright, first star I see tonight, I wish I may, I wish I might, make this wish come true tonight.

From one, came two, then three, four, five, ten, twenty, fifty, hundreds, thousands. Too many to count.

The familiar summer constellations took their places beside a waxing gibbous moon, but I noticed a pair I hadn't picked out before. Stretching east of Bootes, south of Hercules, and north of Scorpius, Serpens, the Snake, and Ophiuchus, the Snakebearer filled their corner of the night sky. So intertwined are these constellations, it's difficult to see where one ends and the other begins. The secret of any good snake handler is to maintain contact at all times so as not to allow the serpent room to strike. There may be *old* snakebearers and there may be *bold* snakebearers, but there are no *old, bold* snakebearers.

I redirected my gaze toward the circumpolar constellations: Ursa Major, Ursa Minor, Cephus, Cassiopeia, Draco and Camelopardalis. Revolving around the North Celestial Pole, these six clusters are not only visible year round, but also throughout each night. While other constellations rise and set like the sun and moon, these never dip below the horizon, but simply rotate around Polaris at fifteen degrees per hour. Long before wrist watches, cowboys used this heavenly clockwork to monitor the passage of time. The Big Dipper's nightly circumvolution of the north star remains as regular as any hour hand. Far into the next millennium, the pointer stars at the tip of the dipper's bowl will reliably clock the hours between sunset and sunrise.

Outside of the forty-two-degree circle in which the circumpolar constellations reside, a million other stars fought for my attention. Bright or faint, flickering or constant, they sparkled against the night like brilliant, white diamonds.

When I awoke the next morning, I was still seeing diamonds, albeit not as brilliant and not as white. They were black, but not the kind you'd ski. These gems belonged to a western diamond back rattlesnake that lay half visible beneath the far end of my sleeping bag. Tightly coiled, its patterned scales rose and fell with each breath the serpent took. I could just see the horny segments of its tail laying flat at the center of the coil. Its head remained hidden somewhere beneath the bag. Although it had been dark when I bedded down, surely I had not settled on top of a rattlesnake. It must have located itself there sometime during the cool desert night.

Cold-blooded creatures, reptiles rely on external sources for warmth. Whether it's a sun-baked rock, a stretch of blacktop, or in my case, a warm body, snakes seek such places to spend their dormant hours. While rattlers can tolerate low temperatures, they prefer to be warm. From southern Canada to Mexico, rattlesnakes are active only when the sun is high enough to activate their metabolism. As night falls, they become sluggish and seek shelter in nearly any nook or cranny.

One would think that such reclusive behavior would limit the number of snake-man encounters, but a sufficient number of incidents during our nation's westward expansion prompted a cry for the eradication of these venomous vermin. Growing up to eight feet long and with fangs loaded with poison, they became the embodiment of Eden's great serpent. They were seen as pure evil by European settlers while traditional Native Americans revered them as messengers from the spirit world. The legless ones were treated with respect and never hunted or killed. It was believed that if you kill a rattlesnake, two will take its place. If those are killed, still more will come until eventually the abundance of snakes will drive a person insane.

One was all it took for me. Aware that snakes are sensitive to the slightest movement, I tried to remain still—a task which became increasingly difficult as the sun rose and warmed me beyond comfort. Already nervous, the addition of ultraviolet rays had me sweating bullets inside the bag. Droplets of water formed on my forehead and trickled into my ears. Like a caterpillar trapped inside its cocoon, I was unable to emerge and fly to freedom.

The rising sun did, however, hold one promise. The sooner it warmed my reptilian friend, the sooner he'd be on his way. Thus began the waiting game.

But patience has never been my strong point. Lacking the snake handling skills of Ophiuchus, I hatched an alternative plan. With two inches of loft in my bag, the chances were slim that the snake could bite all the way through it. If I flipped my legs up and rolled quickly out of range, I might be able to escape .

All right, one, two...wait. I stalled at the critical moment. Try again.

All right, one, two...wait. I stalled again, overcome by a feeling of eminent doom—the familiar sense of dread one feels when about to dive into cold water.

I glanced toward Betsy for motivation and noticed a shoe laying beside her on the ground. The patented "swoosh" on its side conjured up three simple words: JUST DO IT. (Michael Jordan would be paid millions to do a commercial like this.)

With a grunt, a twist, and a lunge, I was free. After the moment of fury, all was silent save for a menacing rattle. In a strange twist of nature, rattlesnakes produce this sound as a warning despite the fact that they are completely deaf. Like Beethoven at the end of his career, they are unable to hear their own symphony. At a safe distance, I watched the viper settle and slither off into the brush.

With a long day ahead, I was already behind. Packing went quickly—the transition from bag to saddle took less than ten minutes. Although the dirt road made for slow going, I didn't mind. Coming off a 110 mile day, my legs enjoyed the easy pace. But the road's condition deteriorated as I made my way deeper into the foothills of the Bighorn Mountains. The ridge line towered above me to the west—a sierra illuminated by the low, morning sun. A cloudless sky prepared me for another hot one. With no town or services for twenty-five miles, I was on my own. A bottle and a half of water bounced along on the bike below me—it would be enough to make it to Arminto long before the hottest part of the day. Nothing could stop me...except a fork in the road.

I coasted to a stop and took out the map. Through experience, I'd become a fair judge of distance when traveling at normal speeds on paved roads, but this was different. Thoroughly confounded by slow progress in unfamiliar terrain, I was reluctant to hazard a guess. My watch read 8:50—a little over an hour in the saddle. Perhaps ten miles, but probably less. Matching topographic features to the map was my only option. Assuming the rise to my left was Roughlock Hill, the map indicated I should take the right fork and continue twenty miles to Arminto. Even a worst case scenario would put me there well before noon.

That scenario began to take shape ten minutes later when I reached the next fork. Rechecking the map revealed nothing new. On paper there was still only one junction. As I recalled, it was also on paper that the Black Hills were set aside for the "absolute and undisturbed use of the Great Sioux Reservation," and that nearly all of my riding thus far had been through land where "No persons...shall ever be permitted to pass over, settle upon, or reside...without consent of the Indians." With little reason to think otherwise, Red Cloud signed the Fort Laramie Treaty believing what was on the paper much in the same way I once believed Superman could fly, Garfield could talk, and a little boy named Calvin was continually outwitted by a stuffed tiger that came to life whenever his mother wasn't around. Experience has taught us otherwise.

I finished the water from the bottle in the cage beneath me and reached back to where I kept the spares only to find that step two of the worst case scenario had taken place. While the empty bottle remained strapped firmly under a bungee cord, the full one was nowhere to be found— undoubtedly shaken free by the washboard. Damn!

No telling how far back. Should I go looking? Should I press on? Unsure, I rechecked the map and noticed Deadman Butte.

Looking up, I could see it directly to the south. According to the map, the road to Arminto passed to its west. Reexamining the fork, it clearly offered a western as well as an eastern option. I should have known intuitively which to take.

The name Wyoming comes from the Delaware Indian language, meaning "mountains and valleys alternating." Along the east face of the Bighorns, the road took due notice. Combined with the washboard, the constant climbing and descents left my muscles weary and my joints shaken. Wrists and shoulders were soon as sore as legs.

The town of Chugwater, Wyoming also has a Native American origin. For hundreds of years, plains tribes would round up herds of bison and stampede them off high bluffs in order to ensure a winter food supply. By the hundreds, the great beasts ran in a frenzy to their deaths. The sound of their bodies striking the valley floor made a loud "chug." The nearby stream became known as, "the land where the buffalo chug," or Chugwater. Although the speck of a town I came to that July morning was called Arminto, by the time I left, I had rechristened it with my own meaning of Chugwater. Gulping until it hurt and then filling my bottles, I must have lowered the local aquifer by at least a few feet.

As hydrogen and oxygen diffused throughout my body, I headed south along a paved county road toward Waltman. Like a milkshake having been in a blender all morning, I poured myself onto a smooth ribbon of asphalt.

When I reached Waltman, I turned west onto U.S. 26 and into a headwind. It came in gusts, blowing across the arid landscape. No longer the benevolent *Tate* I had experienced in Thunder Basin, but the unrelenting Boreas of Greek legend—a wind only Beaufort could love. Downshifting, I climbed the invisible hill.

By the time I arrived at the rest area four miles up the road, I recognized the truth as self-evident. There would be no making Lander tonight. The vision of Michelle's thick bean burritos dripping with cheese faded like a mirage. Eighty miles stood between me and the unreachable feast.

As the temperature broke 100, the undeniable broke my spirit. The sun had reached its zenith, while I hit rock bottom. I pulled into the rest area a defeated man—powerless against the forces allied against me.

Chapter 15

[Past Indian policy has] driven an independent and lordly race into the condition of dependents and beggars.... This Nation cannot evade its Christian duty to save them from destruction and elevate them from their degraded barbarous state.... This evil can only be remedied by the selection of some country that shall be set apart for and devoted exclusively to the use and benefit of the Indians.
—Nathaniel Taylor, Commissioner of Indian Affairs

Before the White Man came we had no lawyers, no jails, no banks, no taxes, and no TV. Women did all the work. White Man thought he could improve upon a system like that.
—Indian Poster

"Don't believe everything you read." The voice was as large as the man to which it belonged. His statements were as short as his crewcut. "It's a pipe dream."

"But the plaque says..."

"Propaganda. Liberal clap trap."

Instead of looking below the surface to fuel the latest generation of rest areas, the Wyoming Department of Transportation has found one high above. Passive solar design is being used throughout the state to heat rest rooms and information centers. The plaque explained how the sun-heated structures were not only environmentally sound, but also economically valid—cutting down on both carbon dioxide emissions and expenditures. The U.S. Department of Energy estimates that "500 times more solar energy falls on the United States each year than is produced by all the oil, coal, natural gas and nuclear energy now used to power our nation."

"Get real," he snickered. "We've got enough coal under Wyoming to last 200 years."

"What about pollution?"

"Look up! What do you see? Blue sky! Not pollution, blue sky."

"Sometimes pollution is not so easy to see. Like carbon dioxide..."

"Carbon dioxide?" He exhaled heavily. "It's harmless. No, no, no, it's less than harmless. Plants need it to grow. If we produce more, they'll grow more. It would be like a plant turbo-charger. Look around. We could use more plants around here."

"But increased carbon dioxide in the greenhouse layer could make it even hotter and dryer."

"Don't give me that bullshit."

"Bullshit?"

"Yeah. It's a theory. It's not proven. I'm talkin' real jobs and real money,

77

not some imaginary global warming. We burn a billion tons of coal a year in this country. It's a multi-billion industry. You take that away and you'll ruin the Wyoming economy."

"Some say the damage from climate change could be even worse."

"I'm not talkin' some imaginary future, I'm talkin' today. I'm talkin' people and paychecks...and you can take that to the bank." He turned and walked to his 4 x 4 truck. The engine roared to life and he sped away.

Less than ten miles from "Hell's Half Acre," I reclined on a thick bed of healthy turf. The irrigated patch of Kentucky Bluegrass was an island of green within a sea of ocher, umber and sienna. Like the common cartoon portrayal of a desert island, a lone tree grew in its center. And like the ragged-looking man in the comic, I leaned against it with the appropriately hopeless look on my face.

If only, like Captain Marvel just a few strips away, I could merely utter the magical word, "Shazam," and have all at once the strength of Hercules, the courage of Achilles, the power of Zeus, the stamina of Atlas, the wisdom of Solomon and the speed of Mercury. At that point, I'd settle for Mercury and Atlas.

Gazing south at the Rattlesnake Range, I ate peanut butter sandwiches in the shade of my lonely tree. I tried to forget both the morning's reptilian encounter and the fact that I'd never make it to Lander by suppertime. With great concentration I might have erased the thought from my mind, but no matter how many PB & Js I ate, my stomach would not forget. Pulling out my journal, I set my alimentary grief to paper.

"Howdy." The voice came from behind a pair of dark sunglasses and under a broad-brimmed Stetson. Two days stubble covered his strong jaw, and a cigarette hung from the corner of his mouth. It was the Marlboro Man.

"You got some huevos ridin' a bike in this heat."

"It's not the temperature so much as the wind."

"Yes sir. I could feel it gustin' against my truck. Where you headin'?"

"Well, the plan was to get to Lander tonight, but I don't think that's gonna happen."

"I'm goin' as far as Riverton if it would help. We can throw your bike in the back."

Like a cartoon character in a struggle of conscience, a small angel alit on my right shoulder while a devil flashed onto my left. The angel spoke for my heart, urging me to cover the miles on my own power while the devil did the stomach's dirty work. "Burritos," he whispered. "Melted cheese. Salsa." Torn for a moment, I wondered if I'd regret the ride. What about accomplishment? A sense of pride?

Maybe so, but at the moment I wasn't proud, just hungry. "Thanks, that'd be great."

His name was Chris Rogers and his truck was as large as his persona. Bright red and shining in the sun, the new Chevy could make even a loyal Ford owner turn his head. Two rifles hung in the rear window. A radar detector lay on the dashboard. He wasn't afraid to use either.

Eighty miles per hour arrived in the blink of an eye—a striking contrast to fifteen. Sage became a bristly blur, roadkill nondescript. The relative wind speed against the truck must have been over 100 mph, but I hardly noticed from the comfort of the cab.

Road signs in most western states are printed with larger than normal letters to allow extra reading time when traveling at high speeds. Even so, I had trouble catching them all. I scribbled frantically in my journal as we sped along: Hiland, Population 27, Elevation 5,998; Moneta, Population 10, Elevation 5,428; Shoshoni, Population 497, Elevation 4,820. They may as well have been Podunk, East Podunk and West Podunk, but I wanted to get the numbers right.

"Was that 497 and 4,820 for Shoshoni, or 487 and 4,920?"

"I doesn't really matter. You can always tell you're in Wyoming when the elevation is higher than the population."

And he ought to know. Rogers was Wyoming back four generations. His great grandparents started a ranch around the turn of the century. "About 4,000 acres. My grandparents worked it through the thirties, forties and fifties, and my mother and father since then. I'm next."

"It's what I've always wanted to do, ever since I can remember. It's a hell of a lot of work—up before sunrise, down after dark—but I love it. It's in my blood."

Somewhat tentatively, I brought up the issue of overstocking and degradation.

"When you come right down to it, this is grazing land. It was that way with the buffalo before we even came along. That's what it's always been. That's what it's meant to be. Open land without cows is a wasted resource. You can't eat scenery."

There was a lull in conversation until Chris pointed out the Wind River Indian Reservation with disapproval in his voice. "Supreme Court decision back in '89 fucked everything up in terms of water rights. Leave it to the Feds."

"What do you mean?"

"You gotta understand, water here is more valuable than land. It's the life blood for ranchers. Ask one anyone around here what he'd take for his water and what he'd take for his land, and nine times out of ten, the water will garner a higher price—often twice as high. Only developers can pay those prices. I heard one over in Utah just bought water rights for ten thousand dollars an acre-foot. No way a rancher can afford that.

"But what do ranchers have to do with the reservation?"

"This 'Res' ain't just Indian. Unlike most, where all the land is tribal, the government opened up parts of this one to homesteaders around the turn of the century. So now you got this checkerboard of land ownership between whites and Indians. The Shoshone and Arapaho have been complaining about it for years."

"So they took it to court?

"The Supreme Court, and the bastards won. They got a bunch of environmentalists and bleeding-heart liberal on their side. Now, in a dry year like this one, they get the water and we get screwed. It's happening to ranchers everywhere. We're the Indians now."

At the junction of U.S. 26 and State Route 789, Chris pulled onto the shoulder. As I climbed out of the cab, he extended his big right hand. It smothered mine.

A sign said "Lander - 24," my watch showed 5:30, and a little voice inside me shouted, "Yahoo!" My grin reached ear to ear. I would make it in time for dinner.

Clearing the confines of fast food restaurants and motels on the outskirts of Riverton, Route 789 winds along Beaver Creek, crossing it twice before setting out alone through the sage-covered mesas.

"Leaving the Wind River Indian Reservation." If only that were true. For thousands of Native Americans, reservation life means many of the same challenges their great grandparents faced 100 years ago: unemployment, alcoholism, and despair. Installation of the reservation system meant the loss of freedom for tribes throughout the nation. Some call it legalized murder, genocide. They see it as a death sentence for an entire race.

Fortunately, the analogy has not been fully realized, although suicide rates among the tribes are the highest in the nation. During the summer of 1985 on this very reservation, nine young men—ages fourteen to twenty-five—killed themselves. For the rest it is merely a life sentence— life on the "Res."

Labeled the "4th World" by some, reservations throughout America are where infant mortality rates compare with those of Africa, where life expectancy is the lowest in the nation, and incidence of suicide the highest. After Nevada—where suddenly penniless gamblers take their lives in moments of despair—Wyoming ranks second in suicides per capita followed by Montana, Arizona, New Mexico and Idaho, all of which have sizable populations of Native Americans.

Reservations are also where homicides—recently due to an increase in gang activity—have risen eighty-six percent over the last five years while the national average has dropped twenty-two percent. They're where diabetes and hypertension—white man's diseases never before found in Indians—are growing problems. They're where child abuse and fetal alcohol syndrome reach epidemic proportions. The most noticeable aspect of the border town of Hudson (Population 392, Elevation 5,094) was the unusual abundance of liquor stores.

I counted four on just the main street before I had cleared the confines of town and headed out over the dry, rolling hills that served as the last barrier before reaching the Lander Valley. Broad fields of alfalfa filled the view clear to the foot of the Wind River Range. Somewhere up there above the wooded slopes of the Bridger-Teton National Forest laid the backbone of America—The Continental Divide.

Admiring the dark eastern slope of the massive ridge, my attention was wrenched back to the immediate surroundings by the pungent smell of death. The air turned foul as the rotting corpse of a pronghorn antelope filled my nostrils. A swarm of flies hovered over the lifeless body like an electron cloud. In a synaesthetic merging of senses, I saw the smell and smelled the site. Gym socks, limberger, raw sewage—all these and more. Indescribable. It persisted long after I had passed. (Be thankful this book does not come with scratch and sniff.)

Not technically an antelope, the western pronghorn has evolved keen eyesight and incredible speed—ideal traits for avoiding predators on the open plains. A recent study at the University of Wyoming revealed the pronghorn rivals the Cheetah as the swiftest land animal on the planet, capable of reaching speeds to sixty miles per hour. How cruel a fate for this Carl Lewis of the animal world to have been struck down by the only thing faster in all the West—a pickup truck. It must have been doing sixty-five.

"Welcome to Lander - Home of the National Outdoor Leadership School." Known most often simply as NOLS, the school is considered the world's premier academy for teaching backcountry safety and minimum impact camping skills. From its headquarters in Lander, NOLS runs thousands of courses out of branches in Arizona, Washington and Alaska as well as in Mexico, Patagonia, Kenya, India and Australia.

As a result, Lander has become a Mecca for wilderness trip leaders. Four-wheel drive Subaru station wagons with climbing stickers on the windows and mountain bikes on top crowded the main street. With according reverence, I bowed my head as I passed the renovated Noble Hotel on Main Street which serves as NOLS headquarters. The lights were off. For the administrators it's a day job.

Chapter 16

There is a numerous class of man who are cast into painful fits of astonishment whenever they find anything, in all God's universe, which they cannot render what they call 'useful' to themselves.
—John Muir

The screen door flew open and through it came a rush of memories. With spoon in hand, she wrapped her arms around me with the kind of hug that takes your breath away. Her petite frame held close to mine. The familiar scent of lilacs rose from her bare neck.

As always with us, I was the first to let go. Michelle smiled. She looked great in her striped apron and running shoes. Besides her cooking skills, Michelle was a forester, rock climber and budding potter—the only woman I knew who looked as natural in work boots and overalls as she did in pumps and a skirt. Carharts or Laura Ashley, she complimented them both.

It's no wonder that a dynamic woman like Michelle ended up in a place like Wyoming, the Equality State—first in the nation (and the world) to allow women to vote in 1889. December 10th is set aside to commemorate the end of suffrage in the state. Leaders in the fight for equal rights are honored and remembered.

Surprisingly, Wyoming lays claim to a number of other significant firsts. It is home of the first national park (Yellowstone, 1872), the first national monument (Devil's Tower, 1906) and the first JC Penney (1902).

"All that's nice," admitted Michelle, "but the real reason I moved here was to have a cowboy on my license plate."

She slipped in a Bonnie Raite CD and I was taken back to a time when we gave 'em something to talk about. I take full responsibility for the break up. Young and foolish, I didn't appreciate her unique qualities. She patient, but eventually her patience wore out. It took her absence to recognize how foolish I had been.

The front door slammed and moments later a long-haired black and white dog entered the kitchen followed by a blond man. They each headed straight for Michelle. She introduced me to her dog, Hueco (pronounced wake-oh), and her boyfriend Dave (pronunciation understood).

"Why don't you take a shower. Dinner will be ready by the time you're done." She handed me a towel and showed me toward the bathroom.

Dried salt from my forehead drained into my eyes, stinging them briefly, but then offering relief to my entire body. Conditioned by a northern climate, I automatically turned the setting to warm, but found a lower temperature far more pleasurable. I lingered under the cool flow for as long as my stomach would allow.

"You about done in there," came a voice through the door. "Dinner's ready."

Enough said. Foregoing a much-needed shave, I dried, dressed, and dashed for the table. It was covered with a bright red cloth and matching napkins. Festive southwestern style dishes were set before each of three high-backed wooden chairs. Wine glasses, water tumblers and miss-matched cutlery rounded out each place setting.

Michelle set a large bowl of Spanish rice at one end of the table while Dave placed salsa and avocados at the other. At the center, a pair of candles flickered beside a white tile within a brown wooden frame. The lone chili pepper glazed upon its surface disappeared beneath an enormous platter of burritos. The rising steam bathed Michelle in an aura of saintliness as she withdrew her mittened hands from the dish.

"Dig in."

For the sake of manners, I took only two to start and used a fork and knife instead of swallowing them whole.

"How's the trip been?" Dave asked across an empty bowl of rice.

"Incredible, but not really what I expected."

"How do you mean?"

"There seem to be a lot of unresolved issues which date back a hundred years or more. Everywhere I go there seems to be some sort of controversy. Just yesterday I was at a diner over in Kaycee and these two guys in suits were talking about the wolves up in Montana. They were lawyers."

"Probably from the Western States Legal Foundation. I've heard they're involved in the fight over reintroduction."

"I gathered that from their conversation. But I really didn't understand why?"

"Western States has been involving itself in a number of land use issues across the West. I guess it dates back to James Watt. Do remember him?"

"Wasn't he the guy who didn't want the Beach Boys to play at the White House because they were too hard core?"

"Yes, that's when he was Reagan's Secretary of the Interior. But before he left the administration, he helped fuel the Sagebrush Rebellion which sought to transfer title of federal lands to states and eventually to private individuals. It didn't work, but a seed had been planted.

"Years later it had a resurrection of sorts, but with a savvy new look. It's replacement, the Wise Use Movement, is highly organized and highly funded. Their agenda reaches far beyond the 'wolf issue.' Ranchers, farmers, loggers and miners are being encouraged to fight against any and all regulations on public lands. One of their goals is unrestricted access to hundreds of millions of federal acres—over an eighth of the continental United States.

"Another goal is to destroy the environmental movement. The leader is this guy named Ron Arnold—a former Sierra Club activist who's gone over to the dark side. Just like Darth Vader. He wrote this twenty-five point plan which includes gutting the Endangered Species Act, breaking up the National Park System, and redefining grazing rights to recognize ranchers who use public lands as co-owners with the government.

"How can they get away with that? When people see what they're up to, they'll never let it happen."

"Looks can be deceiving. They make themselves out to be true blue grassroots organizations with names to match." He counted on his fingers. "Alliance for America, Citizens for the Environment, Blue Ribbon Coalition, and even the Sahara Club. Other groups use buzzwords like 'sensible,' 'sound' and 'responsible' in their titles, but what lies beneath is anything but. They use catch phrases like 'integrated resource management,' 'sustainable development,' and 'multiple use' in their campaigns.

"Talk about wolves in sheep's clothing," I observed. "Those lawyers I saw yesterday were wearing wool suits."

We all smiled. "That's right," Michelle chimed in. "I call it the 'Wide Abuse Movement'."

"I like 'Institute for Innovative Plunder,'" said Dave. "Who would guess that People for the West! is a consortium of mining companies set on blocking reform to the 1872 Mining Law which allows them to buy public land for under five dollars per acre. They're bankrolled by the likes of Chevron, NERCO Minerals, and Westmont Mining to the tune of millions of dollars a year."

"That's a huge investment."

"It's pocket change compared to the billions they've gained, and stand to gain, by successfully thwarting the law's repeal."

"But people are smart enough to look beyond catchy names."

"Of course, that's why they hire PR firms fluent in 'Greenspeak.' Dozens of firms maintain 'environmental specialty' divisions for their corporate clients. The practice of creating *Faux* grassroots organizations is so widespread that the term 'Astroturf Lobbying,' was coined in response."

We all laughed, and Michelle reloaded my plate for a second round.

"Along with 'prefab' grassroots groups, certain firms use sophisticated techniques to convince high-profile citizens to contact legislators on certain issues. Clients pay a fee for each call or letter generated from community leaders. Like anywhere else in America, it takes money to make money."

Planted in the soil of greed and nourished with a steady supply of manure in the form of bull shit, a flower of deception blossoms in an arid land. As I was learning, ranching, mining and logging had become more of a triple threat in the West than Willie Mayes in his prime with the San Francisco Giants. Everyday, the West provided more than this greenhorn had bargained for. A new range war raged in this country, and I was riding to its heart. My preconceptions of the Lone Ranger and Louis L'Amour were dissolved by a region steeped in myth yet mired in reality. I found a different law "west of the Pecos."

The bed was a magnet, and my body an iron filing. An invisible field held me tight, refusing to let go. Or maybe it was something more like glue that bonding my skin to the clean, white sheets. Or perhaps something even greater—a top secret government project, or an alien experiment in which I was the unknowing guinea pig. Whichever the case, resistance to such a powerful and mysterious force would be futile. I succumbed without a fight, rolling over, shutting my eyes, and dozing off.

Ultimately, a greater force arose and I was bound to obey. The power of a full bladder drove me from the bed and down a ladder I hardly recalled climbing the night before. At the bottom, I stood motionless while my eyes adjusted to the late morning light streaming in through open windows. Hueco, the only one home, greeted me enthusiastically. I stretched, yawned and headed for the bathroom. One look in the mirror provided the incentive to shave before I headed into town.

The wide streets of Lander hold memories of a time when ox-drawn wagons had to swing around in a single arc to reverse direction. Classic western facades hearken back to the mythical boom days when every other building held a bank, tack shop or a saloon. But buried like a bad memory beneath a thick layer of asphalt are the corrugation of ruts and grooves—continually muddy by most accounts—that characterized many early western towns. Paving has made travel up and down Main Street a breeze while the inability of Oxen to walk backwards has provided plenty of angled parking.

Gift shops and cafes had replaced the tack shops and saloons as the most common enterprises. I passed windows full of post cards, t-shirts and "Authentic Indian Artwork." A pharmacy, liquor store and book shop were tucked here and there. A shoe store had a hand-painted sign in the window: "Hi my name is Bruce and I love to fix shoes." The marquee of the Grand Theatre touted Kiefer Sutherland and Woody Harrelson in *The Cowboy Way*. A menu posted outside the Pronghorn Diner offered huevos rancheros, grittle cakes and cowboy coffee. I took a table near the front window.

My attention was drawn from the menu by a parade of honking cars and trucks proceeding down Main Street. Men and women hollered from open windows the way only someone who lives in central Wyoming could. I didn't know what to make of it until I heard the clanging of tin cans coming from the bumper of the last truck in line. "Just Married," read the hand-written sign taped to the tailgate.

As soon as the raucous died away at the edge of town, it started to grow again until reaching another crescendo as the wedding party passed a second time. Followed by a third and forth, it made for a wonderful demonstration of the Doppler effect. In the end, it was unclear whether they stopped because they had run out of enthusiasm or gas.

Between breakfast and lunch, activity inside the Pronghorn was minimal. A waitress with bright red hair, and lipstick to match, strolled over with a bored look on her face. Her name tag said Mae. "How we doin', Honey," she chortled as I browsed through the breakfast offerings.

"I'll need a minute."

"Take your time, darlin'," she said with her eyes more on my hands than my face. "I got all day." She stood beside me with her pad in her apron. "Hot out there, huh?"

"Yup."

"On days like this I like to set myself into a nice, cool bubble bath. Just let that water cover my whole body."

I looked up from the menu as she winked at me. Without a wedding ring, I must have appeared the maverick—an unbranded bull. Before I could garner any response, my stomach growled a reminder of the time—nearly eleven o'clock. The "Cowboy Combo" had caught my eye: coffee (free refills), three buttermilk pancakes, two eggs any style, two pieces of toast, and choice of bacon or sausage. All good, except for the last bit.

"Could I please have the 'Combo' with scrambled eggs? But instead of the bacon or sausage could you give me some home fries?"

"Honey," she said with another wink and a smile, "I'll give you anything you want."

"Thanks," I said as she stood waiting for more of a response. My stomach grumbled in anticipation—no time to flirt. "Thanks...*a lot.*"

She got my message, but it wasn't long before I got hers. When she returned and slid the plate before me, two limp strips of bacon laid across my eggs and there was no sign of home fries. Although Mae thought she'd won, the last laugh would be mine. Finishing the meal, I spread the bacon on the counter and dug deep into my pockets for a pair of copper Lincolns. Setting a single penny on each fatty strip, I got *my* two cents in without saying a word.

Chapter 17

*"Big men may talk and humbug the country...about a railroad to the
Pacific, but if I live a thousand years we will never see the resemblance
even of any such thing...Men who could build a railroad to the moon
perhaps could build one over these mountains, but I doubt it."*
—William Wilson

*The thought of penetrating into the recesses of this wilderness region
filled me with enthusiasm. I saw visions.*
—John C. Fremont, 1839

The temperature had breached the century mark by the time I left the
Pronghorn. I returned to Michelle's place and put in a call to some other
friends who had moved to Utah. The answering machine picked up on
the second ring. I told it I'd be passing through in four or five days, and
would call again with more details.

Too hot to ride, I curled up on the couch and slept until Michelle
returned from work. We ate avocado and tomato sandwiches while she
warned me about the road between Rock Springs, Wyoming and Vernal,
Utah. "That climb is painful when I do it in my truck!"

Dave came home from work and they pulled together what they
needed for their weekend in Jackson Hole. Hueco jumped into the back
of the pickup with the camping gear. Michelle wished me luck as they
pulled out of the driveway. "I'm sorry we have to leave in such a hurry,
but we've had this planned for a long time. Feel free to stay as long as
you want—just lock up when you leave."

As they drove north into a stiff wind, I pulled out the map. Although
I'd be crossing the Continental Divide from east to west, Fremont Pass
lay south of Lander. With the prospect of a healthy tail wind for most of
the afternoon, I packed quckly, scribbled a heart-felt note for Michelle,
and hit the road.

Taking back streets through town, I joined U.S. 287 on the south side
where it wastes no time getting down to the business of climbing out of
the valley. The land grew arid with elevation. Tall grasses and
cottonwoods gave way to sagebrush and Rocky Mountain juniper. Ten
miles south of town, I turned onto State Route 28 at the sign for South
Pass. Road cuts through low hills revealed thick layers of crimson
sandstone. The deeper cuts offered protection from the low, western
sun. I savored the coolness of shadow as I climbed slowly toward the
Continental Divide—2,000 feet above and thirty miles away.

A century and a half ago, the Divide was more than simply a barrier
to the gold fields of California, it stood as a bold challenge to Manifest

Destiny. Backbone of the continent, there was no way around it, under it, or through it. Over was the only option.

That's what made South Pass so important to early pioneers. Gentle grades on either side of the 7,412 foot pass offered prospectors the easiest wagon route over the Rockies.

Born of gold fever, South Pass City thrived on the hundreds of thousands of pioneers that streamed through it like a mountain creek during spring runoff. But as the gold ran out, the flow became a trickle and the commerce of South Pass City dried up. Consigned to mothballs as a State Historical Site, it commemorates the Gold Rush days as well as the Wyoming Territorial Legislature's bold move to extend the vote to women.

Despite the tail wind, I struggled up the slope wondering if I'd make the Pass before dark. Alternating between standing and sitting, I could not find a comfortable rhythm. The sun dipped below the ridge line, but ample light remained on the road for the time being.

Within half an hour, things had changed. Shadows thickened with no sign of the summit. I judged the climb ahead by oncoming headlights. First appearing as a single glowing beacon in the distance, with time they became two eyes piercing the darkness, until finally—rounding the last corner—the twin beams struck me with an explosion of light. At close range, it didn't matter whether they were high or low, I was blinded all the same. Left with few options, I closed my eyes and held my line.

Moments later, I would find myself struggling to readjust to the blackness of a moonless night. Head down and eyes fixed on the white line, I trusted it to lead me safely. I pressed on through the cooling mountain air that raised goose bumps on my bare arms and legs.

Suddenly, the climb ended. Gaining the backbone of the continent was easier than expected. Perhaps sleeping in and enjoying half a day off made the difference. Except for my empty water bottles, I was satisfied with my position.

Noticing lights and a structure not far ahead, I pushed on in search of hydration. Arriving at the foot of an inclined driveway, I looked up at a house and large metal storage building illuminated by a yellow spotlight. At 10:15 I opted for the latter so as not to disturb anyone. It looked substantial enough to have an outside spigot—perhaps to wash vehicles on the wide apron of asphalt around the structure.

Entering the arc of the single spotlight I was greeted by a violent growl. Barks echoed across the ridge as I fled down the driveway. Howls continued as I turned onto 28 and coasted downhill into darkness. "No Cujo!" a voice called out. "No!"

The next set of headlights suggested nothing more than another brief annoyance. Like the others, they first appeared as a single, blurry dot in the distance, slowly growing and dividing like a cell undergoing meiosis. I watched the familiar progression from prophase through telophase. But soon after the elongated luminary had differentiated itself into two distinct orbs, there was a sudden moment of blackness, the screeching of tires and the sound of impact.

The Blazer had come to a complete stop by the time I reached it. The sound of its idling engine droned above the fallen body. The driver, a tall, thin man, stood at the edge of the beams. His female companion remained in the passenger seat.

I laid Betsy down on the shoulder and hurried across the road and into the headlights. Catching my first glimpse of the downed animal, I stopped dead in my tracks.

"I never saw it," said the man from the shadows.

I took a step closer. The steaming body heaved in a failed attempt to stand. Its head and shoulders swung back to the pavement and came to rest. Its tawny fur quivered as lungs heaved moist vapor into the cool air. I took another step forward and knelt by its side.

"Be careful."

I placed one hand on the mule deer's neck and cradled its head with the other. A mixture of blood and spittle drained from its open mouth.

"Is it going to be ok?"

I didn't answer, couldn't answer. My eyes were fixed on those of the deer. They were filled with a terror that shot into my soul. I could feel the life draining from its body—leaking through my fingers. There was nothing I could do. With one final, labored breath, it was gone.

"Is it...?"

I nodded without looking up.

"What should we do?"

"Contact the highway patrol. You'll probably need to go all the way to Lander."

"I've got a cell phone. Do you know the number?"

"No, I'm just passing through."

"So are we. Should I try 911?"

"Good idea."

He was in the car for less than a minute. "I'm not getting a signal. They need to put up some more towers around here. You think we should drive into Lander and report it?"

"That'd probably be best. Give me a hand and we'll drag it onto the shoulder."

As he crouched beside me under the glow of the headlights, I saw his frightened face for the first time. The moment his fingertips met the soft fur, he recoiled. "I don't think I can do this."

"Yes you can."

He hesitated, and then crouched again beside me. Slowly, he extended his hands toward the deer, making gentle contact high on a forelimb. His fingers wrapped around the leg as he let out a deep breath. He turned his head and gave a slight nod to signify his readiness. A single tear clung to his cheek.

We dragged the limp body out of the headlights and across the shoulder, laying it to rest at the edge of the barbed wire fence it had so nimbly vaulted minutes earlier.

"Thanks for your help," he said, extending his hand. I took it in mine and felt a quiver not unlike that of the dying deer.

"Be careful," I said as he turned toward the humming Blazer.

"Yeah."

The red tail lights disappeared around a bend, leaving me alone in the darkness. A gust of cold air brought me back to the mountaintop. Walking back to where I had left Betsy, I eased her upright and stepped into the saddle before setting off in search of a gap in the fence line.

Not far ahead a side track branched off on the north side of the road. A locked gate did not deter me. Laying the loaded bike on its side, I dragged Betsy under the bar and wheeled her another fifty feet to where a tall metal post grew out of the gravel. Leaning her against it, I dug through the panniers for long underwear and a pile jacket. The north wind picked up and the temperature continued to drop. As a pregnant moon rose in the east, I slipped into my bag and settled in for what would become a long, restless sleep.

In silence, the first streaks of long anticipated light cut the darkness. Stars faded into the steely blue sky. A pale pink ribbon of clouds illuminated from below hung on the eastern horizon. Every day the dawn works the same magic—those precious moments when all the power of life is in the sky—but this morning was special.

Sky, cloud, rock and trees—everything radiated color in the time of transition between night and day. My sleeping bag turned a bluer blue, its stuff sack a redder red. The emerald needles of pine and spruce drew out the redness of the rock in the pale light of predawn. The indirect glow brought out subtle hues that disappear in broad daylight. If only for a few minutes each day, the true colors of our world are revealed. I gazed through rose-colored glasses from my perch atop the Divide.

Beside me, the rusty pole on which Betsy leaned drew my eyes upward to a weathered, white sign: "PRIVATE PROPERTY." Beyond it, the Great Divide loomed like a sleeping bear, revealing another truth—I had not yet reached South Pass. My rosy vision faded alongside the vibrant hues of dawn as the first direct rays streamed over the eastern horizon.

The warmth it brought, however, provided some restitution. Although night had left the mountain, it's legacy of cold had not. The nocturnal memory faded slowly as I began to climb fully bundled. Only when I reached the Pass did I feel the need to shed a layer. I stopped to disrobe, but stayed for the view. On the backbone of the continent, I looked east and west thinking of the man for which it is named. Not a hair over five feet tall, John C. Fremont was as short in stature as he was tall in accomplishments. No giant myself, I appreciate his brevity.

Wider than expected, the pass hardly looked the part. The slopes both coming and going were as Fremont described them, about equal "to the ascent of the Capitol hill from the Avenue at Washington." Far to the north rose the high country of the Wind River Range. To the south lay the rolling Antelope Hills.

A historic marker described briefly the significance of South Pass in settling the West. After the Oregon Trail opened in the 1840's, countless wagon-loads of pioneers took advantage of this dip along the ridge line. Had it not been for South Pass, some historians claim the United States would have been significantly smaller. The cultural weight of over 300,000 American settlers, scholars say, allowed for the ultimate annexation of southern California from Mexico, and parts of Oregon, Washington and Idaho from the British.

Perched atop the Divide, I could see—across the arching plain of sage and greasewood—the two major watersheds of North America. Ignoring evaporation, water that falls east of the ridge line flows to the Atlantic Ocean while to the west it's destination is the Pacific. The ridge marks the division of the continent in its truest sense—not by an arbitrary line on a map, but by the very nature of the land. Native American mythology often refers to North America as "Turtle Island." The Continental Divide is simply the crux of the shell.

Intrigued by the situation, I took the opportunity to relieve myself along the backbone of America—my first transcontinental piss.

But as I'd come to learn, things aren't always as they appear. Theories and even logic have a way of evaporating in an arid land. A sign marked the Great Divide Basin, an anomaly where water flows to neither ocean. So flat and dry, the only way for a raindrop to find its way out of this shallow valley is to reverse direction—a hydrological U-turn. In a reverse of gravitational logic (and a popular song by Blood, Sweat and Tears), what comes down must go up.

As one would expect, the road flattened out and pointed like an arrow across the sage-covered plain. Light traffic and the absence of wildlife gave me a sense of solitary being. Other than a bug that flew into my mouth, I was alone under the sun.

Farson: Population 325; Elevation 6580—still in Wyoming. At the junction of 287 and U.S. 191, the east wall of the Farson Mercantile advertised Groceries, Feed, Post Office and Ice Cream. As the only store in town, I assumed that's all the locals needed. Had it not been for the ice cream, I'd say they were pushing it.

Eden (Population 220; Elevation 6590) is perhaps the most appropriately named town in the state. Through waves of heat rising from the asphalt, tall trees appeared like an oasis across the arid basin. Under a mid-day sun, the steaming canopy seemed to writhe in fire. Thick willows and towering cottonwoods lined 191 through town— Wyoming's answer to Hollywood Boulevard.

South of Eden, rolling hills were punctuated by rising temperatures. Feeling the effects of the previous day's climb and a poor night's sleep, the next thirty-seven miles to Rock Springs would have done me in had the last fifteen not been downhill.

From humble beginnings, a sudden boost to the Uranium industry in the late seventies turned Rock Springs into boom town almost overnight. As money flowed in, it didn't take long for this once sleepy town to feel the effects. Drugs, gambling and prostitution replaced fishing, bingo and horseshoes as the most popular local pastimes. Allegations of Mafia involvement fueled the fire that Barbara Walters caught on videotape in a 20/20 news story titled "Sin City."

Sin, vice, corruption...in Wyoming? With a reputation like that and a population of 19,050, I wondered if this the right state? After all, the elevation of Rock Springs was below 6,000 feet.

Even before the mafia arrived, the Interstate had begun to corrupt Rock Springs. Billboards advertised convenience stores, fast food restaurants and motel chains, while "Out of Business" signs hung in the empty windows of local shops. How can the Corner Cafe compete against McDonalds with its golden arches and "BILLIONS AND BILLIONS SERVED?" How does Mom and Pop's Variety compete with 7-11 and its Super Big Gulp? How can the Country Inn compete with Motel 6 and Tom Bodet's voice saturating the airwaves? Who'll leave the light on for them?

I passed under I-80 and headed toward the center of town where a two-foot trench had taken the place of Main Street. Were the pawn shops on either side at war? Yellow D.P.W. barricades blocked side streets, many of which had also been torn up either, I assumed, for repaving or to install an intricate canal system that would restore Rock Spring's shattered economy by making a popular tourist attraction—"Venice of the West." Although it was hard to imagine gondola rides among the neo-western architecture, it wouldn't be the first time a western town adopted a piece of Europe to promote tourism. I'm sure Lake Havasu City would even give them a deal on a slightly-used London Bridge.

Pushing Betsy along the sidewalk, I had no intention of stopping until I saw the sign for Newman's Second, Third and Fourth Hand Shop. "Buying and Selling BLUE JEANS and More."

Inside the door, a long folding table sagged under the weight of a mountain of Levi's and Wrangler—no sissy designer denim here. No Guess or P.S. Gitano, and even Brooke Shields may find that Wyoming comes between she and her Calvin Kleins.

Not in the market for jeans, I stepped into a back room that qualified as the "and More," part of the hand-painted sign out front. A row of dusty cowboy boots filled the floor space under a long rack of hanging clothes. A series of hand-made shelves supported a random collection of miscellaneous junk. Naturally, I was drawn to it. From rusty belt buckles and broken jack knives to mismatched knitting needles and odd balls of yarn, the shelves held something for anyone willing to make do. Board games missing pieces, a lamp without a shade; decks of forty seven, a broken garden spade; mismatched woolen stockings, ties out of style; assorted pins and needles, a worn-out nail file; chairs that need re-caning, a broken-handled mop; all these treasures seem to find their way to Newman's shop. There was no string too short to be saved.

A scratchy voice from behind me. "Afternoon."

I turned to face an elderly gentleman standing in the doorway. He smiled pleasantly, exposing an incomplete set of yellow teeth. A pair of thick glasses clung to the bridge of his crooked nose, held together by masking tape. He leaned slightly on a wooden cane who's finish had long since worn off. Like his shop, everything about the man seemed previously owned.

"You've got a nice place here. How long have you been in business?"

"I guess it's been twenty years now. Started up right after I quit my job over at the dump. Just couldn't stand seein' people throw away perfectly good stuff—clothes, books, vacuums, toasters, mixers, you name it—usually with just a switch that's broke or a cord that's shot. What a waste. If there's one thing I can't stand, it's waste."

Sensing a streak of Yankee thrift, I pursued the subject of providence. "What can you tell me about the grazing on public land?"

He hesitated, sizing me up for a moment. "Where you from?"

"New Hampshire."

"Back East, huh?"

"Yup."

"You ride here on that bicycle?"

"I took a bus to North Dakota first."

He gave me a long look up and down. "I want you to keep this between you and me."

I nodded.

"Now I'm not saying this is me, but some folks call it 'Welfare ranching.' If a fella's got a lease on Forest Service land or BLM..."

"BLM?"

"Bureau of Livestock and Mining," he said with a smirk.

"No, really."

"Land Management."

"Right. Now I remember."

"So this fella's got a lease on public land. He pays about two dollars per animal unit per month—they call it A.U.M. Now that same animal would cost him eight or ten dollars on private land. I've heard the fees don't even cover the cost of administerin' the program and maintainin' the land. For every dollar spent, the government gets back about twenty cents. "

"Twenty cents?

"It's like walking into a restaurant and having the government pay for most of your meal while other folks have to pay full price. And some of those gettin' the free lunch are the richest ones in the place! "

"How rich?"

"You got some billionaires listed in Forbes magazine. You got companies like Union Oil, Getty, Vail Ski Corporation. They use ranches as tax shelters."

"So the rich get richer?"

"This is America. But there's still room for the little guy to hustle a few bucks. I've heard a couple of savvy fellas are subleasing their grazing rights at a profit."

"Is that legal?"

"'Course not. The whole thing ends up costin' taxpayers around $50 million dollars a year. Again, I'm not saying this is me, but some folks would call that a waste."

"Fifty million! Why doesn't Congress raise the fees?"

"Mind if I swear?"

I shook my head.

"Them people got no morals. They don't. They'd sell their own mothers to ARCO or Mammoth Oil if they thought there was money in it. Have 'em rendered down to crude. Politicians ain't nothin' but...Shit, now ya' got me mad.

He went on to explain that most federal permits won't make or break a rancher. Less than ten percent of permitees on public land control more than half of the total acreage. After corporations, the next largest percentage of permitees raise livestock for supplemental income. Forth-generation ranchers struggling to survive on the same land their great grandfathers worked are as rare as those who wouldn't shoot a wolf on sight.

"Now, you understand this is a sensitive issue around here. Don't go spreadin' it around that I was talkin' this way. I'd lose some of my best customers."

Spotting a leafy canopy over the flat-roofed buildings to the west, I made my way along cracked sidewalks to Bunnings Park. Surrounded by a low brick wall, it filled an entire block. I passed under an arching iron gateway and followed a paved walk to a neatly painted pavilion. Sturdy wooden benches sat beneath the ample shade of tall oaks. Curiously, a portable soda fountain hummed next to the pavilion and a buffet table and grill stood nearby. I'd stumbled across a tenth year reunion of Rock Springs High School.

The sounds of happy children filled the air and I reminisced about a time when a ball, a friend and a sunny day were all that mattered. Clusters of young parents gathered here and there, one eye on the kids and one on the lookout for old friends. Hugs were exchanged among women, hand shakes among men, and a few hearty pats on the back for those especially sensitive men. With volleyball and horseshoes as a backdrop, the wholesome scene made me wonder if Walter's "Sin City" had outgrown it's moniker?

Steering clear of the festivities, I laid Betsy against the shady side of the pavilion and opened a pannier in search of lunch. But before I had a hand on the peanut butter, a tall, thin man with wispy blond hair asked about my ride.

"That's somethin'," he said when I told him how far I'd come. "Where you headed to next?"

"Utah."

"Watch out for those Mormons—they're a wild lot."

He invited me to join him at the buffet table where pasta salad and coleslaw provided a welcome break from PB and J. I helped myself to a second helping after he had gone off to join a volleyball game.

The family atmosphere warmed my heart, but by late afternoon I craved something more. I thanked my host and headed into town looking for excitement. A six pack of Harleys parked outside C.J.'s Lounge showed me where to find it. I leaned Betsy against a "Motorcycles Only" sign and stepped inside.

Wyoming's answer to Hell's Angels leaned against the bar. Five bearded faces and the bushiest mustache I'd ever seen turned toward the light streaming through the open door. My Patagonia shorts and white t-shirt garnered nothing but stares from the row of black leather. Someone said something under his breath and the rest snickered. I asked the bartender—an attractive blond woman—if I could please bring my bike inside for safe keeping. She smiled and answered yes.

"Hey, what about me, Chris? Can I bring mine inside too?"

A chorus of agreement arose from the sextet.

"Very funny Jake."

I leaned Betsy against the wall next to a jukebox, and ordered a beer. With a frosted mug in hand, I found a seat at the far end of the L-shaped bar. The dark oak was scratched and gouged. Cigarette burns riddled the vinyl arm rest. A large screen TV hung from the ceiling nearby.

It had been weeks, but I still remembered the routine: power, volume, channel. Who would have guessed surfing in Wyoming would be so easy. Flipping through the channels, I came across ESPN as Phil Ligget began his half hour summary of the day's stage of the Tour de France.

Stage fourteen was 118 miles from Castres to Montpellier. The pack stayed together for the first seventy-five miles, successfully thwarting all break-away attempts. Finally two men, Rolf Sorensen of Denmark and Neil Stephens of Australia broke away and it soon became evident that one of them would win the stage—if they worked together. Differences in team, nation and language were set aside as the unlikely allies joined forces in pursuit of a common goal. But as the finish line grew near, the race became a tactical game of cat and mouse. Both men knew that Sorensen was a better sprinter and every attempt that Stephens made to get away was unsuccessful. Needing the Australian to pull him to victory, the savvy Dane hung in his slipstream, conserving energy for the inevitable sprint finish. In bicycle racing—as in life—there are times when one man can do all of the work while another claims the glory.

With every intention of leaving after the Tour coverage, a commercial caught my eye: "Redsox vs. Royals - 8 PM Eastern on ESPN." Converting to Mountain Time, that was a half hour away. I filled the gap with another beer and a pair of phone calls.

After checking in with my folks and making plans to meet my friends Sean and Sharon in Bicknell, Utah, I picked up another beer before returning to the tube. Chris told me she admired my courage.

"What's that supposed to mean?"

She smiled and handed me the beer.

The first inning had begun when I returned to my stool. No score through three, but the Sox homered in the fourth. At that point I was on my fifth.

As the evening wore on, bikers filled the bar—none interested in the game. The jukebox cranked heavy metal tunes, reducing me to watching, but not hearing the action. By the seventh inning, a sixth beer had stretched my limit. The game became a blur of strikes, balls and Ozzy Osborne. The Red Sox were up, but I was down. My liver called for relief but the bullpen was empty.

Chapter 18

Your advise, father, is in good time, for here a boy is truly in the very gates of destruction, as all kinds of vices hold unlimited sway in the cities and mines. But I hope and trust I shall be able to leave this country as pure and innocent as I came in—and that ain't anything to brag on, is it?
—Lucius Fairchild, 1850

Darkness, but not that of open desert. A sweet smell, but not that of sage. A confining darkness, a human smell.

A light cotton sheet, a soft mattress, the light hum of an air conditioner. Each clue produced more questions than answers. A dry throat and splitting headache were my only certainties.

As my eyes struggled to gain focus, I looked for additional clues around the darkened room: a digital clock flashed 4:23, a narrow shaft of light leading to a door left slightly ajar. Standing slowly, the blood rushed from my head, doubling its already intense disequilibrium. I sat on the edge of the bed until the spinning stopped—or at least slowed enough for a second attempt. Vertical again, I stumbled toward the source of light. Nearly tripping on a pair of shoes, I slipped through the doorway and into a fluorescent deluge. With my eyes clenched shut, only the feel of cool tile beneath my feet told me what room I had entered.

Groping blindly, my hands found a sink and grasped it firmly while I waited for sight to return. As my cheek muscles relaxed their grip, a slight separation provided the first visual confirmation. Through a thin screen of lashes, I found myself staring back at me. Neither of us were smiling.

Bending over to wash my face, I shot upright as a pair of arms wrapped around my waist. What the...? Who?

Jerking my eyes back to the mirror, they met by another pair gazing back from over my shoulder. Long, blond hair shrouded the angelic face. A smile emerged and before I could utter a word, she leaned forward and kissed my cheek.

Speechless, I turned to face her naked body. She threw her arms around my neck and gave a squeeze followed by a peck on the nose. "What're you thinkin'?"

The question men dread. If I tell her the truth, she'll throw me out, and if I say, "Nothing," she'll say "You have to be thinking *something.*"

Think man, think. Think of something good. "You look great naked." She blushed and turned away.

Dodging that bullet, I returned to the bedroom to find myself staring down the barrel of a much larger gun. By the light of a table lamp, I paused to look at a collection of photographs mounted on the wall: family, dog, group of friends, camping trip, graduation, wedding...

"You're married?"

"Don't worry. He's off hunting this weekend."

"When's he due back?"

"Sometime today, but it'll be late. He stays out for as long as he can. Bruce just loves shooting things."

"That's what I was afraid of."

"Don't worry," she repeated. "Come back to bed."

Four Tylenol and a tall glass of water helped my headache but did nothing to settle my nerves. I lay awake, heart racing, muscles tense. As the lyrics from Kenny Roger's "Gambler" ran through my head, I thought it best to make like another famous Rogers—1972 Olympic marathon champion, Bill—and run like hell. "You gotta know when to hold 'em, know when to fold 'em, know when to walk away, know when to ride."

As soon as Chris had fallen asleep, I slipped out of bed and crawled along the carpet searching for my clothes. They appeared in a line leading away from the bed in reverse order of how they must have come off: boxers, shorts, t-shirt. But where were the shoes? Repeated sweeps of the floor proved fruitless. At 5:30 I decided to abandon the search. Missing in action, I gave them up as casualties of love.

Guessing my way through doors and down hallways, I found the living room where I pulled back a curtain and peered outside. The dim light of predawn revealed no sign of Bruce, but Betsy lay quietly in the back of Chris' pickup. Gently turning the deadbolt and easing the door open, I slipped into the cool morning air. Closing the door with equal care, I crept barefoot across the driveway.

After lifting Betsy from the bed, I slipped on my riding clothes and cleated shoes. I coasted to the end of the driveway, but pulled a U-turn once I hit the street and returned to Chris' truck. I tore a page from my journal and scribbled a quick note. Folded over and tucked under a wiper blade, the message was short and sweet.

Weaving through a maze of manufactured housing, I made my way toward the rumbling sounds of I-80. It would serve as my benchmark for finding my way out of town. A large, green sign marked the spot: 191 South - Exit 1 Mile. A frontage road carried me safely to the junction where I crossed over the interstate and left "Sin City" behind. Having broken at least one commandment during my brief stay, I guess the name could stick.

Barren hills and lonely buttes defined the landscape south of town. The sound of the interstate dissolved into the wind. Between the shaded slopes of the Aspen Mountains to the east and the cool blue waters of the Flaming Gorge Reservoir to the west, I pedaled the rolling hills of southern Wyoming for the last time.

Sunlight skipped across the choppy surface of the man-made lake, its reflection tickling the sheer canyon walls. Dancing diamonds sparkled through the mellow hues of ocher, umber and sienna. Within this cruel desert landscape, a billion gallons of water could only be a mirage. Wind-formed monoliths and sharp-toothed pinnacles looked on in disbelief.

Bold-faced black on school bus yellow, the sign—one of thousands throughout the West—warned of "Open Range," unfenced areas where motorists are likely to encounter livestock in the roadway. The ineffectiveness of this particular sign, however, was foretold by the odor. Foul, fetid, putrid, rank—a witches brew of rotten eggs, skunk's tail and gym socks. The bloated corpse threatened suffocation.

Stretched taut over a distended stomach, the brown and white hide was a stink bomb waiting to explode. I held my breath for what seemed like a safe distance only to discover a withered calf on the shoulder ahead. Fortunately, this dogie's odor was proportionate to its size. The next sign—"Loose Stock"—appeared only to add insult to injury.

Mustangs, broncos and pintos had once been used to round up cattle on the open range, but a new breed of horsepower is playing a different role. Despite the losses to four-wheeled stallions, ranchers have yet to call in the Western States Legal Foundation to protect themselves against the Ford Motor Company.

From my collected observations and an unofficial survey, animals fall into four groups in Wyoming: stock, game, wildlife and varmints. Stock are domesticated animals raised and slaughtered for food. Game are wild animals killed for food or sport. Varmints are wild animals that are just killed. And Wildlife is what's left over for the tourist value.

Three of the categories earn highway signs: "Loose Stock," "Game Crossing," and "Wildlife Viewing Area." Perhaps the fourth would read, "Varmint Shootin'."

In a strange reversal of the Mann Act (crossing the state line for immoral purposes), I entered the Beehive State. The welcome sign had been edited by an unidentified liberal with a can of spray paint to read, "Utah - Still the Right (Wing) Place."

Traffic picked up south of the border—SUVs, campers and beefy pickup trucks hauling power boats to and from the boat launch. Within two miles, I had reached Dutch John, a cozy hamlet curiously named for a Dutchman named John.

Despite a hangover, I made good time—sixty-five hilly miles in four and a half hours. Michelle's warning of the climb may as well have fallen on deaf ears. At a break in traffic, I turned left into the parking lot of a catch-all market/outfitter/convenience store/gas station. The clerk wore a tee-shirt with large block letters, "This is not Lake Powell."

Often confused with its big brother to the south, the Flaming Gorge National Recreation Area is a popular destination in this corner of Utah. Etched from the Uinta Mountains by the Green River and dammed by the Army Corps of Engineers, the ninety mile reservoir of deep, clear water snakes through sharp canyons and multi-colored ravines. With over 350 miles of rugged shoreline supporting picnic areas, campsites, hiking trails, boat ramps, marinas, visitors centers, lodges and an historic ranch, Flaming Gorge has something for everyone. For me it was water.

A stream of cool, clear liquid issued forth from a rusty faucet in the grungy bathroom. Icy smooth, I downed a quart before filling my bottles for the road. With just forty-five miles separating Dutch John from Vernal, I felt optimistic about getting there around noontime. As I would soon learn, the topography had something else in mind. Michelle's warning was about to come true.

A pleasant downhill run through the low hills surrounding the reservoir fueled my false hopes of an early arrival. Rounding the last corner, the Flaming Gorge Dam appeared: 502 feet of cold, gray concrete. Implacable and mute, the concave facade stretched between gently hued canyon walls. Even in a land as big as the sky, this dam would not go unnoticed. Hundreds of feet across, the massive bulkhead held my eyes as I coasted slowly toward, and then over it. To my right, an enormous body of water stretched out for miles, to my left, nothing but air. Only from the very edge of the downstream side of the dam can one see the Green River stretching out below like an emerald necklace sparkling in the sunlight.

Vehicles—both recreational and sport utility—filled the parking lot on the west side of the dam. Their occupants lined the restraining wall, marveling at the cornerstone of the Recreation Area. The water's surface teamed with power boats, jet skis and water skiers, but with a name like Flaming Gorge, my thoughts turned to what lay beneath.

"Technically," a dam employee named Mike told me, "it's a reservoir. But 'lake' sounds better in tourist brochures."

"Isn't that like calling pronghorns 'wildlife' during tourist season and 'game' during hunting season."

"It's all in the spin."

Our conversation was interrupted as a Ford Windstar with New York plates squealed into a parking space beside us. While the engine continued to hum, the driver's door swung open revealing a balding man with a camera around his neck. He hurried to the restraining wall and snapped a quick photo while yelling over his shoulder, "Hey you kids, get back in the car. You can see it when we get home." He returned to the mini-van, reversed out of the space, and sped away.

"I see that all the time," said Mike, who went on to explain his theory of late twentieth century tourism. "It's like a rolling cocktail party where you meet all of the guests, but get to *know* none of them. A whirlwind tour of budget motels, gift shops and 'Kodak moments' does not qualify as knowing a place."

As the Windstar sped off to the next "Point of Interest" described in their tourist guide, I vowed to strive for a deeper understanding of the land through which I traveled. The type of understanding that is a way of life for traditional Native Americans.

For them, the land is more than just miles to cover. It holds a greater significance which is often expressed in place-names. The Apache, for instance, take great pleasure in simply speaking names such as *deeschii'bikoh*—"valley with elongated red bluffs." More than simple labels, many place-names are complete sentences providing succinct descriptions of the terrain: "water flows down on top of a regular succession of flat rocks;" "big cottonwood trees stand spreading here and there." It is believed that the use of such vivid nomenclature effects a more direct censorial bond between humans and the land. Rather than emanating from the syllabic pronunciation itself, anthropologists suspect that the benefits spring directly from the mystical powers of the very places so described. While the Apache name for the upthrusted region of northern Utah is unusually, *Ute*—meaning "people who live higher up in the mountains"—holds power beyond its three letters. I was about to find out what the Apaches meant by "higher up."

Eons old, the Uinta Mountains towered above me looking none the worse for wear. Uplifted during the Laramide Orogeny between 60 and 40 million years ago, the Uintas are representative of the dramatic crustal activity the region has experienced. Sediments making up the Green River formation suggest that lakes developed between the uplifts before a final period of tectonic activity created the topography of the Colorado Plateau as we know it.

The road wound upward through exposed cliffs streaked with soft pastels and earthy hues. My hopes of reaching Vernal by mid-day withered like a raisin in the sun. Down shifting, I began the serpentine climb through blue spruce and quaking aspen. Drivers coming from the other direction smiled and waved, some laughed.

Leaving the saddle at first only for short spurts to break up the monotony of the climb, as the morning wore on I found myself standing out of necessity. The slope demanded more than even my small chain ring could deliver. With the sun at its zenith and switchbacks every hundred yards, north, south, east and west became confused. Only one direction held its meaning—up. With each bend, I wondered if it would be the last. No such luck. A Sisyphean labor of sorts, would my boulder ever reach the top?

After too many disappointments I didn't even bother looking ahead. Instead, I concentrated on my breathing and cadence. I became lost in a rhythm of pumping legs and beating heart. In a Zen-like meditation, I just might reach Nirvana on my way to the mountaintop.

Effective in some respects, the limitations of this method became evident after a particularly close call with a Winnebago. I abandoned the practice and began to take in more on my surroundings. The crowded, green slopes of Mount Lena rose to the east high above the Green River. Entering Ashley National Forest , a sign indicated that a memorial to firefighters lay ahead. The parking area was full, perhaps in response to a recent tragedy on Storm King Mountain in Colorado where fourteen smoke jumpers lost their lives. That fire had been one of many that raged throughout the West as a result of the severe drought conditions the region was experiencing.

This reality hit close to home moments later as the last drops from my first water bottle dribbled onto my parched tongue. I thought about how I might ration the next two more carefully—make them last the rest of the morning—when the words of the old man in Dickinson rang in my ears: "Carry a map and drink your water while you're still alive."

Despite the altitude, the temperature continued to rise. Where a combination of dry air and constant wind had kept me comfortably dry across the Wyoming plains, the slow, arduous climb through placid air resulted in a sweat-soaked T-shirt. The damp cotton clung to my body like a leech. As a thin cloud crossed the sun, I removed the aromatic smock.

A light breeze tickled my bare skin as I neared the top. Easing its slope, the road wound through mountain meadows in full bloom. Ditch banks, hollows and swales teemed with elk thistle, Indian paintbrush and American bistort. Open fields ran thick with Perry's primrose, yarrow, phasilia and buttercups. The celebration of color stretched to aspen-covered hillsides where flat-stemmed leaves shimmered in sunlight and shadow as if applauding the floral performance. The light-colored undersides of the heart-shaped leaves exposed themselves with the slightest southern breeze. Their chance in the limelight would not come until the autumn when they would turn yellow and take center stage.

Among brooklets, hillocks and glades, a series of false summits raised my hopes only to dash them with more climbing. Finally, it appeared. With a fist raised in victory and a sigh of relief, I reached the long awaited crest at 8,482 feet. Calves, thighs and hamstrings gave a collective sign of relief. I treated myself to a sitting ovation.

Coasting the rest of the way to Vernal, however, turned out to be as likely as building a railroad to the moon. It would take five more miles of pedaling into a headwind across the rolling corderilla to find what I was looking for—"5% to 8% Grade - 10 Switchbacks Next 9 Miles."

Like exam week in college, I faced test after test. Having passed Freshman Hill Climbing, I found myself enrolled in Descending 101—hopefully not a crash course.

Engaging the big chain ring for the first time in ages, I took off down the mountain, leaning into the curves like a criterion rider. Where cars were absent, I avoided breaking on the hairpins by crossing the double yellow and maintaining my speed into the next straightaway. Outside, inside, outside—I took full advantage of the road's width.

In a reversal of "Ten Little Indians," the Highway Department counted down each turn with black on yellow signs: "9 More," "8 More"; "7 More." Hot winds rose from the canyon below, surrounding my body and filling my lungs. In a paradox of symmetry, it became as hard to breath on the way down as it had been on the way up. Descending the southern slope was like opening an oven to check on chocolate chip cookies, but finding no sweet smell.

I could see to the foot of the Uintas where rolling hills—dotted only with withered sage—melded into a forbidding landscape. Chalky badlands, wrinkled with deep gullies, craggy canyons, and dry gulches awaited at the bottom of the 3,000 foot descent. "3 More," "2 More," "1 More." And then there were none.

Chapter 19

*My soul feel hallelujah, it exults in God, that He has planted this people
in a place...I want hard times, so that every person that does not wish to
stay, for the sake of his religion will leave. This is a good place to make
Saints...*
—Bringham Young, 1849

*The road was so lined with wagons...that one would be scarcely ever out
of sight of some train. Dust very disagreeable but not to compare with
the stench from dead carcasses which lie along the road, having died
from fatigue and hunger.*
—John D. Lee, 1849

A short climb cut into a steep escarpment brought me onto a broad
table land. Vernal lay ten parched miles away. An hour past its zenith,
the sun had burned off the clouds that had urged me to remove my shirt
an hour earlier. Ten thousand degrees at its surface, it felt as though the
radiant temperature had dropped only slightly across the 93 million
mile journey to Earth. By comparison my trip to Vernal was minuscule.
Even at a speed considerably less than 186,282 miles per second, I could
make it safely without a shirt.

After riding 100 miles across a desert and over a mountain, fatigue
came on like a fifth of rum. My head spun, my body wobbled.
Dehydration coupled with low blood sugar lead me into a condition of
physiological collapse known to cyclists as "bonking." Standing on even
the shortest climbs, I found myself zoning in and out of reality. Light
blue signs along the roadside only contributed to my muddled state of
mind: "Shellfish Lived Here;" "Crocodile Teeth...;" "Giant Squids...."
Who? What? Where?

Lost in time and space, I found myself riding through the lyrics of a
song by 70's super group, America: "The ocean is the desert with its life
underground and the perfect disguise above." I may have lost my mind,
but at least my "horse" had a name.

The site of Vernal did little to help my confusion. Like many towns in
the West, Vernal is living in the past, but not the 1970's like Wright,
Wyoming or the 1870's like Custer, South Dakota. The history of Vernal
reaches back to...pre-history.

Dinosaurs still reign in northeastern Utah and Tyrannosaurus Rex is
king. Where Jurassic Park meets Dodge City, his animated likeness hung
from every lamp post in town. Bright orange banners displayed the
grinning Rex outfitted with cowboy hat, gun belt and chaps. Talk about
a long, tall Texan!

Advertising everything from motels to laundromats, "terrible lizards" adorned billboards and store fronts alike. Dinosaurs of every size, shape and description crawled the wide main street: smiling dinosaurs, snarling dinosaurs, reading dinosaurs, bowling dinosaurs, biking dinosaurs, fishing dinosaurs, swimming dinosaurs and even one wearing a chefs hat and flipping a pizza. Gift shops, motels, and All-You-Can-Eat restaurants embraced the timeless advertising campaign.

As I'd come to learn is true for most towns in Utah, the streets of Vernal were laid out on a highly organized grid. A map of town looks like graph paper with streets placed at at regular intervals along a central axis. The intersection of Vernal Avenue and Main Street served as the origin—point 0,0. One block in any direction would bring you to 1st street North, 1st street South, 1st street East or 1st street West. Travel in any direction and you'd find 2nd Street, 3rd, 4th and so on. In a bind, town planners use 1/2's and 1/4's, but that appeared to be the limit of their creativity. What it lacks in character, the system makes up for with ease of navigation.

Asking for directions to a market at Laverne and Shirley's General Store took me back to Algebra class. Like a Brontosaurus-sized graphing problem, I took the abscissa to the ordinand, and hung a left. Shameel, shamozzle, it was that easy.

X marked the spot of the Lion Foodmart, and better yet, bananas were on special—five pounds for a dollar. As Bringham Young said 150 years ago when he led the Mormons to Utah, "This is the place."

With enough yellow fruit to feed the monkey house at the San Diego zoo, I headed for a paradoxically long line at the "express checkout." As I waited, an attractive young woman took the place behind me. I turned and smiled. She smiled back, but then removed herself to an even longer line at another register. Moments later the same turn of events occurred with a middle-aged man. Perplexed, I suddenly caught a whiff of my gamy t-shirt and understood. It was riper than my armload of fruit.

After paying, I headed for the nearest motel pool. Rationalizing my use of the facility by purchasing two over-priced sodas from a machine in the lobby, I kept my conscience nearly as clean as my body.

After the dip, I found a small park behind the County Courthouse where shade trees offered relief from the mid-day heat. From a distance, the lone picnic table looked like a great spot to spend the afternoon, but up close it offered a warning: "Don't Touch," the sign cautioned, "Wet Paint - Unless It's Dry." A quick tap confirmed the latter. I pulled my journal from a pannier and spent the rest of the afternoon writing, dozing and peeling bananas.

As evening approached, I packed up and headed west on Main Street with the intention of covering ten to twenty miles before settling into the desert for the night. That's when fate intervened. I heard the calliope at 6th street, but didn't see the striped tents until 7th. The circus had come to town.

On the athletic fields of Vernal Middle School, the Spaulding Brothers One-Ring Circus readied itself for a seven o'clock show. Unable to resist, I locked Betsy to a "No Parking" sign, grabbed my bags, and headed for the (not-so) Big Top. The ticket seller—who later appeared on the tight rope—let me stash my gear in a nearby trailer during the show. Thanking her, I stepped inside and back in time. The sights, sounds and smells turned me into a six year-old, and I spent the next hour and a half in heaven. Dancing bears, leaping dogs, jugglers, clowns and acrobats. The calliope, the ring master, and of course, the elephant.

For early settlers of the West, "The Elephant" was a term for peril incarnate—any unexpected challenge. Their equivalent to Murphy's law, it could manifest itself as a storm, a drought or a broken wagon wheel—anything that could possibly go wrong. No one knows exactly how the saying got started, it simply popped up as pilgrims struggled to find something to blame for their incredible misfortune. Out of the frying pan and into the fire, "The Elephant" lurked around every bend, more than willing to turn bad to worse. Capable of working its mischief in subtle ways as well, "The Elephant" sapped a traveler's stamina with little things like blisters, a burnt dinner or even a poor night's sleep.

I awoke that morning staring up its trunk. In a town where dinosaurs reign, I came face to face with a pachyderm. Too much popcorn, peanuts and cotton candy kept me tossing and turning, but that was only the tip of the tusk. The real problem was the monkey on my back.

Red, hot and sore, the sun's rays had taken their toll. From shoulders to waist, my back was on fire. It welcomed the cooling touch of my hands as they reached around to sooth it. With 20/20 hindsight, I berated myself for not replacing my shirt after the previous day's clouds had burned off.

Seventh Street West led back to 191 where I stopped at McDonald's to wash up and fill my water bottles. In the restroom, I took off my shirt and turned away from the mirror to have a look. In New England, the shade might be compared to a lobster, but here it was pure Entrada Sandstone.

Equally sore, but for entirely different reasons, my legs took the short stretch of construction on the way out of town as the perfect excuse to start the day slowly. Spinning past orange and white D.O.T. barrels and up a low rise, I passed silently into open desert. Scattered red rock mesas spread across the gently sloping terrain. The High Uintas rose mightily to the north, while every other direction lay clear to the horizon. A slight headwind rose out of the southwest.

A blooming cactus offered its sweet smell to the morning breeze. A jackrabbit darted across the highway. A mourning dove cooed softly. But the subtle chorus of a desert at dawn gave way to irrigated fields as I neared the Whiterock River. Soft umber hues faded into a lush, green carpet. The smell of fresh cut hay took me back to summers on the farm of a family friend in New Jersey. Acres of green corn, whitewashed chicken coops, and fields of fireflies at dusk on the Fourth of July. Receiving less than half the annual precipitation of the Garden State, Utah would seem unlikely to arouse such memories.

Death comes quickly and without warning in the desert. It's not something you notice at sixty-five miles per hour with the windows up and air conditioner running. The grim reaper is no stranger in a land where survival is an everyday affair. From the silhouette of a vulture against the clear, blue sky, to the stench of roadside carrion, death is omnipresent. A letter from John Tjostem to a colleague in 1897 reports a snapping turtle flattened beneath the wheels of a heavily loaded wagon. The incidence of roadkill along the frontier has been rising ever since.

Unlike the New England states where roadside casualties are collected by Highway Departments, most western states choose to leave carrion where it falls, ignoring the potential income from such an abundant resource. In a clever scheme to find alternatives to a state income tax, New Hampshire has turned porcupines into profit and black bears into bucks with its annual roadkill auction (intended for taxidermists, not restauranteurs). While the Granite State raises thousands of dollars each year, others squander this valuable commodity. Nationwide, an estimated 350 million animals lose their lives to motor vehicles annually. The plains states alone could balance the budget, while the rest of the country could go to paying off the national debt. Considering the size of Utah and the abundance of flattened fauna I'd already seen, the state could make millions.

Don't ever let anyone tell you the desert is void of life. Its biological richness littered the shoulder of Route 191. A mental list:

    2 raccoons
    3 snakes
    3 skunks
    9 deer
    5 rabbits
   13 birds (assorted varieties)
    2 cats (both quite bloated)
  ±10 unrecognizable lumps of flesh

Of particular note were a severed deer's head, a disemboweled raccoon, and a rabbit's foot that didn't prove lucky to its previous owner. I love the smell of roadkill in the morning.

Perhaps the warming sun was baking my brain, but I developed an odd obsession with the list. In a twisted holiday spirit, I looked forward to each casualty with the excitement of a child on Christmas Eve. With Grinch-like fervor, I wondered what Santa would leave for me next? Would it be Donder or Blitzen...or even Rudolph? Long hours in the saddle will make you do strange things to pass the time.

As the morning wore on, the trickle of out-of-state license plates grew to a steady stream. Tractor trailers and RV's forced me further and further onto the shoulder where a narrow band of washboard—sometimes called rumble strips—forced me to decide between continuing along the foot-wide strip of smooth pavement to its left, or retreating to a gravel-strewn band half that size to its right. I decided to hold my line until a series of close calls with a Mack, a Peterbuilt, and a Winnebago changed my mind. Thanking each with a one-fingered salute, I crossed the washboard and settled for dodging gravel along the narrow strip.

Studies show that one out of every 450 cars on U.S. roads is responsible for a fatality—one out of seven for an injury. Every fifty minutes a new car comes off the assembly line that will some day become an instrument of death. Although fond of citing statistics, I did not want to become one.

While traveling major routes has its disadvantages, there were bright spots among the roadkill and near fatalities. I first noticed the couple as they crested a rise about a quarter mile ahead. At that distance the figure appeared as a lone cyclist, not a pair. Tucked behind the leader, the second rider remained hidden while taking advantage of the energy-saving slipstream. Like migrating geese, they took turns cutting the wind, creating a synergy of effort that allowed the pair to cover more ground together than either could alone.

Teamwork, cooperation in the name of community. It was the type of alliance Bringham Young called the United Order. He envisioned it. He preached it. He lived it. How else could the Mormons have made the desert bloom?

The couple wore matching red, white and blue jerseys. They waved and smiled as they passed. "Where ya headed?" one called.

I hesitated. "West."

There remained a light headwind through Gusher as I passed into a slim segment of the fractured Uintah and Ouray Indian Reservation. After the systematic removal of the Ute tribe from Colorado in the mid-1800's, President Lincoln was pressed to establish a permanent reservation. He contacted Bringham Young in 1861 as to the suitability of the Uintah Valley. Young reported it to be so completely useless that its only purpose was to hold other parts of the world together. Translation: perfect for an Indian reservation.

An addition of land by Congress in 1882 brought the size of the reservation to more than 4 million acres, but over the ensuing century three quarters of that would be taken back. Looking at a map, the heart of the reservation has been torn out of it. It's a jigsaw puzzle with half the pieces missing.

With advances in irrigation, the best agricultural lands along the Duchesne River were sold to individuals as "surplus." The far western section of the reservation was appropriated for the Strawberry Reservoir while the northern section of forests became the High Uintas Wilderness Area. Most recently cheated of water rights in 1965 by the Central Utah Project, current conflicts center around the control of public lands surrounding the disjointed reservation. Arguments between tribal members and local Anglos have resulted in threats of boycott of local businesses and a bomb scare at the tribal headquarters.

Through Ballard, Roosevelt and Myton, the distinction of property boundaries was clearly exhibited by fences along the roadside: chain link, split rail, but mostly barbed wire. Patented by Joseph Glidden in 1874 and mass produced thereafter, it changed the way cowboys would operate forever. A cheap and easy way to mark boundaries and constrain herds, barbed wire sprang up across the West faster than any weed. It eliminated the need for constant vigilance in monitoring cattle and changed the role of the cowboy from herdsman to handyman. His primary role became one of monitoring and mending endless miles of hateful "bob." Buckaroos used to riding the range found themselves "riding fence." By the time Frederick Jackson Turner declared the frontier officially closed in 1893, barbed wire had already transformed the West.

The message of private property picked up alongside the headwind between Myton and Bridgeland. Every tenth fence post on the north side of the road wore an old tire with "No Trespassing" painted alongside Good Year, Uniroyal or Michelin. Alfalfa grew thick under sprinklers fed by the Duchesne River across the road from the dusty colors of thistle poppy, apache plume and prickly pear cactus.

Cattails and marsh grasses grew alongside irrigation ditches, providing habitat for red-winged blackbirds. Protecting their nesting grounds, the feisty passerines harassed me from above. Strongly territorial and polygamous, their behavior bore a strong resemblance to that of certain other local residents.

Chapter 20

If one is so inclined to wonder at first how so many dwellers came to be in the loneliest land that ever came out of God's hands, what they do there and why they stay, one does not wonder so much after having lived there. None other than this long brown land lays such a hold on the affections.
—Mary Austin

In this area...it may be doubted whether...agriculture will prove remunerative.
—John Wesley Powell, 1878

Thick wedges of potato with the skins left on, deep fried and smothered in ketchup. I sat at a picnic table in the shade outside Karen's Korner Drive-In, delighted by the kwality of the fries. I was devouring them like a swarm of grasshoppers descending on the Mormon fields of Salt Lake when a Dodge Caravan with Illinois plates pulled into the lot. As effective as a flock of seagulls, a trio of screaming kids drove me from beneath the canopy and back into the Utah sun.

Downtown Duchesne consisted of little more than a string of dusty square buildings stretched over a mile-long section of U.S. 40. Achromatic store fronts gave little indication whether merchants were open, closed, or even still in business. To its credit, Duchesne had a nice park where I spent the day reading, rehydrating and resting—my personal three R's.

Sitting at a shaded picnic table, I heard a low mumbling voice coming from behind me. Turning slowly, I discovered the source of the sound. The wrinkled old man with a long, white beard was about to color my vision of Duchesne.

He wore black denim pants and faded black boots. Out of the pocket of his light brown shirt stuck a box of Swisher Sweets cigars. He held one, unlit, in his left hand—putting it occasionally to his chapped lips, but not lighting it. A brown baseball cap covered his thin, white hair. Beneath a pair of crossed golf clubs was the message, "I'm not over the hill, just on the back nine." Three pins on the cap read: "Retired, but not tired. RSVP;" "Veterans Helping Veterans - 1994;" and "We the People..." A pair of dark glasses hid his eyes.

"Name's Dave Baum," he said extending a hand. "Lived here all my life, save for a tour in Europe during World War II and a couple months with an oil company in the Middle East. It ain't much, but it's all I claim as home."

Although he dropped out of school in kindergarten, Dave presented himself as anything but uneducated. For two and a half hours I listened, struggling at times to hear his low voice above the persistent wind.

"Like my grandfather," he began, "I've always helped the little people. My wife and I never had kids of our own, but we adopted whoever came along. We owned some land up on the ridge where we built our house and I sold lots cheap to newlyweds who wanted a place of their own. If their money was tight and they could only afford a small lot, I threw another one in for free—you need space to chase the cat around the yard. Settin' out to adopt a few, we ended up with a town-full."

He moved around the picnic table and took a seat. "It's just like with my grand dad. He was a man of morals and never ran another man down. I grew up with him and he taught me through example. He didn't talk much, but when he'd say, 'Looky here boy,' you can bet I was all ears. Yes sir, he was a rare man.

"Grand dad used to take supplies up here onto the reservation. It was his business but he never made any money. When he'd see some Indian kids playing outside with no shoes on, he would stop in and have a chat with the family. He'd motion over to the wagon and give 'em a pair of shoes. The mothers would always say, 'Ike, we can't afford it.' And he'd reply, 'Yes, but someday you will, and there's no sense in me hauling all of this back to town with me.' He always lost money because he gave so much away. He was a charitable and compassionate man. It didn't matter if you were red, white, blue or green.

"The way I see it, if we were all color blind, we'd have a lot less problems. To be fair, you need to ask yourself before you do something to someone if you wouldn't like to have them do it to you. I don't feel I'm above any man, because everyone has talents. The only strange thing about other cultures is your own stupidity and ignorance of them. And the only difference between the Indian culture and the white culture is that the Indian culture is a little bit better.

"All my relatives had nothing but real human friendship and respect for the Indians. My grand dad taught me how to hunt in the Indian style. When we saw an animal he would say, 'You gonna eat it?' And if it were a squirrel I'd say, 'No', and he'd say, 'Then don't kill it.'

"An old Indian friend once said, 'If you want to go up into those hills, go ahead. But when you do, don't leave anything but tracks. And try not to leave too many of those because you might have somebody trailin' ya.'"

After an hour of story telling and waving an unlit cigar, Dave paused. "Mind if I light up?"

I shook my head and he continued. "Never been able to go into a church and get much satisfaction. I'd rather get on my pony and ride up into the mountains to see his creation without any distraction. I don't think there's a God, I know there is. But I don't know who he is or where he is. I'm just thankful to have my time in his fine creation."

Dave got sentimental while he talked about many of his friends who had died recently. "I'm tired of going to funerals."

He was quiet for some time after that, but left me with one last piece of advice. "You don't have to be crazy to be happy, but I've found that in this old world, it sure helps."

By early evening the temperature had dropped but a steady wind continued to blow out of the west. Since I'd be heading south and up a canyon, it wouldn't be a factor. Before hitting the road, I set off in search of a market.

Reversing direction on Route 40, I spotted an IGA and pulled in behind a Chevy pickup with six bodies in the front seat—mom, dad and four little ones. Stopping to let them pass, I practiced my best track stand—no easy feat when fully loaded. Four tiny hands waved as they passed. But before I could follow, a Ford Bronco squealed into the lot behind them. "Federal Aid Hell—It's *Our* Money," read a sun-faded bumper sticker.

With a shorter list, I was in and out with peanut butter, bread and bananas before the family was even through the produce isle. On my way back to the junction of Routes 191 and 40, I caught the attention of a trio of teenagers in the front of a bright red Ford F-150. "Tree hugger!" they yelled for reasons I could only guess.

I hesitated, waved and called back, "Thank you!"

Passing into another fragment of the Uintah and Ouray Reservation, this section of 191 follows an old Indian trail. A slight headwind persisted within the canyon walls, but it provided more pleasure than pain. Combined with light traffic, the conditions were right to take off my helmet. Cool air descended from higher up the mountain, ruffling my hair and lifting my spirit. I alternated between standing and sitting as I climbed alongside the dry bed of Indian Creek. Through low, desert terrain the constant grade allowed me to cover the first twenty miles without shifting gears.

Broken fences, abandoned cabins, and an abundance of trash at roadside marked this section of the reservation. There was no sign of current habitation from Duchesne to the National Forest boundary—marked as much by a cattle guard and warnings of "Loose Stock" as by the welcome sign. Grazing under permits issued by the federal government to private ranchers, heifers and their calves became the most visible inhabitants of Indian Canyon.

With elevation, a silty trickle appeared in the creek bed, flowing feebly between eroded banks where normally common willow, alder, aspen and cottonwood were all but nonexistent. Hoof marks riddled the fragile soil at stream side.

Unlike the actively moving ungulates native to the region, cattle prefer to remain near their source of water. The result in arid lands is that they concentrate around the few and often fragile riparian areas which support eighty percent of the region's endangered species. Research has identified cattle grazing—more than any other single factor—as most harmful to habitat and species native to the southwest—especially near sources of surface water. Poorly-managed herds degrade water quality, spread non-native plant species, compete with wildlife for forage and often cause erosion problems.

The loss of stream side trees, particularly cottonwoods, has led to declines in populations of game birds, songbirds and cavity-nesters alike. Populations of sharp-tailed grouse, masked bobwhites, bluebirds and woodpeckers have decreased in heavily grazed areas. Even raptors and waterfowl are not immune to the impacts of cattle. Mallards, Canada geese and sandhill cranes have suffered damage to their nesting grounds, while the lack of roosting sites has driven hawks and eagles away.

When not moved often enough, cattle trample the same patches of ground over and over, compacting the soil and reducing its ability to absorb the infrequent rains. Interfering with the ground's ability to absorb and store water in times of plenty and release it in times of scarcity, the result is a cycle of flood and drought instead of a naturally constant flow. A report from the General Accounting Office has determined that six times the biomass is produced along streams where cattle are excluded. No longer viewed as gentle beasts grazing peacefully on the plain, cattle have nibbled their way to the heart of controversy in the West.

Wide-eyed bovines monitored my progress—their presence as constant as the signs warning of it. "Open Range" and "Loose Stock" must be the first words local children learn to read. Look! See the spotted cow run.

Startled at my silent appearance, the yearling shuddered with sudden fright. Her hooves slipped on the smooth asphalt as she tried to run for cover. After a moment of spinning her wheels, she gained enough traction to engage first gear. But instead of trotting off into the brush as all the others had, the bone-headed bovine headed up the road.

Too good to pass up, I let out a "Yeehaw," and followed her along the blacktop. Riding her hip, I discovered the ease of manipulating her speed and direction. Like the Mexican Vaqueros who first perfected roping and riding, I felt the power of control. Get along little dogie, get along!

After a quarter mile, she appeared to have had enough. I pulled alongside and drove her into the brush. Breathing heavily, she came to a stop in the sage, turned, and let out a disgruntled MOO!

As darkness settled into the canyon, I found an isolated cluster of willows near the creek. I walked Betsy through the nibbled sage, stepping cautiously through a mine field of manure. I stretched and ate as big-eyed calves came to investigate. More daring than their mothers, they stared in wonder—as any youngster would—at something strange and new. In the end, the persistent bleating of their mothers brought them back. "Don't get too close," they warned. "You don't know where it's been."

Chapter 21

Desert is a loose term to indicate land that supports no man; whether the land can be bitted and broken to that purpose is not proven. Void of life it never is, however dry the air and villainous the soil.
—Mary Austin

Two things kept me in the sleeping bag: the frigid air inches away; and Indian Creek Pass 2,000 feet above. Given my ample supply of synthetic fabrics, the temperature should not have been an excuse. Arctic sheep had given up their polarfleece for my warmth. That left the pass. Although I'd covered part of the 9,100 feet the previous afternoon, my legs and back still suffered from the Uinta climb. I stalled as long as my bladder would allow.

Slipping out of the bag, I scrambled into as many layers as possible. Within minutes, I was fashionably assembled in hundreds of dollars worth of recycled plastic bottles. Certain I'd end the day in t-shirt and shorts, I set off as a synthetic Eskimo. A granola bar washed down by the last of my water made for a scant breakfast, but I was more interested in hitting the road.

The gentle incline I had enjoyed the previous afternoon grew into a genuine grade within a mile. The low, moan of an approaching diesel engine told me I was not the only one forced to downshift.

Although the sun had not yet breached the canyon wall to the east, its first rays appeared along the upper slopes ahead. With the allure that drew the Forty-Niners to California, the golden glow held a special promise for me. I rode anxiously toward its wealth, greeting the warming beams with a smile as broad as a prospector at Sutter's Mill. Over the next three miles, I rode in and out of shadows created by the sawtoothed eastern ridge—a cycle of boom and bust not unfamiliar to most of the West.

As the sections of sunlight outstretched those of shadow, the first feelings of wetness occurred on my lower back. Warm, moist air rose from my collar, steaming as it met the cool mountain morning. Between two stops, I had peeled down to a jersey and shorts, but retained the fleece gloves as my fingers were not enjoying the bonanza of warmth flowing through the rest of my body.

In a surprisingly brief interval, I reached the summit and crossed from the Uinta Basin into Price Valley. A sign warned of the descent: "8% Grade Next 8 Miles." In the shade of canyon walls—and at speeds of upwards of forty miles per hour—I cooled rapidly. Despite the gloves, my fingers were the first to feel a refrigeration that worked its way up both arms. Pausing at the shoulders, the icy grip forced a sudden shiver down my spine before penetrating my core.

Ruefully thinking about those I had just discarded, I noticed the canyon walls had ample layers of their own. Sedimentary strata of ocher and crimson, they became thicker as I sank into their midst. The Price River grew like a dark serpent alongside the curving road. Together we descended into the labyrinth.

Free of cars, I used the entire road on each turn, hugging inside corners and coming out wide into straight-aways. Goose bumps of excitement sprang up alongside those of cold. Aspen, pine, spruce and fir gave way to juniper and pinon. "Deer Crossing" signs replaced those warning of "Loose Stock." Mounted on yellow diamonds, the stocky profile of a bovine could not hold a candle to the nimble silhouette of a leaping deer.

The quiet summer morning brought mule deer out in abundance. Their presence became as regular as the signs warning of it. Rounding the last curve I saw the familiar yellow diamond but with an unfamiliar black image. It wasn't a deer. It wasn't a cow. It was more of a... As I approached, a thick torso came into focus, and then a long trunk and short, stubby legs. An elephant? But the legs were more like wheels, and the trunk angled like a palette jack. A forklift?

Completing the corner, the answer spread out before me as chain link fences and telephone poles replaced stands of juniper and walls of sage. Parking lots filled what had been open country, and I was bracketed by cinderblock buildings instead of the Roan and Book Cliffs. A man in overalls crossed the road in front of me.

Sight overpowered my other senses. I was shocked by the sudden change. I never heard the bells. It took the flashing red lights and striped gate swinging into view for me to understand. Tomorrow's headline flashed through my mind, "BICYCLIST HIT BY TRAIN." Unable to break in time, I swung into a gravel parking lot beside the tracks. Skidding to a stop in a flurry of dust and pebbles, I watched as the Amtrak screamed through the intersection. A short train, just six cars, but enough to do me in.

The ringing and flashing stopped and the gate rose. Opposing lines of traffic crossed the tracks while I remained on the gravel trying to harness my runaway heart. Deep breath in, slow out. Repeat. After a few minutes I had counseled it back to a normal range and set off again. I bounced over the tracks and continued south as U.S. 6 joined 191.

Swelling to four lanes, the road serves as a major thruway between I-70 and the Provo-Salt Lake City area. By mid-morning, the road teamed with tractor trailers, but the wide shoulder and a strong tail wind provided safe and speedy passage. A gift from the north, the wind carried me alongside the Price River and into the historic mining town of Helper—a small community named a century ago for the locomotive engines it dispatched to assist freight trains struggling their way up to Soldier Summit, another twenty miles into the mountains. One hundred years later, Helper lived up to its name with a healthy push from behind. Like a locomotive on a downhill run, I barreled through Spring Glen and Carbonville, stopping briefly in Price to re-stoke my coal car.

The teenage girl behind the counter at the 7-11 yawned immensely as she rang up a box of frosted strawberry Pop-Tarts and carton of orange juice and put them in a plastic bag.

"Don't bother," I told her. "I don't need one."

"Whatever," she said, crumpling and dropping it in the garbage.

I hesitated. "You could've reused that for someone else."

"Whatever."

After 230 miles together, I bade farewell to U.S. 191 and headed southwest on Utah 10 into a Georgia O'Keefe painting. Raw and bony, like a sun-bleached skeleton, the Castle Valley was the driest region I'd yet encountered. It made central Wyoming look like the Amazon basin. The legendary explorer Jedediah Smith described this part of Utah as, "a country completely barren and destitute of game."

A bee hive adorned the route sign, but I could not picture an apiary in the arid lowlands between the Red and Wasach Plateaus. Although sparse, it was a far cry from the image most Americans have of a Sahara-like expanse of shifting sand and isolated oases. The word "desert" itself, from the Latin *desertus*, is a misnomer—not meaning hot, windy, or even dry, but rather uninhabited, devoid of life. To the contrary, most of the American Southwest abounds with rocky plateaus, dry water courses and a surprising diversity of plants and animals keenly adapted to their environment.

Unlike the East where the struggle for survival is one of competition with other organisms to fill a particular niche, in the desert the contest is with nature itself. Competitive exclusion takes a back seat to the indisputable limiting factor—water. When a cactus dies, it is usually not the result of a Darwinian conflict, but rather because it simply out grows its roots ability to obtain sufficient moisture.

While desert hares, kangaroo rats, lizards and snakes seek shelter during the hottest part of the day, desert plants—called xerophytes from the Greek for "dry plants"—are put to the test. Unable to burrow or hide under a shady ledge, these plants have made remarkable adaptations to survive in this unforgiving region.

Able to endure extreme changes in climate, shrubs like cliff rose, yucca, sage, chamisa and blackbrush separate themselves from neighbors by

117

ten or more feet of uncontested ground. Some plants develop extensive lateral root systems which quickly absorb surface moisture, while others utilize a long tap root to reach deep underground sources. During the infrequent rains, many plants absorb water like a sponge—storing it in leaves and stems—allowing them to continue their growth during dryer periods. During the worst of droughts—while grasses shrivel and die—xerophytes simply lay dormant, putting normal activity on hold.

Desert animals also employ a wide range of dry weather survival techniques. Physiological adjustments include the careful regulation of blood and urine, the ability to adjust metabolism, and adaptations in behavior. While most animals drink when given the infrequent opportunity, both the kangaroo rat and black-throated sparrow can live their entire lives without ever taking in water other than that which is included in the foods they eat. Going one step further, a few species of rodents not only never drink, but eat only seeds which have no moisture content. Considering that they emit small amounts of moisture to the air around them and that their blood is liquid, the question arises: How do they do it? The answer is held within their digestive tract where the starch contained in the seeds they eat is broken down to its elemental components. Like any carbohydrate, it contains, along with the carbon and hydrogen implied by the name, some oxygen. By recombining these elements, a rodent which never drinks can supply itself with all of the water it needs.

Meanwhile a host of desert amphibians, like the spadefoot toad, spend much of their lives burrowed deep underground with their metabolism nearly at a standstill. It is only with the infrequent—but often torrential—downpours that they make their appearance known. In a rush to mate, the desert air fills with a chorus of extremely horny toads. For a night or two, the sounds of the desert are replaced by those of a marsh. Time is of the essence for these arid-land amphibians. As the temporary puddles brimming with eggs shrink under the hot desert sun, tadpoles develop tiny arms and legs at a rate unparalleled by their wetland cousins. In a race against the clock, it's do or die for every generation of spadefoot toads.

Yet neither the plants nor animals who call the desert home would consider the conditions painfully difficult. Each flourishes in its own way in what is, for them, not an unfavorable environment. Jack rabbits, lizards, cactus wrens and pinon pines are as well adapted to the southwestern climate as moose or sugar maples are to that of New England. Who's place is it to say that thirty-five inches of rain per year is "normal," and nine or ten is not? Only to the outsider is there something "abnormal" about conditions in the desert.

Indeed, only a foolish outsider would be under the scorching mid-day sun. Without even the sense of a cactus, and feeling rather grass-like (shriveled and dying), I shifted gears, ducked my head, and found a rhythm that would carry me across the arid plain. Along the gently rolling terrain, my brain sought diversion where it could.

With little else to occupy my mind, I became hyper-aware of the road surface. From smooth, black asphalt to cracked, gray concrete to bumpy, pink macadam, it changed its appearance more frequently than a ninth grade girl on her first morning of high school. Like a hundred mile crazy quilt, a patchwork of pavement strung Route 10 together. Within a single mile it was possible to experience as many as three varieties of surface material. If you don't like the road surface in Utah, wait a minute, it'll change.

As conspicuous as strippers at a bingo game, emerald canopies heralded the approach of Huntington, Castledale and Clawson in succession—each town built along a tributary of the San Rafael River. But I pushed on toward Ferron where towering cottonwoods signaled the town long before its sun-bleached buildings came into view. The sound of rustling leaves was as welcoming as the "Approved Drinking Water" sign at the edge of town. I stopped to tank up and buy a loaf of bread at Jeanies Food Mart just after 11:30. Having ridden eighty miles, I was ready to call it a day, but something—perhaps that "Approved Water"—urged me to continue on to Emery, another fourteen miles away.

Looming over my right shoulder, Nelson Mountain provided the motivation I needed to push through the waves of heat radiating from the blacktop. The landscape, once again, was characterized by cacti, salt pan and thirsty arroyos. The Muddy River held only dust.

At the edge of a wide mesa, Emery clung to Route 10 like a child to its mother's leg. North of the road, a dozen dilapidated cabins stood in a field—either for tourist value or because nobody had ever bothered to tear them down. The latter seemed more likely as not a single gift shop, restaurant or gas station lay along Emery's cheerless main drag.

Freshly painted bleachers stood ready for the first pitch. Bright, white bases marked the diamond. The infield was raked, the outfield mowed. A low chainlink fence stood at 250 feet along each foul line and 275 in straight-away center. More than a ball field, this was a shrine. How many little leaguers had worshipped here—uttering prayers at the plate with a three and two count?

A sign on the backstop listed the activities planned for the upcoming 24th of July celebration—Utah's Settlers Day. Along with a little league tournament, events included a fun run, parade, fireman's breakfast, story telling, horseshoe tournament, dance, fireworks, "and more."

I left Betsy under a roofed picnic area along the third base line and proceeded toward a mint green cinderblock building near the left field bleachers. The smell of stale urine met me at the door. I turned away to inhale a fresh breath before entering the shadowy chamber. Above the urinal, someone had written "Coors Light" in magic marker with an arrow pointing down. The color matched.

Barely adequate for draining liquid, the vulgar rest room could hardly be trusted for supplying it. I grabbed my water bottles and crossed the street to a small, yellow house where the sounds of a man at work emanated from the garage.

"Hello?" I announced in a voice shy of a holler.

"Yes?" the man replied, emerging from underneath the hood of a car. "Can I help you?"

"Just wondering if I could fill my water bottles."

"There's a spigot 'round the side."

As he pointed, another voice came from inside the house. "Who are you talking to Hank?"

"Nobody, Martha."

A woman appeared in the doorway and the Burns and Allen Routine began. Playing the perfect straight man, Hank provided set-ups for Martha's bizarre stories and outrageous non sequiturs.

"This fella rode his bicycle from North Dakota," he said. "He's lookin' for some water."

"All the way from North Dakota?" she responded. "Goodness, you must be thirsty. Let me get you a tall glass of ice water."

Hank rolled his eyes as Martha passed through the screen door and back into the house.

"You a Dakotan?"

"No, I'm from New Hampshire. I took a bus to North Dakota, and started riding from there."

"You've been busier than a cow's tail in fly time! Why'd you take a bus to North Dakota if you wanted to come to Utah?"

"It's a long story."

Hank rolled his eyes again, but it was hard to tell if it was in response to me or to the loud crash that came from inside the kitchen. "I'm all right," cried Martha. "Just brushing up on my tap dancing."

"Never a dull moment," Hank confided. "Last week she went to the Post Office and came back four hours later with a waffle iron. What am I gonna do? I love her."

We shrugged in unison as another clatter came from the house. Martha stood at the screen door—her hands full—trying to pop the latch with her elbow. Missing repeatedly, her bent arm crashed against the loose plexiglass. The rattle echoed through the garage.

"Hold on Honey, I'll get that for you."

"Thank you Dear. You're a regular Prince Spaghetti."

The tray in Martha's hands held a large glass of ice water and a paper plate piled high with fresh fruit. Alongside the sweating tumbler, juicy slices of pink watermelon and glistening green grapes made an ideal still-life—"Cyclist's Dream."

"Get this Martha. This fella took a bus from New Hampshire to North Dakota so that he could ride his bike down here."

"That's silly." She turned to me. "Don't ya know there's a bus station up in Price? Or did you get lost, honey? I once got on the wrong train up in Salt Lake. I was supposed to meet Hank in San Diego—back when he was stationed there—but two days later I ended up in Chicago. I kept wondering why the sun was rising in the west, but nobody else seemed concerned about it. The railroad people were real nice, though. They gave me a free trip from Chicago all the way to San Diego. Do you remember that Hank?"

"Of course dear." He smiled and turned to me. "Where you headed?"

"I'm going down to Loa to see some friends. What's the best route?"

"Just stay on 10 until you get to I-70. Go under the Interstate and take the first right where the sign says Fremont Junction. Follow that for a mile and turn left on 72."

"Oh, the road from Fremont to Loa is just beautiful," said Martha.

"It's a heck of a climb..." Hank began .

"But the 'Quakies' are simply breath-taking."

"Quakies?"

"Aspens," they responded in unison. "Quaking aspens."

As the conversation continued, Hank mentioned something about a spring, but they disagreed on the location. Not wanting to cause any more controversy, I thanked them and headed back to the park. Although it was clear that Hank deeply loved Martha, the neatly trimmed grass, carefully weeded garden and homemade lawn ornaments—a Holly Hobby style wooden girl swinging from a tree branch and a lumberjack whirligig—indicated that he spent quite a bit of time working alone in the yard. Sometimes the best thing for togetherness is spending time apart.

Back at the park, I started in on the watermelon, savoring each bite as the sweet juice dribbled down my chin. Nibbling it down to the rind, I lost myself in the flavor of childhood memories: Fourth of July picnics; summer camp cookouts; seed spitting contests. Laying on the soft grass of a ball field on a hot summer day chewing on a thick slice of watermelon. Frederick Turner once wrote, "The meaning of America still resides, somehow, in the West." I had to agree.

"Sorry," said the man with a large hammer in his hand. He stood high on a ladder repairing the chicken wire backstop. "gotta get ready for this weekend."

"No problem," I replied. "Time for me to get up anyway."

A wake up call in more ways than one, I took it as a hint to do a little maintenance work of my own. Betsy's front derailleur had given me problems earlier in the day, but the quick fix I had employed would not hold up long. Upon closer examination, the clamp that held it in place had slipped. The derailleur no longer held a position parallel to the chain rings. A simple repair, five minutes were more than enough to set things straight. But I spent another half hour carefully examining the rest of the bike for potential problems. A squirt of 10 W 40 on the rear derailleur, chain, and free wheel would have the drive train running like a well oiled...Pow!

The blast jerked my head like a line drive into left field where a tractor had just turned off the road beyond the foul pole. It parked behind the fence and backfired again as a man in blue overalls and red cap turned off the green and yellow John Deer. He sat motionless until joined by another man in a beige pickup. As the truck came to a rest beside the tractor, the men exited their vehicles and played a twenty minute game of horseshoes. The clanging of metal upon metal carried across the field. These were no beginners—quite literally a couple of ringers. At the game's conclusion they shook hands and drove off.

Rested and rehydrated, I prepared to do the same. Hank and Martha topped my bottles and we said our goodbyes, but the friendly tail wind which I had enjoyed earlier had shifted ninety degrees and buffeted me from the side. With heavy legs, I proceeded south along Utah 10 framed by the Coal Cliffs to the east and a distant Musinia Peak—seven feet shy of 11,000—in the west. Like the mountain, my legs came up short.

When you ride a lot, you get to know yourself and your bike in a deep, intuitive sense. You know what gear you should be pushing under a wide range of conditions and roughly how fast you're going at any given time. A cycling computer is not essential to this bond between man and machine. If anything, it may even weaken the bond by providing digital output on speed, distance, R.P.M.'s and maximum velocity. With this precisely calculated information at your fingertips, there is no need to develop a deeper understanding of your partnership. Like technology in many parts of our lives, it separates us from the immediate experience.

I don't consider myself a Luddite, but I do believe that technology can stand in the way of authentic experience. I've gone through any number of cycling computers over the years (most have died on me), and I am confident in saying that they change the feel of a ride, especially a long one. I get wrapped up in the numbers instead of the road itself.

Trying to increase my average speed for the ride from 17.8 miles per hour to 18.0 takes away part of the pleasure in just being out there. If that's my focus, I might as well be on a Lifecycle at the gym.

Marathoners describe a similar sense of knowing their bodies while racing. They can tell the difference between a 5 minute pace and 5:05. It's nothing more than a sense of, "Yes, I'm in my zone and all it well with the universe."

For me, this sixth sense takes into account hills. Even when I downshift and may be crawling up a steep grade, in my mind it's all right because I can see the slope. Without even consciously thinking about it, my two-wheeled intuition absorbs the information and adjusts. It's sort of a granny gear clause.

The same process accounts for rough roads, descents (both steep and mellow), and stop-and-go riding in areas with stop signs (although most cyclists regularly ignore them) and traffic lights. In all of my experience, however, this sense has never been able to account for wind. Sometimes a tail wind pushes me to a point where I know I'm riding beyond my limits. It's a sense of euphoria, empowerment, ecstasy. This is good.

But sometimes a headwind can come like an invisible menace, slowing progress to a crawl on a flat straightaway or even a slight downhill. When this happens, my entire sense of self—the oneness with my bike—is lost. Perception and reality do not mesh. I find myself grinding it out, yet hardly moving while a smooth ribbon of asphalt stretches out invitingly. No flat tire. No brake pad rubbing. Nothing wrong with the bike. It must be the pathetic rider. What a loser! It's a sense of helplessness, dejection and despair. This is bad.

"Welcome to Sevier County." The spelling may have differed slightly, but the pronunciation was right on. The eleven miles to Fremont Junction took nearly an hour. Passing under the interstate and turning directly into the gale, I called it a day at 110 miles.

With growling stomach and howling thighs, I pulled off at the foot of Mount Alice, just inside Fishlake National Forest. Walking Betsy through low, withered sage and silver gray rabbitbrush, the soil disintegrated beneath my feet. A cloud of dust followed me into a grove of shaggy-barked junipers where I found a shady spot among a cluster of lousewort and unpacked my gear. A sweet scent drew my attention to the spreading phlox nearby. The purity of the large, white petals offered hope beside the gnarled junipers.

Between courses of peanut butter and jelly, I noticed increasing numbers of red ants crawling over the ground and investigating my legs. Scurrying hither and yon, the scene appeared as chaotic as a city during rush hour. Running from one whole to the next and back again for reasons unknown, each ant formed a fraction of a cog in the colonies complexly integrated machine.

I sat back and watched with interest until suddenly...Ow! That little bastards bit me. Ow! Another one. Brushing them off only aggravated the others to respond by digging their tiny mandibles into my already suffering legs. Too tired to move, I slipped into my bag for protection. In ancient times, the seeds of the nearby lousewort were used to destroy lice. Laying captive, I wondered about its effectiveness on ants.

Chapter 22

A great American myth is embodied in wild lands, and it is myth, ultimately, that holds a people together.
—Ann Weiler Walka

Wilderness is an anchor to windward. Knowing it is there, we can also know that we are still a rich nation, tending to our resources as we should—not a people in despair searching every last nook and cranny of our land for a board of lumber, a barrel of oil, a blade of grass, or a tank of water.
—Clinton Anderson, former Senator of New Mexico

If future generations are to remember us with gratitude rather than contempt, we must leave them more than the miracles of technology. We must leave them a glimpse of the world as it was in the beginning, not just after we got through with it.
—Lyndon Johnson, signing the Wilderness Act, 1964

I could move my eyelids, but little else. The sun had risen. I could feel its warmth penetrating my sleeping bag. I didn't bother checking my watch—the thought of raising my arm was too much to bear. Unable to use the cold morning air as an excuse to linger inside my cocoon, I searched for others.

My legs ached, my heart raced, my spirit sank. My only solace came from knowing that I faced a relatively short thirty-five mile ride. I tried to forget the fact that Fishlake Mountain lay in my path. At that moment I didn't know if I could stand up, let alone climb a mountain. With the knowledge of a short day ahead, I used all my power to stay in the bag. Only the sun's warmth, and the corresponding increase in ant activity, drove me out.

With a strange feeling of Deja Vu, I ate a granola bar for breakfast and washed it down with the last of my water. I leaned my head back and squeezed the plastic bottle with a vigor of urgency. Both hands pressed the liquid onto my morning tongue. My eyes were closed when the top popped, so I didn't see the cascade, but I surely felt it pouring down my chest. I reacted swiftly, but not swiftly enough. My fingers relaxed around the empty bottle as the small puddle between my feet disappeared into the sandy soil. The last of my water slipped away toward the roots of thirsty junipers, destined to be squandered a second time.

Called *phreatophytes*, or "water-wasting" plants, junipers are despised by farmers and ranchers throughout the Southwest. The gnarly evergreens have long tap roots that soak up more moisture than most trees twice their size. Juniper forests are condemned for choking out

125

forage for cattle and reducing groundwater yields. Standing in their midst with a parched throat and empty bottles, I felt the same ill will.

Saddling up, I chose a gear that matched my energy level. Although the grade did not warrant it, I remained in my small chain ring all morning, spinning even where the valley opened up into wide, level meadows appropriately called "flats." Each one had a name: Frying Pan Flat; Sign Board Flat; Pancake Flat. Coming upon one as yet unlabeled, I offered one of my own: Dehydrated-Bicyclist-the-Morning-After-Riding-110-Miles-Over-a-Mountain-and-Through-a-Desert-and-then-Sleeping-on-an-Ant-Hill Flat. If that proved too long for the USGS to print on maps, they could simply call it "Pretty Fuckin' Flat."

As the grade increased, fortunately so did my spirit. Dwelling less on my miserable condition, I noticed more along the road. Like a Richard Scarry book, everything was labeled. Besides the flats, there were signs for draws: Willow, Burro, Water; creeks: Paradise, Goat, Last Chance; and springs: Pine and Aspen. Despite the aqueous indications, none held any water. More than a few early settlers in the region had surmised that the rivers must have run underground, "'cause they sure ain't on top."

There were signs for cows and signs for deer. Not much traffic, but plenty of signs for "Parking Areas" and "Scenic Pulloffs." But alas, there was no sign of the top.

With elevation, twisted pinon and juniper (what local folks call P-J forests) gave way to the aspen groves promised by Hank and Martha. Clusters of silvery-barked "quakies" shimmered with the slightest breeze. According to Ute legend, the aspens were once the proudest of the trees. When the Great Spirit came to visit the earth, all of the plants and animals shivered in awe while the aspens stood stiff and proud. Outraged at their indolence, the Great Spirit cursed them to forever tremble whenever any eye is laid upon them.

Since male and female flowers occur on separate trees, it's rare to see a solitary aspen. Because females are few and far between, most aspens do not grow from seeds, but rather sprout from the roots of established parents. Competing for sunlight, water and space, they crowd each other until the weaker die and the stronger go on to replace the aging parent trees. Ferns and bunch grasses take advantage of the lull between generations—growing thick among the silvery trunks.

A succession of switchbacks indicated the top must be growing near, but reaching the summit without finding water would be a hollow victory. Along with the sound of aspen leaves rustling in the breeze, I could hear the expansion joints of the guard rail shifting like tectonic plates under the warming sun. As I'd learned over many days, late morning marked the critical temperature—around eighty degrees—to set the joints into motion.

Through the first switchback, I saw nothing that could qualify as a spring, even a dry one. As I began to lose hope, it appeared on the outside corner of the second hairpin. Salvation! From dry earth sprang forth water—beautiful, life-giving water. Dismounting, I knelt beside the spring and prepared myself for baptism. "Our Father who art in Heaven, hallowed be thy..." manure? What cloven-hoofed beast had left its mark beside my christening chamber? Tainted. Sullied. Impure. Paradise lost, it was nearly my last temptation.

As I leaned over the tainted pool, horrific tales of the gastrointestinal parasites filled my mind replete with cramps, nausea, and explosive diarrhea. I pulled out a bottle of Potable Aqua and scanned the directions: ...one tablet...seal lid...shake well...ten minutes.

A miracle—one oxygen atom bonded to two hydrogens. Agua, aqua, atl, ab. Maji, mizu, moyam, ma. Wasser, woda, waha, wai. Vatten, vada, voda, viz. Millions of such miracles splashed over my tongue, down my throat, and diffused throughout my body. Like the brine shrimp we used to order through the mail, water brought me to life. I pushed on with renewed vigor.

The summit rewarded me with a tantalizing view of Wayne County. The still, blue waters of the Forsyth Reservoir in the distance gave me hope that it would be less severe than Sevier. Optimism replaced doubt as I followed the ribbon of asphalt out of the mountains and into the desert below. Passing the all-encompassing Riverside Inn, Restaurant, R.V. Park and Lounge in Fremont, I found myself looking for its namesake. A yard wide and a foot deep, the narrow irrigation canal beside the road was the only surface water I could see—hardly worthy of the title.

It's amazing what passes for a "river" in Utah. I looked with disbelief at the channelized trickle beside me that wouldn't even pass as a creek in New Hampshire, let alone a stream. But in Utah it received full river status. Like the diminutive man who's name it bears—five foot John C. Fremont—the "river" has overachieved.

With water and will, the fields of Fremont were made to bloom. Verdant as any I'd seen, they stood out as bright emeralds among miles and miles of gray sage. Streaming sprinklers threw water in long arcs across thick carpets of alfalfa. Cascading droplets sparkled in the sunlight, giving each field its own rainbow. But a pot of gold would not be found beneath the leaves of alfalfa—water itself is the bullion of an arid land. Like miners staking claims on a mother lode, cattlemen hold water rights up and down the river. The Fremont has long since been tapped to its fullest extent. Subsidized or not, water is the undeniable cornerstone to human settlement in the heart of Utah. This is where water reigns.

Route 72 wound through the fields and stockyards of Fremont, passed a state fish hatchery and came to a T-junction with Utah 24 at the north end of Loa. Turning south, I rode down Main Street looking for Aspen Achievement Academy. As I'd been told over the phone, the large, brown building with "MARKET" painted on the front was easy to spot along the modest boulevard. Even as the County Seat, Loa's residents numbered less than 300.

Due to an increase in the popularity of alternative treatment programs for troubled teens, Aspen had recently moved its office to the former market. Boxes of books, files and folders were stacked in the foyer, but I hardly noticed the clutter in my excitement to see the familiar faces of old friends.

A receptionist directed me upstairs and down the hall to the second office on the left. I stepped through the doorway and into their arms. Just what the doctor ordered, Sean and Sharon were Prozac to my spirit. Take two hugs and call me in the morning.

Sean offered to treat me to lunch at Jeneal's Drive-in, but Sharon had some calls to make. She would join us as soon as she could.

Less than a quarter of a mile away, we decided to walk. Crossing the street we proceeded south along the rocky shoulder where the sight of an auto parts store triggered Sean's memory. "I've got to stop in here and check on something," he said. "It'll just be a minute."

"No problem," I replied, remembering his interest in auto repair. "I'll wait here."

Standing in the shade of the overhung roof, I scanned the vicinity. Typical of small towns in rural Utah, Loa had a small, independent market, a gas station, and a state liquor store.

As in New Hampshire, the state owns and operates liquor stores, but that's where the similarities end. A hundred years of Mormon influence has resulted in a complicated system of state stores and private drinking clubs. While some finer restaurants have full liquor licenses, they may only offer spirits upon request. Bars and taverns are permitted to sell only 3.2 beer. It's a far cry from New Hampshire where a state liquor stores stands beside the "State Safety Rest Area" just north of the toll booths on I-93.

Sean stepped out of the auto parts store with an awkward look on his face. Mid-way between rage and hysteria, I couldn't tell whether he was going to blow his stack or keel over laughing.

"I can't believe it," he moaned with a smile on his face. "He didn't order the new radiator like I asked. He told me I didn't need it—that I could fix the old one myself. Have you ever been in a store where the clerk tries *not* to sell you something? It happens all the time around here. Money is tight for most folks, so they look out for each other. They expect that you have about what they have, and a dollar saved is worth every penny. It's a far cry from New York where everybody is trying to rip you off."

"So he didn't sell you the radiator because he wanted to save you money?"

"It's crazy! For the first time in my life I can afford to buy a new radiator, but the shop won't sell me one. Old Charlie just smiled and said, 'You kin fix t'other, goddammit.'"

"Goddammit?"

"It's a standard part of the vocabulary around here. If you want someone to take you seriously you have to end your sentence with 'goddammit'."

"That must take some getting used to."

"Life in rural communities is very different and most outsiders just don't get it. People got along fine for a long time without much outsider impact. There wasn't any interest in this area for a decades. Through good times and bad, families managed to get by. These people are skeptical of outsiders, governments from away, and legislation that locks up land that has been traditionally used for extraction.

"We try to be sensitive. We're careful about some of the things we say. Outside of my house and the Aspen office, I never use the E word."

"The E word?"

Sean stopped walking, looked around cautiously, and then leaned to whisper in my ear. "Environmentalist."

"Environmentalist?" I repeated in a normal tone.

"Shh. It has a bad connotation around here. Mormons aren't allowed to swear. They can't say 'asshole,' so they use 'environmentalist' instead."

"You're kidding."

"Yes and no. It took me months before I had the guts to ask for a vegetarian taco at Jeneal's. I got tired of eating French fries every time we went. When I finally asked, she looked at me funny and said, 'How can you have a taco without taco meat?' But I talked her into it. She makes a good meatless one now."

The truth. We enjoyed our lunch at a shaded picnic table outside the small restaurant. Making sure there was no one within ear shot, I asked Sean about the difficulties of being a vegetarian environmentalist (local translation: hippy asshole) in rural Utah.

"Cows have more rights than people," he joked. "They can sleep and crap within 200 feet of water."

"Tell me about it. I've seen them everywhere, especially on public land. What's the feeling about that around here?"

"Well, the debate over wilderness designation has come to a head this summer. The BLM manages about 22 million acres in Utah, and the question is how much of that affords designation. Even though polls show a majority of folks would like to see 5.7 million acres set aside, Utah's Congressional delegation introduced a bill that would designate just 1.8 million acres of the most economically unappealing land in the state. The kicker is that the bill would then release all the remaining BLM land in the state from future consideration as wilderness."

"Incredible."

"What's more..." Sean cut himself off as a pair of men in cowboy hats exited Jeneal's and walked to a pickup truck. "What's more, the 1.8 million acres designated would allow construction of roads, dams and power lines—all of which are against the spirit and letter of the Wilderness Act: '...where the earth and its community of life are untrammeled by man...'

"What year was that anyway, '68?"

"No, earlier. More like '65."

"Try '64, boys." Sharon joined us at the table with a traditional taco. She was decidedly not a vegetarian. "Why are you talking about the Wilderness Act?"

"We're just discussing the clash of vision and values we've found out here."

"Clash?" said Sharon. "Have you told him about the Utah Wilderness Education Project?"

Sean shook his head.

I ventured a guess. "Wise Use?"

"How'd you guess? This is *not* an organization that takes pimply faced junior high school students on educational field trips into the redrock desert. The name is merely a front for an organization representing the Farm Bureau, the Petroleum Association, the Mining Association, the Woolgrowers Association, and the cattlemen. Their goal is simply to influence debate over the Wilderness Bill.

"That's quite a backing," I observed.

"Yeah," admitted Sean, "but UWEP is an upstart compared to the Wilderness Impact Research Foundation."

"Wilderness impact?"

"Their goal is to educate the public about the damage that wilderness causes society."

"What?"

"It's true. And do they have backing!" Sean counted on his fingers. "Rocky Mountain Oil and Gas Association, the National Forest Products Association, the National Cattleman's Association, the American Motorcyclist Association, the Northwest Mining Association..."

"That's a lot of associating."

"We've been following the debate fairly closely up at Aspen." Sharon added. "In one press release they claimed that if the existing wilderness study areas in southern Utah were given official designation, it would cost the state $9 billion a year."

"Who would believe that?"

"You'd be surprised. There's a new group down in the Escalante area that's fighting wilderness designation any way it can—threats, intimidation, even vandalism. They call themselves People for the USA."

"One county official took a bulldozer and bladed a primitive road into a proposed wilderness area because he disagreed with the feds on jurisdiction."

"And you should read the editorials in the county paper. I was down there last week and picked up a copy. One guy claimed that environmentalists were a bad influence on children, and another lamented about 'worshiping the creation instead of the creator.'"

"But the best," interrupted Sharon, "was the man who said he felt 'raped, pillaged and plundered' by environmental groups. He ended his letter by asking 'tree huggers' where they had been for the last 125 years."

"I think I know some Native Americans who could ask a similar question."

As the debate over wilderness intensifies, an increasing number of people are coming to its defense. Wilderness, as UWEP and PFUSA would have us believe, does not lay in opposition to liberty, but rather stands beside it. They are brothers.

Yet only recently has this become a respected point of view. Throughout much of our nation's history undeveloped land was seen as something dark, mysterious, evil. Even the revised 1978 edition of Roget's Thesaurus, lists Wilderness as "wasteland, waste(s), wilds, badlands." For an antonym it suggests "see HEAVEN."

It was just a matter of time before these archaic ideologies were left behind, allowing us to realize that it is through our relationship with the land that we have developed those qualities that we, as Americans, hold dear: resourcefulness, perseverance, individualism; also generosity, optimism and hope. So deeply is wilderness ingrained in our collective imagination, that we often fail to notice it's presence.

Wild lands are all that connect us to a long history of life on Earth. They are not something to be feared and conquered, but rather embraced and celebrated. When traveling through them, we leave society behind and take no one but our true selves. When close to nature, everyday garnishes become insignificant. We accept our limitations. We embrace ourselves and the world. There are lessons we learn in the wilderness that are learned nowhere else, for Mother Earth—Gaia—is the greatest teacher of all. Who else has been tenured for four and a half billion years?

When we lose wilderness, we lose the *idea* of wilderness. And when we lose the idea of wilderness, we lose our character as a people. There are those who may never set foot on a trail or spend the night in the backcountry, but still write angry letters to Congress simply because they want to know that wilderness exists. For some unexplainable reason, a plumber in New York City, or a garbage collector in Atlanta, need to know that a seemingly useless gorge in Utah is protected.

America, simply put, is among the last industrialized nations on earth that retains undeveloped tracts of land substantial enough to be called "wilderness." Wild lands have seen our nation through good times and bad. From the first wobbly steps of sea-weary pilgrims, to Neal Armstrong's "great leap for mankind," wilderness has been beside us and within us. "Love it, hate it, or ignore it," writes Donald Snow, "wilderness is in our American soul." It is the embodiment of the national myth—that which ultimately binds us as a republic.

Part 3
Cowboys

Chapter 23

*We deem it hardly necessary to say...that a cowboy is a fearless animal.
A man wanting in courage would be as much out of place in a cow-
camp, as a fish on dry land.*
—Texas Live Stock Journal, 1882

"If there's one thing I've learned since we moved," Sean said as he drove me to the house in Bicknell after lunch, "it's that we need to find balance. The land appears boundless, and most folks who live here have little perspective on using it up. They were brought up to believe that resources are to be harvested and made useful. Instead of place they see space. Many Westerners resent laws written by Eastern E's, most of whom have never set foot in cattle country.

"On the other hand, perhaps a trip to the crowded Atlantic seaboard would do ranchers a bit of good. With a common experience, both Easterners and Westerners could better see eye to eye. After all, isn't there a common goal—a healthy, productive environment?"

"I hear what you're saying, but can it work?"

"It's got to," he said pulling into the driveway. "What are the options?"

"*The Monkey Wrench Gang?*"

He smiled. "You ought to talk to our neighbor. Elmer can tell you what a rancher thinks—he's been at it for nearly seventy years."

His skin had the look of tanned leather soaked and dried in the sun for decades—rode hard and hung up wet. Deep lines across his face attested to a life outside. Crow's feet—a whole flocks worth—rumpled his cheeks and the corners of his eyes. Dark, precancerous moles covered his nose. But behind his deeply furrowed brow was a sharp mind.

"When I was a kid," he began, "we'd drive steers up to Salt Lake for twelve dollars a head. It'd take us two weeks there and almost another back. Made fifteen dollars a month working sunup to sundown, even Sundays. Woulda worked longer if the trail boss coulda figured out how to stretch the hours of daylight. Once they got electricity in that barn it was time to find another outfit—I didn't want to be workin' all night too.

"Yes sir, things were mighty different back then. Weren't no trucks reliable enough to take 'em out after the herd. Did all our work on horseback. A good saddle was your most important piece of equipment—

used to cost a month's wages. I'd say a good one now'll run you over two.

"I remember when there was more open space—fewer fences and gates to slow you down. A fellow could lose himself in country bigger than his problems. There really ain't no open range any more. It's all been surveyed, mapped, and fenced. Yes sir, things have changed."

"With new equipment, barbed wire, and pickup trucks, do you think the cowboy will ever be replaced?"

"No sir, they'll never invent a machine that takes as much abuse."

"What about...the land? How much abuse can it take?"

He paused, and for a moment I thought I had ended the conversation. I sat nervously. Tension joined us on the porch. You could have cut it with a Buck knife.

He broke the long silence with a sigh. "In the old days the way you were competitive was to run more cattle than your neighbor. The land was so big nobody thought twice about it. Most of the range degradation happened before 1900. They say at the turn of the century, there were 30 million sheep and 15 million cattle on open range. They say that's twice the number of wild ungulates—deer, antelope, buffalo—that were grazing the land in 1800. Of course that was before my time," he said with a chuckle which turned into a hacking cough. His wrinkled face grimaced as involuntary contractions shook his entire body. Thumping firmly on his chest with his right hand brought the spasm under control.

"As I was sayin', that was in the days before men knew how to manage the land. I'll admit they made mistakes, but I'm tired of being blamed for 'em. Times have changed—the Taylor Grazing Act saw to that. Even the cows have changed. Plump Herefords have replaced those scrawny longhorns who never really produced much of anything besides horns, tails and appetites.

"I agree that too many head can damage an area, but the land needs to be grazed. What these people don't understand is that cattle are a tool for range management. Grasses need to be grazed to remain healthy. These lands have evolved over many, many thousands of years of hooved animals being in the ecosystem. And so it's formed a symbiotic relationship—which means they coexist with each other. They do better when both are present. They need the impact of the cattle. They need something to graze on 'em to clear away the old grass. Otherwise it becomes dormant, I mean stagnant, and nothin' happens on the range. Cows break up the soil for water absorption and they spread fertilizer around.

"Some folks call it 'Holistic Resource Management.' It's spelled with an H, but it's not like a 'Hole,' it's 'whole,' with a W. I'm not into this new age stuff, so it took me a little while to figure that out. I'll admit I was skeptical at first—like most folks—but now I'm beginning to understand. There's a fella by the name of Allan Savory down in New Mexico who's come up with this theory that overgrazed areas can be restored by *increasing* the size of herds."

"Increasing? What's holistic about that?"

"This fella, Savory, is from Africa, but he's a white man. He's a biologist, and he used his observations of zebras and wildebeest on the plains of Africa to develop his ideas. The dry air and seasonal rains make the African plains much like ours, only we don't have the great migrating herds anymore. But we used to. And it was with those great herds that the American grasslands evolved.

But just as cattle were introduced to the American West using management techniques developed in the humid East, the same thing was happening in Africa using European practices. In both cases the result was disaster. They tried to use cookbook formulas, and failed miserably. You've seen it."

I nodded. "So how is this any different? You haven't told me how it works."

"I'm gettin' there. Just cool your heels a minute."

"Sorry."

"So these wild herds—in both Africa and here—they naturally bunched together against the threat of predators. They grazed an area intensely for a short period of time, fertilized the soil with their dung, trampled the ground, and moved on. They wouldn't return until the grasses were tall and green again. You follow?"

I nodded.

"On the other hand, domestic stock tends to be dispersed over an area for a longer period of time, grazing some plants again and again while avoiding others. This may work where rainfall is predictable and abundant, but that just ain't the case here. We need a system that works for us, and Savory is offering one.

"It's important for you to understand that ranchers want to take care of the land. We have to—we depend on it. That's where land management comes in. Lusher grass means fatter cows, which means more profit for a good land manager. It pays off where it really counts—in the wallet. I'm talkin' about things like keeping the cattle moving, and placing salt licks away from water. Without the large grazers that once lived out here—bison, antelope, deer—cows need to be on the land."

"What about...public land?"

Elmer was among the majority of western ranchers who do not graze animals on public land. Just one out of six cattle growers holds a lease to either BLM or NFS acreage, accounting for less than two percent of national beef production. But he stood by them.

"Like I said, the land needs to be grazed. Public land is no exception. But what's happening is that traditional uses of these lands are coming into conflict with what you might call 'recreational uses.' Of course it's all federal land, so the question becomes how to cut the cake among the interested parties.

"It's like these two mountains we got here." Elmer pointed to the highlands both north and south. "When the Geological Survey first named 'em on the maps, they mixed 'em up. On the first 'topo' of this area, Boulder Mountain was the one covered with ponds while Thousand Lake Mountain hardly had a speck of blue. At first the Survey didn't want to admit the mistake—they got pride like the rest of us. But they had to come around sooner or later, and they did. Now we got maps with boulders and lakes on the right mountains."

If only it were that easy. If only it were that clear. After my conversation with Elmer, the western cattle issue was no longer a battle between good and evil, right and wrong. It wasn't nearly as black and white as the Holsteins I knew from New England hillsides and Ben & Jerry's ice cream cartons. Having given a fair hearing to the other side of the debate, I was thrust into a gray area as wide as a set of Texas longhorns.

Chapter 24

For behold, I reveal unto you a new and everlasting covenant...if any
man espouse a virgin and desire to espouse another...he cannot commit
adultery for they are given unto him...and if he have ten virgins given
unto him by this law, he cannot commit adultery, for they belong to him,
and they are given unto him; therefore is he justified.
—Joseph Smith, 1843

Mormons are born with a shovel in hand and irrigation in their blood.
—Stewart Udall

Sharon honked as she pulled into the driveway. The white Toyota pickup ground to a halt on the loose gravel. She got out and waved. I thanked Elmer. He nodded and raised a finger to his hat.

"You got any laundry?" Sharon shouted across the yard.

"You bet," I answered, shaking hands with Elmer and joining her beside the truck.

"Grab your stuff then, and let's go."

"Go where? Didn't I see a washer and dryer in your kitchen?"

"Been broken three weeks. It's not easy getting a Sears repairmen way out here."

With a single movie theater in the entire county, that didn't come as a surprise. But what it lacked in service technicians and cinemas, Wayne County made up for with complimentary religious literature. Free copies of the *Book of Mormon* were everywhere—in the post office, in the laundry mat, and even in Spanish (*El Libro de Mormon*).

The Aquarius Laundromat stood adjacent to the Aquarius Motel and Cafe, and down the street from the Aquarius R.V. Park. My suspicions of a remnant hippy population—or at least a diehard Fifth Dimension fan club—were put to rest as Sharon explained the name. Serving as the southwestern boarder of the valley, the Aquarius Plateau curves around the lower canyonlands from Powell Point in the east to Boulder Mountain to the west. It is the dominant topographical feature of the area.

"You won't find too many hippies around here," she observed. "Most folks tend to be on the conservative side. This is the state who's legislature refused to accept the Equal Rights Amendment in 1973, and had a man shot by firing squad in '77."

"I haven't been in a state this conservative since...I left New Hampshire."

"Don't get me wrong," Sharon said as she shuttled a load of socks and underwear from washer to dryer. "The Mormons are friendly and considerate...and they have the most beautiful blond-haired children.

Most families we know have exactly four, or are working on it. Up north, we often hear of families with ten or more."

"Ten?"

"Mormon's are about as much into birth control as atheists are into Sunday School."

"What about polygamy?"

"Having multiple wives is pretty much frowned on these days. You'll find it up in the mountains here and there—maybe a man with two or three wives—but you won't see it in most towns. And you'll never find anyone with twenty-seven wives like Bringham Young."

"Twenty-seven?"

"Some folks call him 'Bring 'em young.' His motto was, 'I never refuse to marry any respectable woman who asks me.'

We spent the rest of our time at the laundromat shuffling loads, folding t-shirts and sorting socks. We loaded the warm, fragrant clothes into the back of the truck and returned to 100 South where Sean was playing catch with Tyler the dog.

"Let's get some supper," he said as we pulled up. "I'm famished."

"How about the Sunglow?"

The name rang a bell, but it wasn't until I opened the plastic-coated menu that the faded, plywood billboard at the edge of town came back to me. "Home of the World Famous Pickle and Pinto Bean Pies." I'd have to save room for dessert.

The smell of coffee and grease met us at the door as we stepped into an American classic. Back to back, a row of brown, leather booths ran along picture windows on three sides of the restaurant. Opposite the doorway, a lunch counter ran the length of the rectangular seating area. Evenly spaced clusters of napkin dispensers, salt and pepper shakers, and ketchup bottles lined its surface while a row of empty red upholstered stools stood ready before it. A wide, short window in the wall behind the counter passed into the kitchen. Through it passed a constant banter of short-order talk: "Gimme a pistol, whiskey down. Hold the skins."

The pass-through was flanked on one side by a rack holding small boxes of cereal, and to the other by a glass pie case. A sign above it read: "Fresh Baked Daily."

A variety of beheaded "game" lined a strip of brown paneling between the top of the windows and the white ceiling. We found a booth under a pronghorn. I opened the menu and chuckled at the Dinner Specials: "Fried Chicken $3.75; Spare Ribs $4.75; Children $2.50."

Within moments, a smiling waitress far too young to call me "Honey" distributed plastic tumblers of ice water and took our orders. Her name tag said Dawn.

Sean went first. "I'll have a BLT without the B."

Without skipping a beat, she continued, "Fries or baked?"

"Fries."

"Salad or 'slaw?"

"Salad."

Sharon ordered a burger and fries. I opted for grilled cheese, but my mind was really on dessert.

Scanning to the bottom of the menu, I was relieved to discover that the "World Famous Pickle and Pinto Bean Pies" were actually two different varieties. The comma after pickle on the billboard had gone undetected.

Dawn found my confusion hilarious and shared it with another waitress behind the counter as she opened the case and served me up a whopping slice of pinto bean. My eyes grew as wide as the king-sized dollop of homemade whipped cream.

Incredible! It called for both a standing ovation and an encore performance. Truth be told, I stood up to go to the bathroom, but I did order a second piece on the way.

Over coffee and empty pie plates, we talked the talk of old friends—catching up, reminiscing and sharing our visions of the future.

"That's part of the problem," Sean said in response to my comment about the increasing popularity of the region. "People who used to just come through during the summer months are starting to build vacation homes or move here permanently. Everyone wants a part of the West."

"But what is it that makes the West the West?" asked Sharon. "Open spaces. But when you fill 'em up with housing developments they're not so open anymore."

"It started up in Salt Lake and Provo, and now it's spreading across the state. It's the same pattern of low-density development. They often call them 'ranchettes.' You spread these five or maybe ten acre lots across a beautiful valley, and pretty soon the beauty is gone. Almost anywhere there's scenic beauty and private land, houses are popping up. It's like a virus on the land."

Incubated in the petrie dish of suburbia, careless handling has allowed sprawl to invade the rural West where an inadequate immune system has left it vulnerable to infection. The idea of land use planning had never been considered in a region celebrated for its rugged individualism. What's to keep a rancher with substantial land holdings from selling out to a developer for a lump sum he would never see by running cows? Raising houses in the pastures is simply more profitable than raising cows.

For the first time since I'd learned about the abuses suffered through

negligent grazing practices, the American cowboy appeared as a part of a possible solution rather than the heart of the problem. Maintaining the character of the West, Sean and Sharon agreed, means, in part, maintaining its most enduring character.

"What you've got to understand," Sean offered emphatically, "is that people are a part of this land. Always have been, and always will. You're talking about people's livelihoods. You're talking about tradition.

"Despite what's happening up in Salt Lake, Provo, and all the rest, the essence of the West remains in the well-defined relationship between man and nature. Popular myth describes the cowboy as many things, but in reality he's a ranch hand, a laborer. Of course there's a long history of overgrazing and abuse, but most ranchers I know are working hard to repair the damages. Managed properly, I see cows as perhaps the only thing that will save the sense of space which defines this region."

"Those are strong words coming from a vegetarian..." I lowered my voice to a whisper, "...environmentalist."

The empty street glowed by the light of a full moon. Its pale illumination spread across the plateau, smoothing and softening the rugged landscape. By moonglow, one sees things through a different light.

Without difficulty, my hosts convinced me to stay for a pancake feed before leaving. Warm conversation over hot coffee, I savored both. Once more they asked me to stay, but I had to decline.

Sean reached into his pocket and pulled out a string of beads. Carefully, he explained its meaning, "These are ghost beads—juniper seeds that have had one end chewed out by a pack rat. To certain tribes, they represent the hogans in which they place their dead. They poke a hole through the opposite end of the seed just as an opening is made in the top of the hogan to let the spirits of the dead in and out.

"One hundred and one beads must be collected and prepared to make a necklace that will protect it's wearer. There is one bead for each of the hundred Navajo spirits and one extra for the coyote who'll try to trick you into thinking that he is a spirit himself.

He extended the necklace. "Sharon gathered these beads and I put them together. We want you to have it."

The three of us embraced. They fit me like a hand-knit sweater—love filled the gaps and mended the flaws in stitching. It entered my heart and soothed my soul.

The sweet taste of friendship lingered as I road south toward Torrey and Capitol Reef National Park, stopping briefly at the Red D Market to buy bananas. Held up, or rather slowed down, at the checkout counter behind a woman whose cart was as full as her blouse, I counted thirty-four varieties of beef jerky on display. From hickory smoked and barbecue flavor to black pepper and teriyaki, Baskin & Robbins had nothing on the Red D.

Route 24 wound south and east of Bicknell, following the contours of the exquisite landscape. A group of sedimentary monoliths loomed ahead, their western sides shadowed before the low, morning sun. Beyond them stood the vertical, red cliffs of the plateau. North of the road, they ran tall and level like the Great Wall of China. To the south they were fragmented, the broad span interrupted at intervals by gulches, ravines and an occasional pinnacle. These cliffs more closely resembled the Berlin Wall mid-way through its collapse. More stable than any man-made rampart or even the institution of communism, it takes millions of years of weathering to bring these cliffs to the ground.

In Torrey, I passed the Capitol Reef Inn and Cafe (four star dining and accommodations), the Chuckwagon General Store and Motel (three stars), and the Brinks Burger Drive-in (unrated). South of town, State Route 12 cut south toward Teasdale, Escalante and Bryce Canyon National Park. Until the road over Boulder Mountain was cut, the Kaiparowits Plateau had been the least accessible region of the continental United States. The towns of Boulder, Escalante, Henrieville and Cannonville were the last in the lower forty-eight to receive mail service.

The Kaiparowits Plateau was also where local legend Everett Reuss disappeared in late 1934. Just twenty years old, he set out on November 11, 1934 from Escalante on the back of a burro, posting a letter to his brother before he left. "As to when I shall visit civilization again," he wrote, "it will not be soon, I think." The young artist encountered a number of sheepherders on his way to do some sketching at Hole-in-the-Wall, near the confluence of the Escalante and Colorado Rivers. He was never seen again, but his legend looms large to this day over southern Utah.

I stuck to 24 and headed toward Capitol Reef alongside the beleaguered Fremont River. Co-opted by irrigators along its entire length, I had difficulty understanding its status as a good trout stream. In a state where eight of the eighteen endangered animal species are finned, perhaps any fishing at all constitutes good fishing. Efforts to preserve aquatic habitat have increased in Utah partly in response to the tragedy that has occurred in Arizona where thirty-two native fish species have disappeared while twenty-one of the remaining twenty-seven are either endangered, threatened or under consideration for such listings.

After three miles of blue sky and purple sage, a pair of motels, a gas station and an information center signaled the edge of the park. I continued up a small rise to where the road bent slightly left, presenting me with a horizontal landscape to the extreme. It was the kind of vista that inspires wide angle camera lenses and those extra-long panoramic post cards that require additional stamps. The Navajo call it "Land of the Sleeping Rainbows."

Dotted by gnarled junipers, the gullied landscape ran to the horizon in every direction like an ebbing, crimson tide. The same vermilion cliffs of the "Great Wall" continued along the northern border, interrupted mid-way by a broad, level shelf. Most clearly marked by the shrubs growing along it, only careful examination revealed a slightly different hue in the sandstone above and below. The far off stratum provided the first clue about what makes Capitol Reef a sedimentary geologist's Disneyland.

Originally deposited in a vertical order, later periods of uplift and erosion have exposed millions of years of geological history along a horizontal plane. Passing through the angled strata of the park is like riding through time. The first layers took me back to the Cretaceous Period—65 to 135 million years ago. The Mesa Verde formation, Mancos Shale and Dakota Sandstone remember the time when flowering plants first appeared on Earth. Shallow seas flooded the Colorado Plateau while coal-forming swamps and lagoons blanketed the shoreline. Lignite is abundant in the Mancos layer while oyster shells identify the Dakota as a marine deposit.

The blue-gray bentonite hills of the Morrison Formation signaled the transition into the Jurassic Period. Rich in dinosaur bones, petrified wood and uranium, this layer is popular among archaeologists and nuclear scientists alike—one seeking clues to a mass extinction in the past while the other prepares a potential element for one yet to come.

Beyond the Morrison Formation rests the chocolate-colored Summerville and greenish-gray Curtis Formations. At some time during their deposition, the first birds took to the skies. These historic strata give way to the striking red Entrada Sandstone known for its unusual formations in both Cathedral and Goblin Valleys. Alternating beds of siltstone and fine sandstone result in an uneven hardness which allows certain sections to resist erosion better than others. While the harder patches withstand the forces of wind and water, softer material is carried away, creating the eerie shapes often called "goblins."

Rich in gypsum, the light brown Carmel Sandstone is evidence of the brief incursion of a narrow seaway during the late Jurassic. It lays is stark contrast to the bright white sands which were once shifting dunes but now lay fixed in the Navajo Formation. The parks name sake, Capitol Dome, is a memory of those dunes. A certain sense of irony, however, surrounded the feature honoring the hallowed halls of Congress which lay within a layer bearing an Indian name.

Deposited by wind, Navajo Sandstone marks a dramatic change from the underlying Kayenta Formation—a marine deposit commemorating a shallow inland sea that covered southern Utah. As I had learned on the outskirts of Vernal, this shallow sea teamed with an abundant variety of life. Ranging from clams and coral to octopi and fish, a rich fossil legacy is contained within the dark red sediments.

Within the Kayenta Formation, Hickman Bridge—largest natural arch in the park—recalls the dual role water played in its formation. From its benthic origins through a period of uplift and riparian erosion, the bridge owes its existence to hydrologic forces. Viewed in its current arid surroundings, however, it seems as out of place as grounded ships now more than a mile from the retreating shoreline of the Aral Sea.

Because of their similar color, it's difficult to tell where the Kayenta layer ends and the Wingate Sandstone begins. Ocher upon umber, it takes an artists trained eye to pick out the subtle change in hue. Nearly undetectable, the boundary marks another significant transition not only from water-born sediments back to aolean deposits, but also the Jurassic Period to the Triassic. Stretching from 190 to 230 million years ago, the Triassic Period includes the day that furry paws first walked on the planet. With humble beginnings as a primitive monotreme resembling the duckbill platypus, mammals have adapted and evolved over the ensuing eons into the most complex and intelligent of any animal group.

It was more by chance than by some deep mammalian connection that I ended my morning ride in the middle of this thick, crimson layer. I stopped because 100 years ago a group of Mormons decided to plant an orchard in a land of rock and sky. They had faith, the kind of faith that can neither be laughed off nor reasoned aside. Wipe away the unfriendly epithets Mormonism has been branded with—bigotry, racism, intolerance—and you'll find a soul as solid and as certain as the rocks it turned into gardens. Defying explanation, it demands respect. To this day, fruit trees carpet the canyon floor from one sheer wall to the other. Fruita is their legacy.

Maintained by the Park Service, acres of cherries, nectarines, peaches, pears and apples are available to visitors at a nominal fee. Pulling into the shade of a grove of peach trees, I felt grateful to the men and women who made it possible. A slight breeze carried the sweet perfume of fresh fruit through the canyon as I stepped off Betsy and leaned her against a fencepost. As I gazed at the breathtaking surroundings, I noticed a pair of deer eating fallen apples not twenty yards away. A family of partridges came into view just beyond them and headed off across the orchard—undoubtedly looking for a pear tree. Wild onion, Mormon tea and larkspur lined the banks of the streamlet that split the canyon. Who would have guessed the Garden of Eden lay hidden in southern Utah?

Unlike Adam, I needed no tempting. The sweet juice of nectarines dribbled down my chin as I devoured one after another. Anything but forbidden, a ranger told me to eat my fill—no charge.

Comforted by eventlessness, I dozed in the cool shade. Any cynical thoughts I may have had about the Mormon's dissolved like sugar in a cup of tea. The boat people of their time, they'd overcome great hardships and made the desert bloom. Utah enchanted me in ways I'd never dreamed possible. Safe, clean and beautiful (forget the road conditions, I'm on a roll), the Mormon's State of Deseret surpassed all expectations.

John Muir had a trick of inverting Heaven and Earth by standing on his head and flip-flopping the landscape. Had I not been so full, this Canaan would have been the perfect place for such a maneuver.

Back on the road, the bicycle again became a time machine carrying me through the layered sediments of the Triassic Period. As with the rest of the Mesozoic Era, this was a time when dinosaurs ruled the Earth— "The Age of Reptiles." Their tracks can be found in the burnt orange Chinle Formation as well as the red-brown Moenkopi layer. This latter stratum also boasts two of the park's main attractions: Chimney Rock, which towers like a lonely smokestack in the desert, and Twin Rocks, so similar in size and shape it's as if an enormous mirror had been placed next to one to reflect its image toward the parking area.

Beyond the Mesozoic Era lies the Palaeozoic—a time favorable to the development of marine invertebrates. Trilobites flourished in shallow Palaeozoic seas like the one that covered this region.Their fossils are common throughout the Kaibab Limestone alongside the road. A tremendous variety of shapes and sizes had evolved during the Pennsylvanian Period, but the trilobites mysteriously began to decline during the Permian until finally, at it's end 230 million years ago, they were extinct altogether. The reasons, as with many ancient extinctions, are unknown.

The sight of an orange cement truck alone in the desert jerked my mind back to the present. Like a Magritte landscape, it was surrealistically out of place. Parked perpendicularly to the road, I could not make out the spray-painted message on the large tumbler until I was much closer: "Cafe 800 Feet." The makeshift billboard was followed by another of a more conventional plywood variety: "Hungry? Stop at the Luna Mesa Cafe - 600 ft." The sun hung low in the western sky as I slowed my cadence to view the offerings.

A covered porch flanked three sides of the wooden structure. Weathered to a mellow gray by wind and sun, little separated the building from the similarly ashen moonscape around it. The only bright colors for miles around—besides the cement truck—were those of the UFO painted between the gently sloping roof line and the top of the porch. A traditional disc-like saucer with a semi-circular bubble on top, it resembled the one George Jetson used to fly on Saturday mornings. The only difference was the bright red, blue, yellow and orange geometric shapes painted on the side as if the Partridge family had done the job. As intended, the proprietor had captured my interest, and my dollars were not far behind.

Whizzzzzz. A sound not unlike that of George's saucer clipped my ear as I walked up a short set of stairs to the porch. Flinching briefly, I regained my composure and followed the blur across the veranda to where it hovered beside a feeder. Beating it's wings in a figure-eight pattern too rapidly to see, the tiny hummingbird appeared as armless as Michelangelo's Venus. The iridescent colors of it's tiny head and trunk sparkled in the last rays of sunlight.

Awe struck, I simply stared, feeling a commonality with a creature who, like me, requires long periods of rest to recover from intense periods of physical exertion. Scientists have measured their heart rates at 1,200 beats per minute—highest of all birds. But the tiny avian creature is no stranger to superlatives among it's kind. The hummingbird is not only the smallest, but also the quickest, most maneuverable and considered by many the loveliest of all our feathered friends. In the blink of an eye, and as suddenly as it had appeared, the hummingbird was gone, leaving me to wonder how such a delicate creature could exist in this forbidding place.

Continuing up the steps and across the porch, I opened the screen door and entered a world of odds and ends. The cafe/gift shop was decorated in early random. Raw plank walls were lined with shelves piled high with knickknacks of every description. Each nook and cranny displayed a memento with little significance to the uninformed. An odd mix of Native American artifacts and X-File memorabilia blended into the standard gift shop offerings of t-shirts, postcards and cheap jewelry.

A broad map of the United States covered most of the ceiling. Beneath it, four wooden picnic tables filled the floor space. A spicy smell emanated through an open door behind an unfinished bar—a pot of chili on the stove.

A barefoot blond girl appeared in the doorway to the kitchen only to disappear just as suddenly. Moments later a bald, bearded man in a Hawaiian shirt and shorts took her place. "Can I help you?"

"I was passing through and curiosity got the best of me."

"The spaceship, huh?"

"That and the cement mixer."

"Great investment."

"I bet."

"Give a holler when you wanna order."

"Whatever's cooking smells good."

"Today's special—bean chili."

"I'll take a bowl."

A minute later the barefoot girl reappeared in the doorway, her hands cradling a large, brown bowl. She walked slowly and deliberately, eyes fixed on her steaming cargo. With the top of her head barely above the bar, she extended her arms up and out to set the bowl upon the counter.

"Thank you."

"Youwecum."

I drained three glasses of water before I reached the bottom of the bowl, but ordered a second serving none the less. Waiting for the return of my pint-sized waitress, I noticed a sign on the wall. "Teepees For Rent - Nightly rates." Unsure at first, the second bowl sealed the deal. For the third time that day, my stomach was bursting at the seams.

Chapter 25

The nation that destroys its soil destroys itself.
—Franklin D. Roosevelt, 1937

The San Rafael Desert spreads like a broad, waterless sea over millions of acres of southeastern Utah. Sparsely vegetated waves of sand roll from the Henry Mountains south of the Fremont River to the Tavaputs Plateau north of I-70. Sixty miles of acrid soil, dusty arroyos and stunted brush lay between Caineville and the town of Green River. The prospect called for an early departure.

By 6:30, I was pedaling into the sunrise. State Route 24 carried me through Blue Valley where steep, dry cliffs—each with a broad apron of talus—ran along the north side of the road. In stark contrast, thick fields of alfalfa lay to the south, brought to life by the meager Fremont. Private land clings to the river like a calf to its mother—suckling precious moisture from the source of life. The volume of water had decreased since I last saw it in Torrey. Agricultural withdrawal has caused the river—like a rattle snake eating a kangaroo rat—to be narrow at both ends and wider in the middle. Only a relative trickle of the Fremont ever reaches the Colorado.

Careful monitoring has revealed that a full ninety percent of the water diverted from the Colorado River watershed is used to grow hay for livestock which supply four percent of the nation's meat production. Under an agreement between five western states and Mexico, the Colorado is the most carefully managed river in the world. So thorough is the accounting, that the river once called the "Grand," now disappears into the sands of northern Mexico miles shy of the Sea of Cortez.

Stingy sage and rabbitbrush grew scarce as I continued east into a moonscape of gray bentonite hills. Lizards sunning themselves on the edge of the asphalt peeled away like the crowds lining a stage of the Tour de France. Biting flies pursued me as tenaciously as the paparazzi hound the wearer of the Yellow Jersey.

A vast network of ATV tracks weaved in and amongst the ashen mounds of the Pinto Hills. The slopes were scarred by the distinctive double lines left behind by pleasure seeking four-wheelers obviously confused about the difference between "recreation" and "wreck creation." With little rain to wash the scars away, their legacy will remain for decades—a testament to the fragility of the desert as well as the frivolity of man.

Without warning, a trio of junk art dinosaurs rose out of the barren landscape. "Welcome to Hanksville." Welded from scrap metal and painted with white Rustoleum, skeletal versions of Stegosaurus,

Tryceratops and Tyrannosaurus Rex stood beside the Poor-Boy Motel. My smile remained as I passed a sign for the Jurassic RV Park. Beyond Stan's Burger Shak and Johnson's Stage Coach Market, I pulled into Jeem's Cafe at the far end of town: "We Cater to Bus Tours." It was nearly empty.

"Have a seat. I'll be right with you," said a slim, brown-haired waitress as she passed me, her arms hidden beneath plates of eggs and homefries. She dealt them to a table of men, turned and wheeled back. "Oh, you again."

"I was just hoping to fill my bottles and maybe get a couple of coffee rolls for the road."

"We can do that. Here, I'll take 'em into the kitchen." She extended her arms.

"I can fill 'em in the bathroom."

"Nothin' doin'. We got a filter on the kitchen tap. Hand 'em over."

"Thanks."

She was back before I even had time to give the place a good once over. "Here ya go. That'll be a buck fifty for the rolls and ten dollars for the water."

"What?"

"Can't take a joke, huh? Must be from the East."

"It's that easy to tell?"

"'Fraid so. Where you headed?"

"Green River today, and then Moab."

"Shoulda guessed. You gonna have enough water?"

"I hope so—got all my bottles full."

"Radio said it's gonna be a scorcher today—hundred and five. Hang on right there," she said and disappeared back into the kitchen. She was gone longer this time, and her weather report made me want to get back on the road as soon as possible. The mercury was already pushing eighty at eight o'clock.

"Here you go," she said walking toward me with a ketchup bottle in each hand. "Consider these your reserve fuel supply."

"Thanks," I said accepting the converted water bottles.

"It's an stunningly beautiful land," she said, "but it can also be cruel as hell."

Three miles north of Hanksville, the confluence of the beleaguered Fremont and Muddy Creek gives birth to the aptly named Dirty Devil River. Like liquid sand, it flowed under the highway bridge and southeast toward the Colorado. The next forty miles would be entirely void of surface water.

Desert of one kind or another makes up a third of the land mass of our planet. Satellite images indicate this fraction is increasing at an unprecedented rate. Worldwide, an estimated 15 million acres of once fertile land are degraded each year—an area the size to West Virginia lost beyond hope of reclamation.

Beyond this, another 50 million acres become too debilitated to support even the simplest forms of agriculture. Meanwhile, hundreds of millions of additional acres lie in varying stages of deterioration. The United Nations Environment Program estimates that a total of 8.6 billion acres are moderately desertified with another 3.7 billion acres qualifying as severely desertified. Unlike natural deserts where a diversity of organisms survive as part of a balanced ecosystem, these new deserts come closest to resembling the original Latin term *desertus*, as they are practically devoid of life.

The domestic threat first caught the public's attention in 1934 when windstorms swept across the Great Plains. To regional farmers, it began yet another year of such conditions, but ended in disaster. From Texas through Montana and the Dakotas, strong winds kicked up dust clouds thick enough to cause darkness at noon. During May of that year, the eastern half of the country was blanketed with a massive haze of topsoil blown off "America's Bread Basket" 1,500 miles away. Ships 200 miles off the Atlantic coast received doses of the Great Plains. The erosion was so severe that 9 million acres of cropland were lost forever, earning the region its tragic nickname—The Dust Bowl.

Eventually, the federal government had to intervene. Hugh Bennett of the U.S. Department of Agriculture addressed a congressional hearing on the matter. He expressed the need for a program that would protect the country's topsoil—arguably it's most valuable natural resource. In typical Washington fashion, lawmakers debated the issue until finally, as if a message from a greater power, western dust seeped into the hearing room and spurred them to action.

Recent estimates put rates of topsoil loss in the U.S. at 5.5 billion tons per year. While eighty percent of this has been attributed to erosion by water and twenty percent by wind, the root causes are poor farming techniques, irrigation and overgrazing. One third of original U.S. cropland has been permanently removed from production due to excessive topsoil loss. Half of what remains is losing soil at a rate faster than it can be replaced.

Overgrazing is the chief cause of degradation on millions of acres in the western United States. Eighty-five percent of the topsoil lost from our nation's cropland, pasture and rangeland is associated with raising livestock. Natural systems which have existed in a delicate balance for thousands of years are stressed beyond the point of repair as marginally productive semiarid lands are turned into sterile wastelands. If, as Elmer contends, the land needs cattle to remain healthy, the question becomes how many?

Beyond the entrance to Goblin Valley State Park, I began to notice the union between my rear end and the bicycle seat had worn thin as the desert soil. The Gilsen Buttes saw me fidgeting like a long distance bus traveler trying to find a comfortable position. As Route 24 dipped slightly through Old Woman Wash and climbed a series of low dunes, I took full advantage of standing despite the gentle grades. By the time I had crossed the San Rafael River and passed Jessie's Twist, however, it no longer took a change in topography to get me out of the saddle. I stood on flat sections simply to give my glutes a break. I was up and I was down, up and down, up and down, out across Nine Mile Wash, Five Mile Wash and into Green River.

A stream of sparkles bounced across the horizon like shooting stars caught up in tumble weeds—windshields glimmering in the sun. The familiar rumble of eighteen wheelers started out low and distant, building to a crescendo as I approached. Out-of-state cars hauling campers with stickers from Yellowstone, Yosemite and the Grand Canyon sped toward the next National Park on the schedule. ("We *did* Arches, Canyonlands and Capitol Reef all in a weekend!") For many, the roads in between have become little more than open-air tunnels. The sights and sounds of I-70 reminded me why I'd stuck to the "blue highways."

Although SUV's and minivans have become the *modus transportatus* of American families, the scene inside is timeless. Repeated in all models of station wagon over the last fifty years, each member dutifully fulfills their respective role. A scowling father puts the pedal to the metal, powering through the miles to get to the next motel and a cold glass of beer. Mom alternates her gaze between the wrinkled road map in her lap and the wrinkling husband by her side, unsure whether to mention the fact that they just missed their exit. From the back seat come howls of "Get off my side" from a pair of road-weary children involved in a petty game of territoriality.

I recalled the countless hours I'd spent battling my brother in the back seat of our Pinto station wagon, driving back and forth across the longer-than-you-think-it-is state of Pennsylvania each holiday season. Over the turnpike and through the toll booth, to grandmother's house we'd go. But dad knew the way to put an end to our play with a well-place backhand blow.

To this day, I still can't understand how he could keep one hand on the wheel while reaching clear into the back seat to smack us with the other. With uncanny range and accuracy, he could nab us even while crouched in the apparent safety of the foot space behind the passenger seat. For years my brother and I thought he was Plastic Man, but now we know better. Our sense of awe has been replaced with a little nagging guilt. We can't help but feel at least partially responsible for his constant back pain and monthly visits to the chiropractor. All those years of stretching and bending on the turnpike must have taken their toll.

With a standard assortment of truck stops, motels and fast food joints, Green River typified the interstate town—lots of convenience, but not much charm. Intense heat radiated off the asphalt in front of the West Winds Truck Stop where at least a dozen cars had roof racks with mountain bikes. Pilgrims like me, they were heading east toward the Mecca of off road riding where the trails are legendary: Merrimac, Hurrah Pass, Gemini Bridge, and above all Slickrock. Fifty miles away, the red rock of Moab beckoned. They could be there in under an hour.

Envious but patient, I locked Betsy in the shadow of the overhung roof and stepped into the truck stop. A large sign filled the front window: "All U Can Eat Buffet." Most of the truck drivers looked as if they had, but I deferred. A loaf of bread, a pair of Snickers, and full water bottles seemed enough until, further down the road, I encountered the source of Green River's moderate fame.

Plump, round and pale green, they filled fruit stands up and down the wide main street. Broad pyramids of the luminescent orbs sat beneath colorful umbrellas. The mere utterance of the name is strangely satisfying—Honeydew.

Pulling into a lonely looking stand for a sample, I got more of a taste of local flavor than I'd expected. A large, Hispanic woman greeted me with a smile. She wore a long green dress and held a pink plastic fly swatter in her lap. From the moment I arrived, she seemed more interested in hearing about my trip than selling me a melon. She bombarded me with questions in broken English: "Where you come from? Isn't you so hot? Where you get water? How fast you go? Where you sleep?"

Listening carefully to my answers, she offered one final observation "Loco!"

Given the opportunity to finally make a purchase, I palmed a large melon and brought it to the woman.

"No," she said. "Poco. Poco. Smaller is more sweet." She lifted a melon half the size and exchanged it with me. "Put in river for una hora, then you eat frio. Muy bien!"

I reached for my wallet.

"No," she shook her head. "Es un regalo."

"Gracias."

Sweet, green juices streamed over my palate as freely as the river caressed my toes. The melon was just as she described—muy bien.

Two miles north of town I'd found a wide sandy beach along the Green River. Originally called the San Buenaventura by Spanish explorers, the Green had recaptured the whimsical spirit of a free-flowing watercourse two hundred river miles downstream of the dam at Flaming Gorge. From that plug of concrete aggregate, the river flows unmolested through Echo Park, Split Mountain and the Gates of Lodore before entering the town that bears its name. To the south it continues through Desolation Canyon and through Canyonlands National Park to its confluence with the mighty Colorado at the legendary Book Cliffs.

But the joy ride through the roaring depths of Cataract Canyon is short lived, as the waters of both rivers become slack behind another mass of concrete and steel at the far end of a once-canyon named Glen. Buried beneath hundreds of feet of water lays what many conservationists consider the most stunningly beautiful canyon on Earth. Following its disappearance beneath the waters of Lake Powell (some prefer "Lake Foul"), Edward Abbey describes, "a once lovely wonderland of grottoes, alcoves, Indian ruins, natural stone arches, cottonwood groves, springs and seeps and hanging gardens of ivy, columbine and maidenhair fern. Imagine the Taj Mahal or Chartres Cathedral buried in mud until only the spires remain visible."

"I was the MESSIAH, the EVANGELIST!" beamed Floyd Dominy, dam builder and last of the two-fisted New Deal-era bureaucrats. In the years following the successful completion of the Hoover Dam in 1936, engineers busied themselves with planning a wide range of other possible manipulations of the watercourse. Over the decades that followed, a multitude of dams and diversion projects sprung up along the Colorado and its tributaries.

Pipelines were built to quench the thirst of nearby cities like Las Vegas and Phoenix, while a 240 mile long aqueduct was constructed to carry water to the sprawling megalopolis of southern California. Fostering no regrets, when questioned about the possibility of his dams wiping out wild salmon populations, Dominy responded tersely that those people who rely on fish as part of their diet, "can eat cake."

From where I sat on the bank of the Green, the dams at Flaming Gorge and Glen Canyon were in another world—their effects only detectable by the most observant hydrologists. Aware only of its temporary freedom, the river invited me to join it in a lazy afternoon beneath the cottonwoods.

A slight breeze rustled the leaves and carried a Latin rhythm from a trio of pickup trucks at the far end of the beach. Children danced in the sand while their parents looked on, sipping beers from a cooler. As the sun dipped behind salmon cliffs, two chubby-cheeked boys approached from the fiesta. Barefoot and shirtless, they kicked sand as they walked.

Stopping a safe distance from such a dubious-looking stranger, the shorter one nudged the taller and muttered something I couldn't make out. "No, no. You ask," came the response.

"But mama say you."

"Okay, okay." The tanned boy with rounded belly and protruding navel turned to me. "Hey meester, you wan eat with us?"

Within minutes I was surrounded by happy faces and lively music. The smiles grew brighter as darkness fell on the riverbank. Chattering teeth were only interrupted by chewing.

In a large, wok-like pan set above a roaring fire, hand-rolled tortillas were fried to a golden brown. A pot of beans and another of rice simmered at the edge of the flames. Fresh salsa topped it all off. In one evening I learned more Spanish than I had in three years of foreign language class.

"Mas cervesa por favor!"

Chapter 26

*Above all things, the plainsman had to have a sense—an instinct for
direction...Few men have this instinct. Yet in the few it is to be trusted as
absolutely as the homing instinct of a wild goose...I never had a
compass in my life. I was never lost.*
—Charles Goodnight

A mourning dove cooed softly in the high branches of a cottonwood.
The soothing call caressed my ears. It woke me as gently as a lover's
kiss. Like a pair of sweet lips, the melody lingered soft and low. I savored
the song, drinking it in through my ears. Smooth. Calming.

I heard another call that morning, but not with my ears. It was in my
bones, in my muscle fibers. It tingled in every cell of my body. It was
inaudible, yet loud and clear. It was a call of destiny and it came from
Moab.

I loaded Betsy with care and headed into the rising sun. The desert
glowed violet through my tinted sunglasses. A kit fox scampered across
the road, pausing momentarily on the shoulder to size me up before
disappearing into the sage. The constant drone of traffic on I-70 a half
mile to the south carried across the still morning air.

Old Crescent Junction Road parallels the interstate for the first five
miles out of Green River until being swallowed up by the serpent seven
miles shy of Crescent Junction and my old friend Route 191. From the
overpass I looked down on a constant stream of traffic. Not wanting to
risk another fine, I checked the map for alternatives.

While it indicated no frontage roads, a single dashed line led southeast
to a junction with 191 about ten miles south of Crescent Junction. Along
with avoiding the interstate, a popular geometric theorem would indicate
that this route would also be shorter. Instead of riding two sides of the
right triangle, I'd take the hypotenuse. Pathagarus, however, never took
dirt roads into consideration.

"End State Maintenance - No Services." Eyeing the gravel roadbed as
cautiously as a nervous groom, I rechecked the map before making a
commitment. The road was smooth at first—a honeymoon of packed
loam. But as with any marriage, the bumps came soon enough. Singly
at first, then as twins, triplets and ultimately like a wave of in-laws at a
Labor Day picnic. So thoroughly shaken, it took some time for me to
recognize that the road was not heading southeast as the map indicated.
Tapping my left shoulder, the sun offered an ongoing reminder that I
was headed due south.

East! It should be veering east! Like a bogus prenuptial agreement,
the map had promised the shortest route to Moab, but delivered

something entirely different. For as far as I could see, the road showed no indication of deviating from its present course.

That's when a seductive double-track caught my eye. Curving sumptuously off to the left, a separation—no matter how painful—appeared to be the only option. Instead of riding back to the interstate and searching for a road I may or may not have overlooked, I convinced myself this must be it. Although the washboard was behind me, the loose desert soil offered a different type of challenge. I had to down-shift and keep even pressure on the pedals just to keep the bike moving through the unconsolidated sand.

Winding southeast through sagebrush, thistle poppy and prickly pear cactus for about two miles, the double track grew smaller and smaller, eventually petering out into nothing. At its unceremonious end, I paused and stepped off the bike. "And I—I took the one less traveled by..."

With Frost on my mind and the sun in my eyes, I set off across the desert where overgrazing coupled with the recent drought left the soil dry and crumbly. A loose amalgamation of sand and silt disintegrated beneath the weight of Betsy's smooth, treadless tires. Knobbies may have been able to do the job, but the slicks that served so well on pavement were useless. Recognizing this, I dismounted, changed my shoes, and took a moment to get a bearing.

Unsure of the distance and time required to cover the stunted sea of sage, I didn't want to rely on the moving sun for directions. Still low in the sky, it served temporarily to set a bearing on a distinguishable peak in the La Sal Mountains to the east. Resulting from a shallow intrusion of magma during the late Cenozoic, Mann's Peak has persisted for millions of years. While the sun would change its position throughout the day, I relied on the mountain to stay put.

"We are now ready to start on our way down the Great Unknown," wrote John Wesley Powell as he set off to explore the Colorado River system on May 24, 1869. If the five foot six, one-armed explorer could make it down the uncharted Green and Colorado Rivers unscathed, surely at five-eight—and possessing all my limbs—I could cross this short stretch of desert.

The challenge of propelling the loaded bike through the unconsolidated soil was compounded by my inability to find a comfortable position to push. Standing to either side set the bike off balance, and reaching for the far handlebar brought a bare shin dangerously close to the near-side pedal. After a number of painful collision of flesh on steel, I stopped to consider a different technique.

Through trial and error (mostly error), I settled on a style that called for one hand on the near handlebar and the other on the back of the saddle. Bringing the bike into balance, the technique allowed me to spend more time looking ahead for cactus thorns instead of down at my shins.

I made good progress where the terrain was flat or gently sloping, but the occasional dry gully forced me to lift Betsy over the short but steep escarpments. The technique also allowed me to notice more about the desert. As a result, I discovered one of its rarest jewels.

The rock would not otherwise have caught my attention had it not been moving. Moving? A second glance revealed legs, head and stumpy tail. The color of desert soil, thirteen fused plates made up the concave shell.

Once common throughout the Southwest, desert tortoise populations have plummeted recently due to habitat loss. One of nearly 800 species listed as endangered in the United States, the future of the desert tortoise is uncertain. Like Dr. Seuss's Yertle, this turtle teeters precariously but for completely different reasons. While the Turtle King's own self-interest brought about his ultimate decline, it is the greed of others which threatens the desert tortoise.

Because of its listing, the desert tortoise enjoys certain protections accorded by the Endangered Species Act. Requiring developers to complete inventories and provide environmental impact statements, however, have not ensured the tortoise's survival. Vandals risk up to a year in prison wrenching tortoise burrows apart in an attempt to stop them from reproducing. With fewer turtles to inventory, the permitting process is accelerated and building can proceed uninhibited.

In an ironic backlash, listing has actually accelerated the decline of certain species across the nation because paranoid property owners fear restrictions will be placed on their land if "the government" identifies it as critical habitat. There are those who see the presence of an ivory-billed woodpecker or spotted owl not as birds of paradise but as the proverbial albatross. They would rather eliminate these rare gifts from their land than face government intervention.

And today the great Yertle, that marvelous he
Is King of the Mud. That is all he can see
And the turtles of course...all the turtles are free
As turtles and, maybe, all creatures should be.

By nine o'clock the increasing heat had cultivated new levels of respect and empathy for the desert tortoise. Respect for its ability to live in such an arid land, and empathy because I too felt endangered. As sweat dripped from my brow, Frost again came to mind. "And that has made all the difference." His words haunted me as tomorrow's headline flashed before my eyes: "Bicyclist Lost in Desert: Victim of Poetry."

Never much for tabloid hype, I decided to spoil the story by surviving. After twenty more minutes of the desert soft shoe, I picked up a double track solid enough to ride. It lead me northeast for about a mile to an intersection with an authentic dirt road. I held my breath for a moment. Was it the same I'd left an hour earlier?

Six large cattle troughs settled my fears. I would have remembered them. Anticipating a good dunking, I was met with disappointment. The echo of corrugated steel filled the air as I dropped each lid back in place.

Packed by the wheels of pickup trucks and baked by the Utah sun, the surface was smooth and fast. Combined with a tail wind, it carried me southeast at an encouraging speed. A series of significant dips posed a slight challenge, but not a threat. Where water would otherwise have quickly percolated into the porous soil, it pooled in the ruts at the bottom of each declivity, forming twin bowls of liquiescent ooze the color of tomato soup. Using the conveniently located middle passage, I managed to maneuver through each quagmire unscathed. Until, that is, I reached the last.

The final dip had the dual distinction of being not only the deepest, but also possessing the widest puddles at the bottom. Not quite bridging the gap, they left enough middle ground to give the impression that safe passage was possible. Although not covered by standing water, the sedimentary make up of the gap was sufficiently saturated to form a thick gruel all too capable of seizing Betsy's tires.

Time slowed, as it tends to during the moments before disaster strikes—the milliseconds that stretch and grow as your car approaches the bumper ahead. Caught up in the illusion, I believed I could escape in time. With the desperation of a quarterback on fourth and long with time expiring on the clock, I reached down and managed to free my right foot (the pass is off) only to find the bike falling left and taking me with it (but it's incomplete). A last second pull with my left leg was as futile as a seventy yard field goal attempt as I splashed into warm, red pool—too thin to plow, too thick to drink.

Trapped by the toe clip and held down by the weight of the bike, I stared up from my mud bath into the clear, blue sky. One dot, two dots, three dots, circling. *Cathartes aura*, purifier of the air.

Among the most graceful of fliers, the turkey vulture spends its life searching for death under a seven foot wingspan. Spiraling into heights on invisible currents, keen vision allows the vulture to seek out an endless bounty of dead and dying below. A jackrabbit, a pronghorn, or a man, the bald-headed scavenger does not discriminate. Navajos refer to birds simply as "the airborne," and none commands more respect than the vulture. It is said that intense concentration on the bird's power ensures safe passage through open desert.

Admiring the freedom of the bird of the sun, I felt more like a coyote caught in a leg-hold trap with only one option for survival—chew off the confining limb. Bare teeth ripping into flesh—incisors, canines tearing through layers of muscle. Veins and arteries sticking in teeth like dental floss. Faced with bone, molars come into play, the powerful jaw clenching down and snapping tibia, fibula...

Water seeping into my left shoe snapped me out of the Walter Mitty daydream. Consisting of a mucilaginous red clay, the mud held fast to everything—bike, panniers, helmet, legs and hands. Unconcerned with aesthetics, I worried only about the slick, crimson layer covering my palms and fingers which made it difficult to maintain a firm grip on the handle bars. Using the front of my white t-shirt as a rag, I had them road ready in seconds. The rest could wait until later.

Sparkles of sunlight on windshields announced the highway long before I could hear the roar of trucks. By the time I reached it, the mud that covered me had lightened to a dusty rouge.

Reunited after a week apart, sliding onto Route 191 was like slipping into an old pair of Levi's. From Farson, Wyoming to Price, Utah, I'd worn the two-laner for five days and nearly 400 miles. With the same pleasure of tucking my legs into a warm pair of jeans fresh from the dryer, I pedaled the smooth tarmac toward Moab.

I followed the blacktop south over a gentle rise and into rimrock country where flat-topped mesas are cracked by rough canyons and rimmed by dusty cliffs; where yawning gorges split the earth; where the Rocky Mountains tumble into sandstone deserts. Over hundreds of thousands of years, this high tableland has been etched by the relentless power of rivers which now lay deep within the strata. The result is a landscape that inspires mystery, inspires legend, inspires Road Runner and Coyote cartoons.

To the east I could make out a speck of blue sky—not more than a pinhole—peering through a distant arch along the horizon of low, red hills. Vast walls of Navajo sandstone rose to the west, growing nearer the road as I continued south. Joined by another bulkhead opposite, they formed a canyon which served as the final descent to the Colorado River. In a world stood on edge, I was engulfed by vermilion cliffs. Where Mormon settlers had once spent weeks traversing the tortuous landscape, I coasted effortlessly past Arches National Park and across the muddy Colorado.

Moab lies along a wide bend in the river at the north end of the pear-shaped Spanish Valley. To the first settlers, it was an oasis amidst the towering sandstone hills and expansive tablelands. In a land as harsh as it is beautiful, they called this place paradise, they called it home, but they did not call it Moab.

The small settlement went through multiple names—including Grand Valley, Spanish Valley and Mormon Fort—before Moab became its official moniker in 1879. In the Old Testament, Moab—"The Far Country"—

was an ancient Syrian Kingdom bordering the Dead Sea. The Bible describes it as a lofty tableland surrounded by flat-topped mountains— flanked to the north by the Armon River, to the east by the Arabian Desert and to the south by the Land of Edom. With the Colorado River, the San Rafael Desert and Arizona ("Land of Opportunity") serving as non-biblical, North American counterparts, the geographic similarities are obvious. So why did Postmaster Henry Crouse try to change the name to Uvadalia in 1885?

By the 1950's, Moab had become a town of real character. In his classic, *Desert Solitaire*, Edward Abbey refers to his once-a-week visits to Moab as a trip to, "a dazzling metropolis, a throbbing dynamo of commerce and pleasure." This, of course, was after living the other six days alone in a trailer in then Arches National Monument. Whenever Abbey went to town for beans and beer, he found Moab crowded with prospectors, miners, geologists, truck drivers, cowboys and sheep herders. The talk was, "loud, vigorous, blue with blasphemy." Thirty-five years later, Moab attracted a different breed. Tourists, car campers, mountain bikers, climbers and rafters—the talk was soft, vincible and disproportionately in French and German.

Like the chicken and the egg, it's hard to tell which came first, the tourists or the tourist town. Since Abbey's departure, Moab has grown ripe with R.V. parks, motels, "outfitter" stores, bike shops, river guides and cafes. During the previous year, nine new motels had been built along with a McDonalds and the King World Water Slide. Other attractions include the Hollywood Stuntman's Hall of Fame, Arches Helicopter Rides and the Bar M Chuckwagon Western Show and Cowboy Supper. Cellular phone rentals and jeep tours allow professional parents to check in with the home office while checking out local scenic byways. Abbey's polemic on Industrial Tourism had come true.

The parking lot of the Tourist Information Center hosted an eclectic mix of vehicles. Alongside the standard ration of RVs and minivans were a selection of Subaru station wagons and Toyota pickups displaying varying degrees of rust. Bumper stickers ran the gamut: "We're Spending Our Children's Inheritance;" "Life Begins as 60;" "Question Authority;" "Keep Your Rosaries Off My Ovaries."

Surrounded by carefully tended gardens and flying the stars and stripes, the Information Center could have been the Whitehouse in May. Although it was late July and the structure was more of a light brown stucco, I felt like the President facing an anxious press corps in the Rose Garden when three boys on rollerblades intercepted me amid the peonies. Their pint-sized version of the third degree included questions on where I'd been, why I was in Moab, and how I went to the bathroom. I couldn't finish answering one question before facing the next.

"Shut up, Billy. He wasn't done with mine."

"But Matt, you've already asked three. I've only had one and Dog hasn't said anything."

"Dog?"

"His real name is Doug, but he likes Dog better."

"Ruff ruff," the previously silent boy agreed.

Taking advantage of the lull, I asked a few questions of my own. Billy told me where I could find a market, and added that I should plan to visit at least one of the bike shops in town. "Rim Cyclery is my favorite."

Matt pointed the way toward the town park. "It's got a pool."

Dog stood by panting.

With the inside scoop on Moab, there remained little need to go in the Information Center, but I slipped in briefly to pick up a brochure on the local mountain bike trails before heading to the bakery department at City Market. With a half dozen bagels and a box of day-old donuts, I exited the grocery to find a middle-aged balding man in a tie-dyed shirt and Birkenstocks looking over my bike. "Nice wheels," he said as I approached.

"Thanks."

"You goin' cross country?"

"No, just exploring a bit—visiting friends here and there."

"And of course you had to come to Moab."

"Of course."

"Gonna ride Slickrock?"

"Probably, but the main draw for me is Arches. Ever since I read *Desert Solitaire* ten years ago I've wanted to see the park."

"Abbey, huh?" With a mottled gray beard, sun-scorched skin and a sparkle in his eyes, he looked a bit like old Ed himself. "Poor guy must be rolling in his grave."

"Why's that?"

"The way the Park Service is going to shit."

"How's that?"

"Budget cuts and corporate interests are forcing the whole system into chaos. If you take inflation into account, the Park Service budget is $200 million less than it was ten years ago. Yet the backlog of repair projects reaches into the billions. The total budget is about one half of one percent of the Defense Department. The government spends more on cotton subsidies than on parks!" He threw up his hands to emphasize the point. "So wardens are being laid off, campsites are closed, and maintenance projects are abandoned—all while the number of visitors is skyrocketing.

"A Review Commission has already been established to recommend parks for closure. There are dozens of Congressmen who say parks are like aspirin: 'Two can be helpful, but a hundred will put you in the hospital.'"

"How do corporate interests fit in?"

"Let me count the ways," he smiled and folded his hands. "In most parks, concessionaires provide food, lodging, gift shops and transportation. Instead of the Park Service managing these services, the contracts go to private corporations with experience in the field of tourism—like Aramark and Disney. The catch is they pay next to nothing for exclusive access to park visitors—less than three percent of gross profits. They see as little wrong with paying pennies on the dollar for rent than they do with charging four bucks for a hot dog and two fifty for a coke."

"So in the midst of budget reductions, the Park Service is giving a cut rate to private companies?"

"If concessionaires were to pay ten percent—like they do in most state parks—it would generate an extra 50 million more dollars a year."

"So why don't they just up the ante?"

"The Park Service can't do that on their own. It's up to Congress."

"So why don't *they*..."

"Save your breath—logic doesn't work here. Instead of doing what seems obvious, key politicians are trying to open the parks to an even wider range of private interests under the guise of 'deficit reduction.' They're ultimate goal is open access for mineral and energy production."

The year was 1872 when Ulysses Grant signed into being the first National Park—Yellowstone— and with it the Park Service. "...hereby reserved and withdrawn from settlement, occupancy, or sale under the laws of the United States, and dedicated and set apart...for the benefit and enjoyment of the people." Later that same year he approved the General Mining Law which opened hundreds of millions of acres of public land—excluding National Parks—to mineral extraction. A century and a quarter later, however, a showdown draws near.

Based on the advice of my new acquaintance, I took a right at the Gonzo Cafe and headed down Kane Creek Road to the Colorado to find a place to camp. "You don't want to pay ten bucks to stay in one of those shitty R.V. parks," he'd told me. "There's plenty of BLM land down by the river. Just pick a site and settle in. It's nice and quiet. I lived down there six months last year and nobody said a thing."

Covered in a sweat that only 107 degree heat can produce, I rode into the sinking afternoon sun. Past a church and over a slight rise (five years later to become the site of an aerial tram to the canyon top), the road turned south as it reached the Colorado and entered a steep-walled canyon. In shadow, the crimson cliffs towered 300 feet above the green water. The sky was reduced to a narrow strip of blue, pinching out at a bend in the river ahead. Thick stands of feathery tamarisk lined the banks of the river, partitioning it from the road. They swayed softly in the light breeze that followed me through the gorge. Combined with afternoon shade, the draft made life inside the canyon nearly tolerable. Yet it would take another thirty ticks off the thermometer to make decent sleeping weather.

A mile down the canyon a dusty double track cut into the thick wall of tamarisk. The first of the BLM sites branched off from the track, burrowing further into the tangled jungle but not reaching the Colorado. A network of small footpaths provided the only access to the river.

Passing one occupied site, and then another, I coasted to a stop at a third. Wheeling Betsy into the clearing, I was overcome by the stench of human waste. The foul odor accosted my nostrils as not even the urinals at Fenway Park could.

Tangled in and amongst the densely packed tamarisks, wadded balls of toilet paper riddled the underbrush—violating not only the laws of common decency, but also a number of local health ordinances. The profusion of white flags signaled my surrender to the caustic assault. I retreated to another site to find fewer visible signs of covert action, but the foul odor lingered like death over a battlefield.

Heading back up the double track, I rejoined Kane Creek Road and continued south for a quarter mile before reaching sites on the opposite side of the road where a slight elevation above the floodplain has denied the luxuriously moist soils which allow the tamarisk to grow in such profusion just yards away. Although the mighty Colorado flowed less than 100 feet away, its presence had little if any effect on plant life. Save for a few lonely junipers growing out of the red sandstone, this side of the road was nearly devoid of plant life—a stark contrast to the virtual jungle on the other side.

Again, human impact was high, but tire tracks and scattered beer cans were easier to deal with than feces. I spent a few minutes corralling eleven Hams beer cans out of a juniper bush but couldn't find the twelfth. Scattered newspapers drew me toward a cluster of dusty sage on the leeward side of the campsite.

Beneath the front page I found a used condom, beneath "Sports" I found the last can of Hamms, and beneath "Living" I found the most beautiful flower I'd ever seen. The tulip-like blossom rose to greet me as I removed the burden of yesterdays news. Atop a narrow stalk, three creamy-white petals wore an aura of lilac. At the base of the blossom, a soft ring of yellow melted into one of purple. Three pointed green sepals lay beneath. The Greeks called it *calochortus,* beautiful herb, but now it is known as mariposa—the state flower of Utah. I admired it for some time before returning to unload Betsy, and heading down to the river.

Free of their leather confinement, my feet rejoiced in the feel of the smooth, red slickrock. The gentle contours massaged my soles as I walked slowly across the weathered stone. But the enjoyable feeling soon gave way to the searing heat still held by the black asphalt. Hopping across Kane Creek Road like a cat on a hot tin roof, I found myself out of the frying pan and into the fire. Not exactly fire, but the sharp gravel bed of the double track seemed to burn my feet just the same. I stepped lightly, as if on eggs, until I reached the compacted soil further along.

Entering the tangle to tamarisk, I stooped through a tunnel of feathery green. Hunched over beneath a canopy of branches, I stepped carefully over knotted
roots and fallen twigs before reaching the riverbank. Warm thoughts of childhood mud puddles flooded my memory as my feet sank into the liquiescent muck. Viscous clay oozed between my toes. Greasy mud caressed my road weary feet. I reveled in the primordial slime.

Wild eyes stared up at me from the still, green water between my feet. Three days worth of whiskers darkened his face; a greasy mop of hair hung over his forehead; dried red mud clung to his grungy t-shirt. A maniacal smirk completed the Kazinski-esque portrait. Letting out a howl, the psychopath extended his arms and launched himself into the cool water.

Rejuvenated by the river, I retraced my steps to the campsite as shadow filled the last of the canyon. Only the top of the eastern wall remained bathed in sunlight, and then only for a moment. By the time I had dried off and unstuffed my sleeping bag, the apricot tint of the upper wall had been engulfed by the climbing rouge hue.

Chapter 27

Out there is a different world, older and greater and deeper by far than ours, a world which surrounds and sustains the little world of man as sea and sky surrounds and sustain a ship. The shock of the real. For a little while we are again able to see, as the child sees, a world of marvels.
—Edward Abbey, 1968

Before the sun had kissed the upper reaches of the western wall, I awoke. Shaking off a shroud of sleep, my mood was Joycean—jubilant, life-affirming. Anticipation coursed through my veins. Ever since a favorite high school teacher had given me a copy of *Desert Solitaire* for graduation, I'd longed to see Arches. Through four years of college and another five teaching, I'd dreamed of Abbey's slickrock desert, "the most beautiful place on Earth."

This pilgrimage would be a time to see the place and honor the man who's writing brought it to life for me. Sometimes I muse on the fact that *Desert Solitaire* was published the year I was born—1968. His death in 1989 prompted me to read more of his work, nurturing the seed first planted by that favorite teacher years earlier. Abbey became a mentor I never met. "It is not enough to understand the natural world; the point is to defend and preserve it." His words struck home with me, and I followed them here, where he began his "lifelong love affair with a pile of rock."

Moab showed the first signs of life as I rolled through at 6:30. Short order cooks flipped buttermilk pancakes while river guides loaded rubber boats. But beside cafes and rafting companies, most storefronts were dark. The purchase of t-shirts, postcards and Indian jewelry called for a more civilized hour.

A pleasing coolness hung in the air as I passed the Chamber of Commerce at the north end of town. Crossing the Colorado, excitement welled up inside me. I would soon be there.

"Arches National Park - Next Right." Making the turn onto the entrance road, I was surprised to see a line of cars already formed at the fee station. I took my place behind a Ford Explorer and waited my turn. Beside me, a plaque—identical to those at National Parks and Monuments across the country—honored the memory of Stephen T. Mather, head of the fledgling Park Service for twelve critical years. Under his leadership, the Service came of age as America accepted the preservation of scenic areas as a legitimate use of land. "THERE WILL NEVER COME AN END TO THE GOOD THAT HE HAS DONE."

I handed four dollars to a bearded ranger in a Smoky Bear hat and proceeded to the Visitor Center at the base of a steep access road leading into the park. Carved into the living rock, the road snakes its way to the mesa top like a sidewinder doubling back on itself to complete the climb. "Grades Exceeds 15%."

I shifted my gaze from the intimidating slope to the twenty pounds of gear strapped to the bike. With forecasters calling for another century day, there would be no need for extra clothes and a sleeping bag on a round-trip morning ride through the park. After some negotiation—and acknowledging that the Park Service would not be responsible for any damage, theft, mishandling, or voodoo curses placed on my belongings—I arranged to leave my gear at the Visitor Center for the next few hours. A friendly ranger took my panniers and sleeping bag, stowing them behind the desk. I thanked him and promised to be back by noon.

The climb proved challenging enough without the added burden. Keeping Betsy in her small chain ring, I found myself having to stand on the steeper sections. Whether offering support or simply affirming my insanity, I had assumed the honking was directed at me. What I couldn't figure was why they started so far below me. I didn't recall a narrow, blind curve that may require a warning for on-coming traffic It wasn't until I glanced over my shoulder that a key piece of the puzzle fell into place. He wore a blue jersey and rode a red bike. More importantly, he was gaining. Suppressing any competitive urge, I let him pass only to discover that he was a she.

This changed everything. Clearly an assault on my masculinity, I had no choice but to respond. Standing, I upshifted and dug into the pedals with thighs, calves and hamstrings. I clenched my teeth and squeezed my fingers, but to no avail. Too little, too late, Annie Oakley was out of sight by the time I reached the top. She had vanished around a wide bend which revealed a panoramic view as powerful as her calves.

In a horizontal world, I could see miles across the sprawling valley of balanced rocks, spires and eroded fins. The morning sun set the slickrock ablaze, but Park Avenue remained in shadow. Resembling a city skyline, this geologic thoroughfare runs north-south for about a mile at the top of the entry road. Walls of salmon-colored Entrada Sandstone rise vertically for hundreds of feet above the desert floor just as skyscrapers of concrete and steel flank its namesake. Instead of antennas and lightening rods, sandstone pinnacles and spires adorn the penthouse level.

Pausing between a pair of Winnebagos in the parking lot, I gazed north up the Avenue before moving further into the heart of the park. A strip of black asphalt became my yellow brick road—leading me into a fantasy land of geologic wonders. I wanted to see as much as possible before the temperature forced me out of this Land of Oz.

Two miles of easy downhill riding brought me to the Courthouse Towers, a photographic mecca boasting a pair of massive monoliths and a small arch-in-the-making. Shutterbugs filled the parking lot. Cannons, Nikons or Polaroids hung from every neck. Kodak stock surged on Wall Street.

Content to take the scenery en route, I bypassed the pull off and continued north past Three Gossips, Sheep Rock and the Tower of Babel. Drawing my eyes from the road, their magnificence became a mixed blessing when taken with the steady stream of traffic passing inches to my left.

At the bottom of a thrilling descent, a sign for Delicate Arch drew me east onto a side road and into the parking lot at Wolfe Ranch. Built in 1888 by John Wolfe, a weathered log cabin and corral are all that remain. It's hard to imagine ranching in this arid maze of erosional fins, balanced rocks and towering spires. "Hell of a place to lose a cow," muttered a man nearby.

Locking my bike in the corner of the lot, I changed out of my cycling shoes and headed up the trail toward Delicate Arch a mile and a half away. I climbed quickly over rounded mounds of smooth sandstone, passing the requisite French and German tourists along the trail.

"Sehr Gut!'"

"Se Magnifique!"

Standing precipitously alone on the edge of a large bowl scoured by wind and rain, Delicate Arch stands over fifty feet high like an uncrossed capital A. In New York font, its twin pillars of sandstone splay slightly where they meet the sandstone bed. The eastern limb, that for which it is named, narrows to less than ten feet in circumference just above this union. The proverbial weakest link, hundreds of tons of rock rest like a geologic house of cards above picnickers either ignorant of or confident in the strength and endurance of the stone. With the La Sal Mountains as a backdrop, it's easy to see why this is the most photographed arch in the world.

Examples of arches in every stage of development and all manner or shapes can be found throughout the park. From the magnificent to the bizarre, lonely pioneers had no trouble naming them: "The Nipples," "Organ Rock" (guess which one), "Parade of Elephants", "Paul Bunyan's Potty," "Kissing Cousins," "Mule Shoe," the list goes on. The first cowboys to see Delicate Arch called it "Schoolmarm's Bloomers."

As the morning wore on and my hunger grew, the curving structures triggered deep childhood memories of fast food. The ultimate advertising scheme, by noon the only arches on my mind were golden. To the delight of my stomach, I returned to the park entrance, picked up my gear and headed back into Moab for a date with Ronald.

But Dave Thomas had other plans for me. The lure of Wendy's air conditioned salad bar enticed me long before I had reached the McDonalds at the far end of town. With all of the great "advertising" in the park, Ronald had forgotten the cardinal law of the restaurant business—Location, Location, Location.

A digital clock outside the First Bank of Utah flashed the vital statistics of the day—12:11 PM - 101?F. Inside Wendy's, the cool air felt as good on my skin as the fresh vegetables in my stomach. The colors alone were an improvement over the varying brown shades of peanut butter, over-ripe bananas and whole wheat bread. I loaded up with crisp, green lettuce, lush, red tomatoes and crunchy, orange carrots. With a stomach full of fibrous roughage and more vitamins than my body had seen in a week, I set out for the public pool.

Entering the men's locker room, I caught a glimpse of myself in a mirror. Although yesterday's mud had been washed away by the river, scruffy whiskers remained under the tangled mop. A flaky film of salt clung to my cheeks and spread across my brow. Underneath the stubble and brine, my skin glowed a golden brown.

I retrieved a razor, soap and shampoo from my panniers. By the time I stepped onto the pool deck I was Schicked, Dialed and Pert Plussed. Long looks from a pair of young women in bikinis let me know I was back in the game.

After a quick dip, I spent a lazy afternoon reading, writing and dozing under a large umbrella. By 5:30 I had convinced myself it had cooled off enough to take on the legendary Slickrock Trail.

A plywood sign at the corner of Mill Creek Drive and Sand Flats Road pointed the way: "Slickrock Bike Trail - 2 Miles." The sun weighed heavy on my back as I pedaled east up the slope. On the right, a chainlink fence surrounded the Grand County Recycling Center. On the left, a dozen sprinklers threw arching rainbows over a thousand gravestones. Further along, Sand Flats Road swung south as the real climb began. Downshifting below what the grade called for, I wanted to save my legs for the trail itself.

At the top of the rise, the road leveled out and then dipped alongside the Grand County Landfill. With its panoramic view of Spanish Valley, certain maps identify it parenthetically as "America's most scenic dump." No such commendation hung at its gate—just a modest sign: "Landfill Rules: No Scavenging. No Liquid Waste. No Hazardous Materials. Have a Nice Day."

A small campground ahead on the left marked the base of the final climb. Again I over-shifted to ease the climb, but was forced out of the saddle by the fierce grade. I reached the top wearing more water than I carried, but the thought of ringing out my shirt for a drink was lower than even I would stoop.

Smooth rimrock spread across the plateau high above the valley floor. Sandstone dominated the view in every direction. Hills, cliffs, canyons— all a dusty red. Even the scattered pinyon and juniper wore a dusty coat of rouge. Abbey claimed this part of Utah contained, "more hills, holes, humps and hollows, reefs, folds, salt domes, swells and grabens, buttes, benches and mesas, synclines, monoclines and anticlines than you can ever hope to see and explore in one lifetime." Some call it "the geography of hope." Others curse it as "the worst country I ever saw."

Love it or hate it, any observer is bound to ask what formed it. While most believe a paleo-geologic explanation involving ancient dunes, millions of years, and the forces of wind and water, there remain other beliefs. "When God finished making the world," zealots claim, "he had a lot of rocks left over and threw them down in a pile in Utah." If less than scientific, it certainly described the Slickrock Trail. As raw as a coyote with his skin peeled off, the smooth sandstone refuses to hold a trail. Except, that is, a painted one.

While Yakima and Thule battled in the parking lot for roof rack dominance, Trek, GT, Specialized and Gary Fischer faced off on the trail. I doubted if any of the other riders had ever heard of a Montague. Without rear suspension or even Rock Shox, rolling Betsy onto the trail was like entering a Yugo in the Indianapolis 500.

A dashed white line lead us northeast from the parking lot and into an otherly world. Riding the rounded pillow rock high on the plateau was like riding on a cloud. I'd seen this world before, but only in dreams and out airplane windows. The unmistakable contours were those of billowing cumulus. Where the Kingdom of God touches Earth, a spirit of joy touched my soul. In a holy union of rubber and rock, each pedal stroke was a prayer. Under the late afternoon sun, my water bottle became a cup of salvation—drinking was my communion, splashing my head a baptism. As my spirit lifted to heaven, Betsy's rear brake cable snapped and I came face to face with the clutches of hell.

Too fast, too steep, too sharp—my speed, the slope and the turn coalesced into anything but a holy trinity. My heart stopped but the bike kept going. The safety of the dotted line became a memory as I was centrifugally forced out of the turn. Momentum carried me closer to the edge as I struggled to slow Betsy as the sandstone angled away beneath her tires. My right foot dragged against the rock with the resistance of ten boys on their way to Sunday School, but still the abyss approached. I entertained the thought of abandoning the bike to save myself, but that would have been blasphemy. We were in this together.

Digging in and holding on, we ground to a halt at the brink of extinction. Precariously perched at the point of no return, I gazed into the chasm that fell out of view beyond the sandstone lip just inches away. Like Wile E. Coyote at the moment of truth, I waited for the cliff to break away and send me plummeting a thousand feet to the canyon floor where I'd stick into the sand up to my neck and wait for the obligatory anvil to land squarely on my head. (I should never have bought that ACME brake cable in the first place.) But there was no fall, no anvil, not even a faint "Beep Beep" in the distance. All was silent until my heart regained its rhythm. Carefully, I swung my left leg over the bike and wheeled it up the slope. Retracing the white line, I walked back to the parking lot and down the hill to Moab where I bought a replacement cable and a new set of pads.

A large-bellied German man in a small bathing suit floated across the pool at the Best Western on Main Street. He spoke unfamiliar words to his wife and two children sitting at a shaded table on the deck. "Big Mac," was the only English phrase used in the conversation until one of the children added "French fries."

Chips, taters, spuds—fried potatoes sounded good in any language. As my stomach grumbled in anticipation, I dried off, changed clothes and walked Betsy three blocks to the house that Ronald built. Aside from the "Over fill-in-the-blank Billion Served" sign outside, not much had changed since the time I had been a devoted teenage customer. I remember the days of cruising the strip in my friend's rusted-out Datsun and hanging out at "Mickey D's." Sometimes I wonder how many quarter pound beef patties I consumed during those years. Over fill-in-the-blank thousand served.

Stepping through the double glass doors, a chill ran down my spine from an air conditioner set too low. I ordered large fries with extra ketchup from a pimply teenager and took them outside. The shade on the east side of the building offered a comfortable alternative to the ice box inside. I claimed a table at the edge of the parking lot, sitting on my jacket to pad my aching rump. My pelvic bones bore into the molded plastic seat none the less. Sore, sore, sore—I dwelled on my predicament as bored adolescents cruised Main Street in Fords, Chevys, GMCs. There was nary a Datsun in sight.

As I finished the last few crusty fries at the bottom of the box, an elderly couple approached from their Buick as its engine ticked its last few ticks. Noticing Betsy—now fully loaded after her unburdened trip to Slickrock—they paused.

"Are you riding across the country?" asked the white haired woman through thin lips.

Here we go again. "No, I came down from the Dakotas through

Wyoming. From here I'm headed for New Mexico."

"That's wonderful," she observed.

"Yeah, that's great," added her husband with a dentured grin. "I wish I could do something like that."

"Oh sure Herb, you complain about taking the garbage to the curb. How are you going to ride a bicycle across Utah."

"Like I said Marge, I *wish* I could do something like that. Doesn't mean I'm *gonna*."

"I could have told you that," she responded, turning back to me. "How long have you been riding?"

"About three weeks. I think I'm close to 2,000 miles."

"2,000 miles!" gasped Herb. "You must be in great shape. Do you ever get tired?"

"Sure, but it's all a matter of pacing."

"I think that's just wonderful," repeated Marge.

"Yeah, keep it up," encouraged Herb, "You're doing a great job."

"Thanks."

Whether it's a compliment from a stranger, a reassuring honk from a passing motorist, or a one finger wave of another cyclist, it's always nice to get a little encouragement. But compliments have their limits. The soothing words from Marge and Herb did nothing for my saddle sores and stiff legs. For those I'd have to rely on Vaseline and Advil— what cyclists affectionately call "Vitamin A."

A pay phone outside the all night drugstore reminded me to put in a call to a friend from high school who had moved to New Mexico. Anna picked up on the sixth ring and said she'd be happy to put me up for a couple of nights. "Listen," she told me, "I work days, but I'll leave the door unlocked. When do you think you'll get here?"

"Four, maybe five days."

"That's fine. Have you got something to take down directions?"

On a post card of Paul Bunyon's Potty, I jotted down her instructions.

"Got all that?" she asked.

"Yeah, thanks," I said looking at the scribbled jumble of L's, R's and illegible street names. "See you in a couple of days."

By the time I hung up, darkness had fallen over Moab. Instead of riding back to the river, I scoped out possible hideaways closer to town. A church yard at the near end of Kane Creek Road seemed perfect. With a low wall providing privacy and thick green grass for a bed, I believed I'd found the ideal spot. But as I'd learn, the thick turf came with a price. Two hours past midnight, the timered sprinklers sent me scurrying to a concrete walkway out of range. Leaving plenty to be desired in terms of comfort, at least it was dry.

Chapter 28

*To really experience the desert you have to march right into its white
bowl of sky and shape-contorting heat with your mind on your canteen
as if it were your last gallon of gas and you were being chased by a
carload of escaped murderers. You have to imagine what it would be
like to drink blood from a lizard or, in the grip of dementia, claw
barehanded through sand and rock for the vestigial moisture beneath a
dry wash.*
—Marc Reisner, Cadillac Desert, 1986

Carry water and use your wits.
—Donald Snow

Headwinds. Headwinds. Headwinds. By the time I left Moab, a torrid
gale blew out of the south. Dry gusts whipped the feathery sage. The air
was heavy with heat and dust. Combined with the formidable pitch,
the steady breeze provided a one-two punch that had me on the ropes
from the opening bell. Windblown and winded, I progressed slowly
along the gradual climb out of Spanish Valley.

Statistical data suggests that heart attacks and strokes among desert
dwellers are most likely to occur when the wind is blowing four or five
on the Beaufort scale—eleven to twenty-one miles per hour. Police
departments report that murder rates double during Santa Ana winds.
As I leaned into Betsy's armrests, my goal for the day was simple: no
one dies.

Within minutes a greater power began testing my resolve. As if
pedaling agonizingly slowly were not enough to turn me homicidal,
cracks in the shoulder provided enough jostling to loosen a screw which
held one of the armrests in place. The next bump in the road became
that proverbial last straw as my back collapsed and my chest hit the
handlebars. I struggled to avert disaster as the armrest tumbled to the
pavement. The fact that I could not reach the brake levers was of little
consequence as breaking was hardly necessary. I glided to a stop as my
heart raced and my temper flared. Shit!

Leaning the bike against a speed limit sign, I walked back to look for
the AWOL equipment. No longer had I left when a strong gust set Betsy
off balance and sent her crashing to the ground. Shit!

The black plastic armrest was easy to spot on the wide shoulder, but
the connecting bolt blended perfectly into the gravel and roadside debris.
Shifting from straws and camels to needles and haystacks, I wondered
if cliche would haunt me the rest of the morning. Refusing to waste time
looking, I turned to walk back to the bike, and that's when it caught my
eye.

Over the last two weeks I'd seen enough roadside litter to fill a dozen garbage trucks, but something about this discard caught my eye. It stood out among the twisted sage ten feet from the road. As I waddled through the sand in my cycling shoes, the object and its significance became clear. Caught in the low branches of a brittle sage was a wide brimmed, felt and leather hat. Broken in but not worn out, the weathered Stetson fit perfectly. Worth the price of 3/4 inch bolt and a little frustration, it turned my aggravation into cheer. What's that about "every cloud?"

I strapped the hat carefully on top of my panniers and headed back into the wind. As I struggled against the grade, the July sun climbed effortlessly in the eastern sky. Rising with perfect cadence, the glowing star never faltered. If only my ascension were as smooth.

I reached the broad plateau hours behind the sun. High table land opened into rolling desert accented by towering sandstone fins and road construction. The Utah Highway Department had found an even, consistent stretch of pavement and was doing its best to break it up. "Welcome to San Juan County."

An idling line of southbound traffic stretched to an orange-vested flagman ahead. He controlled the power of ten thousand horses with a single word, "STOP." Humming under a morning sun, aggregates of steel, rubber, plastic and glass quietly obeyed his silent order. Fords, Chryslers, Dodges and GMCs purred as sweetly as kittens suckling at their mother's side.

Tallies show that most Americans devote close to 2,000 hours each year to their automobiles. Driving, parking, or stuck in traffic, the hours in the vehicle are combined with those spent earning money to pay for gas, tolls, insurance, taxes, tickets and monthly installments. Cumulatively, Americans devote a quarter of their waking hours to maintaining their freedom of mobility. That amounts to more time spent with spouses and children combined.

Cool as cucumbers on a drive-thru safari, families spending quality time together gazed out at the threatening surroundings from the safety of air-conditioning. Children watched me pass, their faces pressed up against the glass. What a treat to see a real live bicyclist and a flagman, both at one stop!

I must admit the flagman at the front of the line was not the run of the mill variety. In my collected observations, flagmen generally fall into two categories. Type one is the slim, tanned, college-aged kid in shorts and tank top who can't believe he'll be doing this for the whole summer. Type two is the pot-bellied, pale (except for the arms), thirty-something drop-out in blue jeans and dirty T-shirt who can't believe he'll be doing this for the rest of his life.

Khaki pants and a Madras shirt were a part of neither formula, yet there he was wearing the reflective orange vest like a sleeveless sweater.

In his mid-forties, he was clean cut, cordial and conversational. He looked at me with surprise. "Don't see many riders this far from town. Most bikes are on top of cars."

"I bet."

"Where you headed?"

"Monticello. Can I ride up the shoulder through the construction?"

"Sorry, you'll have to wait with everyone else."

This surprised me. I'd usually been allowed to continue with no hassle.

"Where you from?" he asked.

"New Hampshire."

"East coast, huh? My wife Doris is from Connecticut."

"I was born in Connecticut, but only lived there for a year before my parents moved to Michigan."

"Michigan? My wife Mary is from Michigan."

Is? Is? That was two is's—as in the present tense of to be—in a row? Holy polygamists, Batman! I didn't dare mention any other states for fear the list would continue. How can a guy like me find a good woman when a guy like him is taking more than his share?

Draining the last of my water, I asked if I could fill up from his gallon jug. Despite an ample supply, he hesitated. My simple request hung in the air as if I had asked to borrow a wife for the night. His serious expression relaxed as he realized my current state of malodorous disarray posed no threat to his monopoly on local women. He obliged me by filling one bottle.

After tucking it back into its cage, I looked up to see a parade of cars approaching in the northbound lane. Like NASCAR drivers following a pace car on the opening lap, they patiently held position behind a slow moving D.O.T. vehicle. Reaching us, the orange truck turned off and the race began. Wanna bee Earnhardts, Irvins and Gordons in minivans and campers took off down the track. Within moments they had passed and the man with multiple wives, ample water, and probably another job too, turned his sign from "STOP" to "SLOW."

Pulling out before the D.O.T. truck had even turned around, I had the road to myself. Rolling desert stretched between Flat Iron Mesa and Mule Shoe Canyon like a turbulent sea. Undulating swells of sand reached to every horizon, interrupted only by the towering sandstone fins—an unearthly landscape of standing rock. Like the dorsal fins of giant underground sharks, the tapering stone slabs encircled me. Hitting the first incline, my heart rate matched the crescendo-bound rhythm from the attack scenes in Jaws.

In the trough of a great, sandy wave, Route 191 dipped briefly and then resumed its climb. The line of cars quickly passed and I was alone again. Despite the persistent wind, there remained an eerie calm about the desert at noon. Animals had long since taken refuge from the mid-day sun. Long-eared hares, kangaroo rats, lizards, snakes and countless insects sought shelter underground. Even the plants had sense enough to close their pores in order to retain moisture during the hottest part of the day.

Meanwhile my skin was a sieve to the thirsty air. By the time I cleared the road work I had nearly finished the bottle I just filled. Reluctant to stop again and ask the "type one" flagman at the other end of the construction if he had any to spare, I simply nodded a greeting and continued down a long, gradual descent which carried me past a covey of campers at Wilson Arch and into a broad expanse of desert between Rone Bailey Mesa and Church Rock.

Creeping up the back of my throat and spreading across my tongue, it didn't take long for the cotton to fill my mouth. Swollen, pasty, dry—my tongue felt like a foreign object. The feeling brought back my days as a wrestler—skipping rope under three layers of sweats to make weight.

Aqua, wasser, vada, viz—it filled my every thought. Appearing on the road ahead, a shimmering pool retreated as I approached—a mirage teasing from the edge of my world.

I tried with little success to get it off my mind. The first diversion required guessing the road signs facing the opposite direction, but after hundreds of miles on the road it was far too easy. Next came speculation about passing motorists. What did *they* think about the road, about the desert, about me? Were they impressed or did they simply consider me insane? Did a honk and wave mean, "Good job. Keep it up!" or "You are one crazy son-of-a-bitch!"?

Of all the passing vehicles, there was only one type about which I could be sure. Any car wearing a roof rack and a bike was surely in my corner. That's why I felt safe when the blue Nissan with California plates stopped on the shoulder ahead. A stocky man in T-shirt and shorts got out on the driver's side as I approached.

"How ya doin'?" he asked.

"Not too bad."

"Need any water?"

"You must be a mind reader."

"I thought so." He opened his door and addressed the woman in the passenger seat. "Honey, could you grab one of those bottles out of the back? I think they're under the camera bag."

While she leaned into the rear seat, he turned back to me. "Where you comin' from?"

"Moab this morning."

"That's where we were. Rode the Slickrock Trail yesterday."

"Me too."

"Isn't it amazing?"

"Yeah," I smiled, but mostly to myself, "it's a real heart-stopper."

He nodded in agreement and then turned back to the car. "How about that water? I've got a thirsty man out here."

"Hold on," came a muffled reply. "It slipped under the seat."

After extracting the elusive bottle, she joined us on the driver's side. "You'll like this," she said handing it to me, "nice and cold. Filled it at a spring in Moab this morning."

My teeth and throat ached with joy as the cool liquid poured over them. Despite a rapid-onset ice cream cone headache, I couldn't seem to drink fast enough. Pausing only to catch my breath, I thanked them thoroughly. "You must be my guardian angels."

After a little chit chat about Moab and bicycling in general, they wished me luck and headed off through the humpbacked tableland of tangled pinon and dry washes. I felt refreshed and confident until I reached George Rock and the final ascent up Peters Canyon. The town of Monticello stood 2,000 feet above me and eleven miles away. I counted them down as a child tallies the last days before Christmas. Ten, nine, eight, seven—mile markers tested my patience like the windows in an advent calendar.

A persistent aching in my wrists worked its way like cancer up both arms and into my hunched shoulders. The trapezius muscle on my left side began to spasm. Random pulses shot through the muscle fibers. They came in cycles, building from indistinct quivers to trembling crescendos before starting over again. Sitting up and shaking out my arms helped a bit, but the relief I felt above the waist only brought attention to the discomfort below.

Of course my rear end yearned for a break from the saddle, but the most acute pain radiated up from my feet. Big toes lead the chant, but the little ones suffered the most. Crammed into tight, leather corners, they cried "Wee, wee, wee" all the way up the mountain. Standing on the pedals and wiggling my toes offered as much relief as shaking my arms had—far short of what they desired. That's when I came to understand the real challenge was mental—a sure sign of trouble.

The appearance of a banana peel on the shoulder told me I was not alone in my suffering. Not yet blackened by the scorching sun, the yellow rind offered the prospect of encountering another cyclist who couldn't be far ahead. I pushed on with a sense companionship brought on by a person I had never seen, heard or met. No face, no words could have held the promise of that saffron Chiquita skin.

From that humble beginning, my whole world brightened to the color of sunshine: a school bus full of teenagers drove by, their heads and arms extended out windows, cheering me on; a yellow road sign indicated a brief descent ahead; and vast fields of black-eyed Susans spread for acres in every direction. Gone were the ocher dunes and umber fins of the morning. I'd left the circling sharks of the desert behind and found myself traveling through a calmer sea of gold. The brightly-colored mental life raft carried me the last three miles to town.

"Welcome to Monticello - 7,050 feet." One sign of relief was followed by another: "Chuckwagon General Store." Leaning Betsy against the front window, I noticed two boys gazing intently at her from a booth inside. I smiled and nodded my head, but they just stared. It wasn't until later that I'd learn their true intentions.

Buying a bottle of Powerade, I slipped into the Men's room and flipped on the light. The rusty knob marked C turned easily in my right hand while I held my left wrist beneath the faucet, waiting for the temperature to drop. An appreciation for cold water had taught me patience. As I waited, I took a long look in the mirror. Whiskers sprouted like cholla through a thin layer of topsoil that covered my face. Brushing the hair from my eyes, I noticed a pale, clean band across my forehead—the undeniable mark of a cowboy in Indian country. Over a hundred years ago, western tribes observed this phenomenon among the newcomers to the region, and put it to use in their sign language. Passing two fingers across one's brow was the gesture for white man. Like the brim of a Stetson, my helmet had shaded my forehead during long hours of riding the range.

When the temperature of the water had dropped sufficiently, I cupped both hands and flooded my face. Cool droplets ran down my cheeks and collected at my chin. I took a deep breath and let it out with sigh of relief. Ahh!

Refreshed, I walked back through the store and returned to Ol' Bets only to find the meaning and purpose of the boys' stares. They were gone, but not without leaving their mark. It was not until I had mounted the bike that I became aware something was wrong. It didn't take more than two pedal strokes to notice a problem. Stepping off and taking a look, I pinpointed the problem immediately—both tires were flat. So much for "Welcome to Monticello."

Although the sun had just passed its zenith, the elevation kept the temperature in the low nineties. According to official records, the mercury has never topped 100 degrees in Monticello—a fact not lost on those who choose to make it their home. While the country on three sides bakes under triple digits, Monticello offers relief to natives and visitors alike. Milder temperatures and a shaded park at the center of town were the perfect ingredients for a relaxing afternoon despite the antics of the preteen welcoming committee.

At the official Visitor Information Center, I discovered racks full of information sheets and tourist guides to the Four Corners Region. The host, an elderly gentleman wearing a pale green Forest Service uniform and walking with a limp, asked where I was from. "New Hampshire, huh?" he responded to my answer. "Don't get many of those."

Over the last week he had tallied twenty-seven Germans and nineteen French, but told me I was the sole representative of the Granite State. He gave me a handful of guides and told me to enjoy his "city of views."

Already familiar with the topography north of town, I noticed how the land also falls away to the south and east as Route 666 bounces over low foothills toward the Colorado border, and 101 slides straight into Arizona. Looking over the possibilities from a shaded bench in the town park, I pulled out a map. Either road could take me to New Mexico with about the same mileage—200. But how to decide?

Considering how hot and dry it had been over the last three weeks, Colorado became the natural choice. I was far more willing to take my chances along a satanic highway (666), than to deliver myself directly into the hellfire of Arizona.

Compared to the hellish temperatures I had heard predicted for Arizona, the Abajo Mountains west of town seemed Heavenly—making Monticello a sort of Purgatory halfway in between. Rising another 4,000 feet above town—to an elevation of 11,000—the Abajos are home to locally famous Horsehead Peak. Named for the peculiar pattern of spruce trees growing on the upper slopes, it has provided the town with a point of interest for years. Difficult to discern in the late summer, it takes a winter's snow to supply enough contrast to clearly see the white nose of a blaze-faced stallion. Originally a natural occurrence, the local boy scouts have taken over its maintenance in recent years—making an annual trip up the mountain to cut saplings, clear brush and help ensure the vitality of Monticello's tourism industry.

I looked up from the local paper and a peanut butter sandwich at the young man walking intently toward me from across the park. He wore blue jeans and a red shirt. Short, dark hair covered his brow, and a pair of gold-rimmed glasses rested on the bridge of his distinctive Indian nose. The fuzz on his upper lip looked more like an emaciated caterpillar than a moustache. He introduced himself as Patrick Haskins, "last of the Haskins," and within five minutes had recounted his life story.

"I was born just outside of town and adopted by a white family. Raised right here in Monticello. As far as I know, I'm one half Paiute, no. One half Ute and a quarter Paiute. Oh yeah, and a quarter Navajo. That's what I've been told—just a whole mix of stuff."

Despite his diverse genetics, Patrick was unable to tell me anything substantial about Native American culture. "I don't know any Indians," he claimed. "Most of my friends are L.D.S."

I stared blankly, wondering how all of Patrick's friends could possibly be Learning Disabled Students. Did he go to a special school? Was it something in the water? Had dyslexia reached epidemic proportions in Monticello?

"Latter Day Saints. You know, the Mormons."

"Of course." Hundreds of miles from Salt Lake City, and twenty from the Colorado border, I was still, after all, in Utah. A polygamous flagman I was willing to accept, but the last thing I had expected to find—even in Utah—was a Mormon Indian. (If you can't beat 'em, join 'em.) He was anxious for me to learn more about Monticello and offered an escort to the San Juan County Library and Museum—a rectangular brick building standing in a corner of the park.

Through the breezeway and into the burgeoning shelves, he eagerly introduced me to the head librarian, assistant librarian and an elderly gentleman quietly reading the local paper. Surprised at the interruption, he lowered the front page of the *San Juan Record*, tilted his head, and emitted an inconsequential grunt.

"This guy rode his bike all the way from North Dakota! " Patrick said with as much pride as if he had done it himself.

Repeating his initial response in reverse order, the old man grunted, tilted his head and raised the paper.

Patrick led me across the hall and into the one room museum of local history. "It used to be bigger when it was down in the basement, but the seniors needed more space for their low impact aerobics classes."

Although that statement pretty much summed up the San Juan County Library and Museum, Patrick insisted we look through back issues of the *San Juan Record*, and even at his high school yearbook. "Not Pictured: John Russell, William Davis, Patrick Haskins."

"I can't remember where I was that day."

Surrounded by shelves labeled "LDS Literature," we sat at a small, circular table soon covered with pieces of Monticello's past. Patrick leafed through the yellowed pages of the *Record*, pointing out the price of bread at the Blue Mountain Market on April twenty-third, 1968—the day I was born. Suddenly and without warning, Patrick looked up from the paper and offered an ominous pair of syllables, "Uh-oh."

A large woman trod heavily on white vinyl shoes toward the circulation desk. Orange polyester pants strained at the seams while a brightly patterned shirt refused to stay tucked. Around her neck hung a long silver chain with a large pendant. She carried a yellow purse in one hand and a library book in the other.

Dressed so comically, I thought it must be a joke until Patrick's shaking head told me otherwise. Considering she was the only person in the last two hours to whom he failed to introduce me, I decided to keep my distance.

The tirade began as she slammed the book on the counter. Her husky voice carried across the hushed room. "This book has bugs in it! When I opened it up at home they got all over me. I am holding you responsible."

The head librarian did his best to calm her down, but she persisted. She described how the bugs had infested her house and how it was the library's fault. "I want answers!" she demanded. "And until I get some, I'm not leaving!"

Her tirade gave me the perfect opportunity to do so. Thanking Patrick for his hospitality and waving sympathetically to the librarians, I returned to Ol' Betsy for a little routine maintenance before heading into the Colorado hills. As I left Monticello that evening, it was hard to believe that two days on a bike would take me further east than Patrick had ever traveled in his life.

Chapter 29

*After many nights of heat, long skeins of white stratus will gather along
the horizon, and out of them will slowly be woven forms of the cumulus
and the nimbus. And it will rain in short squalls of great violence in the
loams, mesas, and bordering mountains. But usually the cloud that
drenches a mountain top eight thousand feet up will pass over an
intervening valley, pouring down the same flood of rain, and yet not a
drop reaching the ground. The air is always dry and the raindrop that
has to fall through eight thousand feet of it before reaching the earth,
never arrives.*
—John C. Van Dyke, 1901

U.S. 666 to the Colorado border was anything but a hellish ride. A tail
wind pushed me down the route of an old wagon trail which had once
been crucial to the livelihood of the "City of Views." The road rolls off
the mountain and through a broad expanse of brittle sage accented by
pathetically small stands of bleached pinon and dry arroyos etched into
the unconsolidated soil. The monochromatic landscape wearied my eyes,
forcing then upward for relief.

With the setting sun at my back and the glowing Rockies ahead,
deliverance was readily at hand. Clouds gathered off to the southeast—
billowing cumuli acting strangely suspicious. They churned with an
unfamiliar urgency that made me nervous. Although the wind still blew
from behind and the clouds lay ahead, my thoughts turned to the rain
gear packed safely at the bottom of a pannier. I checked my watch against
a mile marker and then returned my gaze to the heavens where my
fears dissolved into the magic of light and prism. Suspended on the
ghostly trails of virgo, bands of violet, blue, green, yellow, orange, and
red arched across the sky as if hanging from the clouds by hidden wires.
The full spectrum of visible light floated above the drab landscape as
the raindrops which gave it life re-evaporated into the clouds before
ever reaching the ground. Glowing like a ruby-throated hummingbird
hovering at a feeder, the rainbow floated effortlessly between earth and
sky. According to Navajo legend, rainbows get their colors from the
feathers of birds. A sign on the road ahead said it all: "Welcome to
Colorful Colorado."

But colors soon faded with the setting sun, turning the open fields of
southwestern Colorado into an Andrew Wyeth painting. The low ceiling
created an oblique viewpoint of the brown and graying landscape.
Lonely trees spotted the low hills along the elevated horizon, fringing a
sky of slate. Fences stretched along the highway from one lonely
farmhouse to the next.

The message of private property was loud and clear in a region that's long been known as a stronghold of rugged Mormon individualism. Many claim there are none more reclusive than the stubborn inhabitants of southeastern Utah and southwestern Colorado who ask merely to be left alone so that they can take care of themselves. With the prospect of spending the night tucked away in the corner of a farmer's field, I couldn't agree more—at least for the night.

I slipped off Route 666 and up a dirt road like a dark angel slinking past a row of dimly lit houses and into the fields beyond. But my devilish behavior was revealed by the howls of an evangelical dog at the second yard on the left. *"Nil Sine Numine,"* he seemed to be barking the state motto: "Nothing without Providence." Faster than the information superhighway, the message spread up the road from doghouse to doghouse. Within seconds, the announcement of my arrival echoed throughout the neighborhood. A chorus of yips, yaps and barks hung in the air long after I had left the houses behind.

It was the sound of a different animal that filled the cool country air early the next morning. Starting with a single bird somewhere to the east, high-pitched crowing soon echoed from barnyards in every direction. As farm boys cringed in their warm beds at the feathered call to chores, I welcomed the sound of a new day, a new state. More than just a rooster, Colorado was calling.

Despite the crisp air, I was out of my bag within seconds, munching on a granola bar while pulling on a turtle neck. As my head squeezed through the elastic portal, it was greeted with an incredible sight. I paused momentarily as the flaming sunrise first peered over the misty peaks. In its gentle glow, I finished packing and headed out, slow and easy, through rolling fields of beans. Leafy, green legumes covered the gently rolling hills all the way to the mountains. A proud sign at the edge of town said it all about Dove Creek: "Pinto Bean Capitol of the World."

Out of water, I stopped in at the local Suprette: "Beer, Wine, Guns, Ammo, Picnic Supplies." A trio of pickup trucks with gun racks and NRA stickers were parked near the door. One bumper stick said, "Shoot Doves, Not Drugs," another, "If Elvis Were a Bow Hunter, He'd Still Be Alive."

Out-manned and out-gunned, I entered the market unarmed except for my sharp wit which I was not about to unholster. It's hard to ride a bicycle with your funny-bone in a cast.

Bridling my sense of humor, I walked solemnly down a full aisle dedicated to fishing lures. Beyond the wigglers and jigglers (but no gigglers), I found a dingy bathroom where I filled my water bottles in an iron-stained sink. I picked up a pair of granola bars on my way to the checkout where I found myself the only one not laughing.

Delayed behind a pair of broad-shouldered men filling out applications for fishing licenses, I remained unaware that it was I who was the focus of their amusement. "Nice shorts," muttered a bearded man in a plaid flannel shirt (not that that distinguished him from the other).

His friend looked up briefly from his form and gave me a smirk as if to say, "Real men don't wear lycra." As they returned to their applications, I waited patiently, enduring the awkward looks of every customer who came through the door. They must not see many cyclists in "Bean Town."

Still more rolling fields—Anasazi beans, popcorn beans, and of course pintos—filled the gap between Dove Creek and Cahone. I passed the Adobe Milling Company and an old Santa Fe box car converted into the Whistle Stop Market offering "Groceries and Pinto Beans." What else could one need?

Outside of Cahone, gentle, green slopes reached as far as the eye could see. The undulating topography carried me through Pleasant View, Yellow Jacket, Lewis and Arriola—each town smaller than the last. Standing on the inclines and sitting on the descents, I enjoyed the variety of pedaling positions provided by this type of terrain. With a good warm-up, I was soon up to speed. A slow moving tractor on the shoulder outside of Arriola retarded my progress temporarily, but overall I made good time and found myself in Cortez before 10:00 A.M.

The seat of Montezuma County, Cortez was the largest town I'd been through in over a week. Motels, fast food restaurants and gift shops vied for attention along 160 through town, while the Mart brothers—Wal and K—stood on the outskirts, siphoning dollars away from downtown merchants. I stopped briefly at the Colorado Visitor Center and discovered that a centennial celebration was just then being held eighteen miles away in Mancos. With a fair, parade and street dance, the decision to push on was easy.

U.S. Route 160 led me into a dryer region east of Cortez and through the junction with State Route 145 to Telluride (or as conductors on the old narrow-gauge railway used to announce, "To Hell You Ride"). Shaggy stands of pinon and cedar topped the low, red hills streaked with bands of whitish gypsum. Brittle tumbleweeds—known to cowboys as, "Roosian thistles"—skittered along the roadside. Sparse bunches of shadscale and grama grass grew here and there.

Beyond the lower mesas—spiny with hogbacks and dotted with stunted evergreens—I could see the broad, flat tableland of Mesa Verde National Park. Fifteen miles long and 2,000 feet above the valley floor, its rimrock commands the horizon from the Rocky Mountains to the north and east to the Four Corners region to the southwest. Honeycombed with deep canyons, long crannies and arching caves, the mesa holds the greatest mystery of the region. But more on that later.

Named for its abundance of vegetation, Mesa Vurd—as the locals pronounce it—is a high tableland covered by Douglas fir, ponderosa pine and quaking aspen. The lower reaches are dominated by pinon and juniper, while a melange of gambel oak, serviceberry and mountain mahogany make up the transition zone. Oregon grape and yucca can be found in the shaded canyons.

This abundance and diversity of vegetation allow a wide range of animal life to flourish. Mule deer, elk and bighorn sheep roam the upper slopes while turkey vultures, golden eagles and a variety of hawks soar on thermals overhead. These birds keep a keen eye out for any one of a variety of rodents below. A gray rock squirrel, cotton tail rabbit or tassel-eared squirrel would make a nice meal. But for these tasty morsels, the raptors are in competition with a score of terrestrial predators. While not as abundant as in the past, bobcats, badgers, black bears and even cougars have been sighted within the park in recent years.

My personal wildlife experience, however, was limited to a small selection of songbirds. Along the final ascent to the park's entrance I spotted a trio of mountain chickadees and white-breasted nuthatch along with a handful of unidentifiable L.B.J.s (little brown jobs).

Unlike the big trees of Sequoia or the wading birds of the Everglades, the abundance of plant and animal life are not what qualify Mesa Verde as a National Park. The real reason for the steady stream of motor vehicles passing through the entrance gate is the mystery of what local cowboys called "Moqui houses." Ever since their "discovery" in 1886, there has been a fascination with the cliff dwellings and the mysterious disappearance of their inhabitants approximately 700 years ago. This enigmatic tribe is known only by the name ascribed to them by the Navajo—*Anasazi*, "Those-Who-Were-Here-Before-Us," or more simply, "The Ancient Ones."

Above the Mancos Shale, the Point Lookout Sandstone and the Menefee Formation stands the Cliff House Sandstone, where, sometime during the sixth century, a tribe of nomadic hunters settled and began to carve out great structures in the rock. Towers, terraces and whole towns were built in the grottoes. "They called us backwards and uncivilized," observe Pueblo Indians still living in the region, "but our ancestors built the first apartment house complex in the whole world almost 900 years ago."

Making use predominantly of south-facing caves, these ancient architects have been identified as the inventors of passive solar design. They carefully chose caves with enough overhang to shield the interior from the high summer sun but allow the warmth of low-angle winter rays to enter. Similar design techniques are relatively new in modern

American buildings. Somewhere between the Anasazi and the Whole Earth Catalog, architects forgot about the sun.

Although their sun temple was never completed, the Anasazi's respect and understanding of solar cycles and seasonal fluctuations remain obvious to archaeologist and tourist alike. From artifacts, we know they were farmers who also hunted, snared and trapped animals and birds. We know they collected roots, herbs and nuts, and they used both wooden and stone tools. They also made garments from hide and baskets from plant fibers. All this we know, but what remains a mystery is how and why they left after 800 years of continuous habitation. Could the answer lie within their petroglyphs?

Widespread and common from the San Juan Basin and Monument Valley in Utah to Casas Grandes in Mexico, rock carvings tell rich tales of history and myth. Although many characters are common in the glyphs of different tribes, perhaps the most often repeated is that of Kokopeli, the hump-backed flute player. A popular subject of both Navajo and Hopi myths, his likeness is seen among the Rio Grande Pueblos as well as tribes of the California Desert.

Kokopeli did not reach his greatest popularity, perhaps, until souvenir shops infested the region. Common on T-shirts, ear rings, bolo ties, paperweights, collector cups, canvas bags and refrigerator magnets, you can't turn around without seeing him. Although his former likeness had often been vividly phallic, his new image has been down-rated to PG. Castrated in the name of tourism!

According to myth, Kokopeli was a traveling minstrel with quite a reputation as a lady's man. Representing fertility, he not only brought rain to the crops, but also caused former virgins to awake in the morning with the strange feeling of a seed inside their bellies. This may have something to do with the meaning of his name. "Koko" is both Hopi and Zuni for god while "Pelli" is their word for the desert robber fly.

Above all else, however, Kokopeli remains a wanderer, traveling from village to village trading new songs for old. It was in that spirit, and not that I had also recently lost my masculinity (although the first symptoms of penal numbness may have been setting in) that I descended into the Mancos Valley and the Centennial Celebration.

Chapter 30

All in all, my years on the trail were the happiest I ever lived. There were many hardships, and dangers, of course, that called on all a man had of endurance and bravery; but when all went well there was no other life so pleasant. Most of the time we were solitary adventurers in a great land as fresh and new as a spring morning, and we were free and full of the zest of darers.
—Charles Goodnight

I'd missed the pancake breakfast, but hit town just as the parade was turning from First Avenue onto North Main Street. The Boy Scouts of Troop 518—with their olive green uniforms and bright red scarves—marched by in two lines striding shoulder to shoulder. Merit badges, too many to count, passed by with the easy rhythm of swinging arms. A pair of Eagle Scouts at the head of the column proudly carried the American and Colorado flags.

These fine young men were followed by the local Girl Scouts (sans cookies), the 4-H club, and members of the V.F.W. auxiliary 5231. Next came the Mancos Mustang Dance Club sashaying their way down North Main to a country & western tune. On their heels (which they were kicking up) came a red pickup truck pulling a wagon with a banner announcing the "Past Queens." Sitting on hay bales and waving to the crowd were a dozen gray-haired women in cowboy hats and white blouses. No longer the main attraction of the parade themselves, they served merely to announce the coming of the new queen whose approach was further enhanced by the front end of a police escort.

Sirens blaring and lights flashing, a pair of black and white cruisers accompanied the shiny red Mustang convertible which held the current queen. This year's sweetheart was an attractive girl with high cheekbones and long brown hair. She wore blue jeans, a white embroidered shirt and a red cowboy hat as bright as the car. Silver earrings dangled from her lobes and what seemed to be a forced smile spanned the gap between. Sitting high in the back seat, she turned her slim torso from one side of the street to the other, offering the standard rotating-palm parade wave—the epitome of insincerity. As the Mustang passed, our eyes met for a brief moment and I was suddenly transfixed by her dark brown eyes. As powerful as any true monarch, the Queen of Mancos held me helpless with her gaze. But the moment ended as suddenly as it had begun. The bright red Ford continued down the street, leaving me spellbound.

Trailing the second police car, the hook and ladder truck of the Mancos Volunteer Fire Department—complete with spotted Dalmatian—made a wide turn from First onto North Main forcing a group of eager spectators to step back to the curb. Wide, white banners hung from either side of the engine announcing the evening's street dance co-sponsored by the Department and Coors Light beer.

The last, but certainly not least, group to parade down Main Street had neither a banner to announce their coming nor music to accompany their progress. Made up of children too young to be Scouts of either gender, they were no less proud to be a part of the festivities. Having spent considerable time decorating their bicycles with tassels, streamers and crepe paper, they were ready to show off in front of the whole town.

A half dozen boys—probably nine or ten years old—led the way on BMX bikes. Baseball cards affixed to seat stays with clothes pins rattled in their spokes as they jockeyed for position. Competing for the pole, only by the slow moving fire truck ahead of them prevented an all out race.

The girls who followed were much less competitive in their riding— at least where speed was concerned. With their minds fixed on the back seat of a Mustang convertible, they were already practicing their best parade waves despite the obvious risks associated with taking one hand off the handlebars. Weaving up the street like a caravan of drunks, there were the inevitable collisions along the way. Tears were shed but, as far as I could tell, no blood.

Not to be outdone by their older brothers and sisters, a final group of younger children—probably six and seven-years-old—brought up the rear. While some rode bikes with training wheels, others commanded tricycles and big wheels. With smiles as wide as the western sky and faces as bright as a sunset, they stole the show from not only from their siblings, but also from the Queen herself. Great cheers followed them up North Main.

Moved by the overwhelming show of support for pedal power, I decided to indulge in a little harmless fun. Rolling Betsy onto the street, I fell in with the pint-sized wheelers. With shit-eating grin and *my* best parade wave, I pedaled alongside the children past hundreds of strangers. Unphased by my presence, my new companions simply looked up, smiled and continued pumping their legs. Their mission was simply to make it to the other end of the street. To them I was just another kid trying to do the same.

The parade broke up in a large parking lot at the east end of town. Children were reunited with their parents and escorted to the fair grounds at the far side of the local park. Pushing Betsy beside me, I followed the crowds toward the sights, sounds and smells of a small town fair. The aroma of hot dogs, popcorn and cotton candy lingered like a stale circus in the air. Brightly colored trailers advertised everything from the obligatory offerings of corn dogs, sausages and funnel cakes to more regional specialties like tacos, tamales and frito pies. While the latter offered greater appeal, I ended up taking the advise of a man who noticed me reading the menus. "Follow me," he said, leading me past the rolling greasy spoons to a small tent where four gray-haired Navajo women were feverishly at work. The hearty smell of stewing beans replaced that of frying meat.

"If you want a real taste of local food," he told me, "this is the place to get it. Best Navajo tacos in the county are right here."

Through a constant banter in Navajo, the women performed like a finely-tuned quartet. While the first rolled out dough into broad, flat discs, the second fried them in a crock pot of boiling oil. The next woman loaded the fry bread with beans from yet another crock pot, and handed them to the last woman who added grated cheese, lettuce, tomato and onion. The lone male under the tent simply collected money and asked customers if they wanted hot sauce.

Although I'd never had another Navajo taco in Montezuma County, after just one bite I had no reason to doubt the claim that brought me. Thanking my culinary advisor, I returned to the tree where I'd left Betsy and sat down to finish my meal.

Mid-way through the taco, I was approached by a middle aged man wearing a dark blue Kansas State hat with matching T-shirt. A bright red-and-yellow Jay Hawk adorned each. "Weren't you riding that bike in the parade with all those kids earlier?"

I hesitated. Oh shit.

"Don't worry," he said sensing my concern. "I thought it was hysterical. I'm a cyclist myself. Done the 'BAK' three times."

"The BAK?"

"Bike Across Kansas. That's where I'm from—if you couldn't already tell. I've only lived in Mancos for six years. I'm principal of the middle school here.

I nodded politely, wishing he'd leave me to my lunch.

"How long you gonna be in around?"

"Just today."

"You certainly picked a good one. 'Mancos Days' is always a fun time. We got the parade, hot air balloon rides, a rodeo, and the street dance and fireworks tonight. You ought to stick around for them."

"Maybe I will."

"Well, maybe I'll see you later then. I've got to get over for my softball game. Nice meetin' ya."

"You to."

Having finished my lunch, I locked Betsy to a small tree and took a stroll around the booths. As with the food, there were both the generic offerings as well as those with a western flair. Leather belts and bolo ties were as wide-spread a "No Fear" t-shirts and baseball caps. Turquoise and silver jewelry dominated the market place, but Indian pottery, sand paintings and dream catchers were also common. Some booths specialized in leather, offering vests, purses and jackets, while others boasted cotton quilts, bonnets and place mats. With candles, knives, wreathes and western prints to round things out, I could have gotten all my Christmas shopping done in one fell swoop. Getting it all home on a bicycle, however, would be another story.

Settling for a pound of locally grown pistachios, I returned to Ol' Bets and walked her to the softball field. "Kansas State" grounded out to the second baseman as I found a spot along the left field line. The bleachers behind third base were packed and late comers had taken up positions along both foul lines as well as behind the temporary plywood home run fence. Hand painted, each four by eight foot section advertised a local organization or business.

I found a spot between an elderly couple in lawn chairs and group of rowdy thirty-somethings—five of whom sat on the ground, while the sixth perched himself atop a red Coleman cooler full of beer. Coors was the brand of choice, and two trips to the liquor store were required to maintain the supply throughout the afternoon.

They spoke of motorcycles and tattoos, peeling off their shirts to provide visual aids. Eagles, spiders and the Harley Davidson logo were the most common emblems revealed during this hard-nosed version of show-and-tell.

Men's and women's games alternated throughout the day, but no one seemed to pay much attention to the scores. Although I overheard something about a rule allowing only one base for hitting it out of the park after the first round tripper of each inning, it had little, if any, effect on the sluggers who were more intent on showing off their power than hitting for extra bases. As many as four out-of-the-park singles occurred in a row, advancing the first batter home one base at a time.

A group of young boys wrestled for each fence-topper, with the victor dutifully returning the ball to the nearest outfielder who then hurled it back to the pitcher. Only a late afternoon thunderstorm threatened the oft repeated pattern, but it passed to the north without laying a single drop on Mancos.

By seven o'clock my stomach was growling and the Navajo taco women had packed up and left. By chance I saw "Kansas State" walking off the ball field—his team had just lost in the men's finals.

"Tough game," I said, breaking the ice before asking about where to eat.

"That's no big deal. Their team wins every year."

"I was wondering if you could give me some dining advice?"

"Well, Cindy's is nice, and I think they got a cowboy poet tonight. Its over there across the field. See that building with the brown roof? It's the one next to that."

"Thanks."

I made my way around the field as the women's final got underway. Cars surrounded the windowless building, but a sign assured me not to worry. "Our Lot Is Full, But We Are Not. Come On In For BBQ Ribs, Corn On The Cob And Baked Beans."

You can't always believe what you read. The place was packed. Men and women dressed in the spirit of the day occupied every table in the main dining room, while the back section had been reserved for the Mancos Valley High School classes of 1942 through 1947. Business was brisk as waitresses shuffled from table to grill to table, taking orders, serving meals and clearing dishes. Without breaking stride under the weight of a platter full of ribs, a young woman in a red and white checked apron told me it shouldn't be more than a five minute wait.

In the corner to my right I could see the profile of cowboy poet, Walt Gilliland sitting on a table and speaking into a microphone. Dark sideburns crept out from beneath his wide brimmed hat and followed his jaw bone to where it curved below his ruddy cheeks. A long, bushy mustache filled his upper lip and spilled over at each end, hanging down to his chin. Walt's thick eyebrows were enough to make any of the "Former Queens" jealous. He wore an embroidered white shirt tucked into a pair of blue jeans, and swung his boots forward and back under the table upon which he perched. A pitcher labeled "Donations" sat beside him.

The poor acoustics were made worse by the proximity of the microphone to Walt's mouth. His verse became tangled in his thick moustache, freeing itself only to enter the room as a verbal blur which left me searching for meaning in stanzas ending in words like ajinglin', ajanglin', and ashinin'. Despite my best attempts to understand the buckaroo bard, the combination of chattering patrons and cheap microphone made it virtually impossible. Couplets, triplets and quatrains were drowned in a sea restaurant banter.

I ate corn bread, baked beans and a double order of apple pie in the corner opposite Walt. The waitress looked at me skeptically when I answered "No" to her inquiry about what size order of ribs I wanted. She returned to the kitchen and pressed the silent alarm.

Everyone and his cousin had turned out for the 4th Annual Coors Light Fireman's Street Dance. A flatbed trailer was parked in front of town hall and the entire block had been cleared of motor vehicles. I locked Betsy to one of the orange cattle gates that had been placed at either end of the street, and skirted my way around the dancing throng. The street was seething with bodies in motion—twisting, turning, spinning. From the top of the trailer, a quartet of bearded men kicked out a country tune that had everyone going full tilt. Boots astompin', skirts atwirlin'.

When the music stopped, the dancers came to rest like wind-up toys winding down. A roar of applause broke the brief silence before the band wound the crowd's key with another tune. Finding a comfortable spot along the curb, I was content to watch from the sidelines. I'd always been a wall flower, even where I wasn't a mangy-looking, under-dressed, stranger.

The street lights were lit by the time the band took its first break. As someone started a Garth Brooks tape to fill the void, I felt a tap on my shoulder. Turning slowly, I found myself face to face with the Queen of Mancos.

"Weren't you at the parade today?" She caught me off guard. I struggled to get something out. "Yeah...I was."

"I thought so. You had a bike with you."

"Yeah...Betsy."

"Betsy?"

"The bike."

"You named your bike Betsy? That's so cute."

Cute? Cute? I'm being called cute by a girl nearly ten years younger than me. "I think I saw you too. Weren't you riding in the back of a bright red Mustang?"

"Kinda hard to miss, huh?"

"The police escort ensured that."

"Oh, I'm so glad it's over. The only reason I got elected is because my friends knew it would embarrass the hell out of me. They were right."

"Just think, you're now a piece of Mancos history! You can ride every year as a 'Past Queen.'"

"Oh boy! They only let the old ladies do that anyway."

"Well then, you'll have something to look forward to."

"Believe me, I won't be anywhere near here when I'm that age. I can't wait to get outta Mancos. What are you doing here anyway?"

I described my route, my plans and started in on one of a growing number of anecdotes when the band struck up again.

"Wanna dance?" she asked.

I hesitated.

"Come on," she insisted.

"I'm not very good."

"Its easy. Just follow me."

No small task. One moment her hands were on her hips while she kicked her feet out front and the next she was twirling one arm in the air and stomping the ground. Always a step behind, I may have looked

190

foolish, but I didn't care. "Yeehaw!" I shouted, slapping a knee and doing a little improvisation of my own.

By the time the song ended, we were hardly able to control our laughter, still giggling when the band took up the next tune—a slow one. Entranced by the melody, couples embraced around us. Within seconds we found ourselves in a sea of swaying bodies. With some hesitation, I took one of her hands in mine, and placed the other around her waist. She set her free hand on my shoulder as our bodies came together. I whispered softly in her ear, "You'd better lead."

But before she could respond, I felt another hand upon my shoulder— a heavy hand that jerked me around with violent force. The music played on as I found myself staring into the burly chest of this queen's king. Arm and Hammer biceps stretched the sleeves of his t-shirt.

The town clock read 9:30, but it was high noon for me. This town, it seemed, suddenly wasn't big enough for the two of us. Was I about to become another notch on his belt? My happy trails, I feared, were coming to an end as Black Bart seemed quite set on sending me to the Happy Hunting Grounds.

Amid a slew of cowboy allusions, it was the words of an Indian, Chief Joseph, that called out in my moment of need. "I will fight no more forever." This was after all a fireman's dance, not a Ghost Dance. Deciding between one's honor and a pretty woman had never been easier—I chose neither. Bury my heart at wounded pride.

I could smell the alcohol on his breath. "What do you think you're doing?"

Opting against a sarcastic response, I went with the obvious reply, "Dancing."

"Not you, chump. I was talking to her." He brushed me aside. "You know you're my gal. Why do you gotta do stuff like this?"

"You've been so into your softball and beer drinking that you haven't even talked to me all day. I just wanted to have a little fun."

"So you call dancing with this guy fun?"

"Yes, Carl, I do. He's nice, he's funny, and best of all he's not from around here."

"What's that supposed to mean?"

"You figure it out," she said, turning away and pushing her way through the crowd. I took a step to follow, but felt the heavy hand on my shoulder once more.

"You're not goin' anywhere. Billy, Roscoe, you watch this guy. I'm going after Jane." So that was her name. What a calamity!

Carl pushed his way through the swaying bodies, leaving me alone with his friends. Our little trio gave new meaning to "the good, the bad and the ugly." Outnumbering me two to one and outweighing me threefold, I did my best to get along. Even a dude from back East knows a haymaker when he sees one. I scanned the area for escape routes. Under the flatbed looked most promising.

Billy and Roscoe escorted me to the side of the street where we waited until Carl joined us minutes later. "I can't find her. What's this guy's story?"

"We didn't ask him."

As the interrogation began, I wondered if lynching were still legal in Colorado. That's when I caught a glimpse of "Kansas State" over Carl's shoulder and gave him a wave. Sensing a level of anxiety in my arm's motion, he came over to investigate.

"There's no problem at all Mr. Guilford," Carl responded to his inquiry. "We're just entertaining our out-of-state guest." Translation: "We're going to kick this eastern boy's ass."

Although these were clearly not middle schoolers, Mr. Guilford wielded enough influence to get me away. He escorted me quickly to the end of the street where I had hobbled Betsy. "Yes, she's pretty," he offered. "But she is Carl's girlfriend. And now, for whatever reason, he and his friends are all riled up. And when they get riled up, they cause trouble. Now you look like a nice fella and I'm sure you did nothing wrong, but the best thing for you to do right now is leave."

Taking his advice, I unlocked Betsy and was preparing to go when a reach for my hat came up empty. Gone. It must have been lost it in the shuffle. I looked back toward the crowd of dancing bodies and then at "Kansas State."

"Forget it," he said. "Just go."

Like scratched Teflon, I slipped out of Mancos as the fireworks began. Thoughts of romance waned liked the gibbous moon above.

About a mile down my personal "trail of tears," I found a dirt road heading into a wooded glen. About a hundred yards in, I came to a small clearing in a grove of towering conifers. Leaning Betsy against a sturdy trunk, I took heart in knowing that at least one gal who would stick by me.

Chapter 31

My God and my mother live in the West, and I will not leave them. It is a tradition of my people that we must never cross the three rivers—the Grande, the San Juan, the Colorado. Nor could I leave the Chuska Mountains. I was born there. I shall remain.
—Manuelito, Apache Chief, 1865

The Wind has given men and creatures strength...for at the beginning, they were shrunken and flabby until it inflated them; and the Wind was creation's first food, and put motion and change into nature, giving life to everything, even to the mountains and water.
—Bernard Haile

I awoke in the presence of unseen giants. White fir, yellow pine and Engleman spruce were shadows among the shadows. The cubist depths of a forest primeval engulfed me. I lay in the umbra of an arboreal eclipse. I wore the darkness like a blindfold.

"Who?" called a barred owl through the darkness. "Who cooks for you?"

In the Navajo tradition, Owl has the power to tell a man's future. Sometimes he speaks the truth, but sometimes he lies. I listened carefully as he repeated his culinary question.

"Who cooks for you?"

"Yes," replied my stomach. "Who?"

The owl spoke the truth.

Wearing tights, gloves and a fleece top, I climbed east out of Mancos into the La Sal Mountains. For four miles the road struggles up a wide, timber-filled valley, steepening at an almost imperceptible rate as it approaches the head wall. The climb warmed me, but drawing on experience, I fought the urge to remove layers as I crossed the summit. Within seconds, frigid air whipped my ears—but nothing else—as I barreled down the slope fully bundled. A quarter mile up the next climb, however, I was forced to remove the fleece, but left the tights and gloves in place.

Progress was slow, but turning a low gear early is an essential warm up for a long day. It also gave me a chance to admire the wave-like patterns of green on green across the emerald mountains on either side.

Winding its way through the southern part of the San Juan National Forest, Route 160 could just as well have been in Shangri-La. Between thickly wooded hillsides, the valley floor teamed with wildflowers. Asters, lupine and Indian paintbrush bloomed abundantly in the shadow of Menefee mountain. High above, the coming of the sun was foretold

193

by a golden aura bathing Hesperus Peak. The contrast between light and shadow gave the feeling of riding through Caravaggio's finest chiaroscuro.

In the Navajo tradition, one must climb mountains in order to become intimate with the sky. For them, the massive upthrusts that dominate the landscape are more than mere geologic features, they represent parts of the earth's body. Head, heart, limbs and lungs, they are alive—given the power of motion by the winds themselves. The Navajo recognize four sacred mountains which border the reservation in the four sacred directions: to the East lies Mount Blanca, the Mountain of White Shell; to the South, Mount Taylor, the Mountain of Blue Turquoise; to the West, San Francisco Peak, the Mountain of Yellow Abalone; and to the North, Mount Hesperus, the Mountain of Jet Black. Created by the Holy Ones, each mountain has a mythical origin.

Dibentsaa, Hesperus Peak, is believed to have been fastened to earth by a rainbow. First Man and First Woman placed a basket of obsidian on the peak containing a pair of blackbird eggs. The eggs hatched and the blackbirds became the mountain's feathers.

Rather than sacred feathers on the mountaintop, I found a ski area and a handful of mountain chickadees.

Sunlight drowned the eastern slope, but the promise of a twelve mile descent discouraged a layer break. Pushing a big gear through the flat sections, I maintained a speed close to thirty miles per hour, rubbernecking as best I could at one point to read a hand-painted sign at the edge of a large meadow: "I'd Rather See Cows Than Condos."

Arriving in Durango as it barely began to stir, I made my way easily through the uncrowded streets to the City Market. A teenaged boy hosed down the fire lane as a woman in curlers and a bathrobe emerged from the electronic doors. She wheeled her cart toward a station wagon nearby, pausing momentarily at the edge of the damp pavement.

I passed her there, and proceeded through the doors in search of sustenance. Inside the entryway, I was shocked to find—along with the standard supply of shopping carts and weekly fliers—an espresso bar.

Wondering whether highly caffeinated shoppers spend more money than their more sedate counterparts, I made my way through a maze of artificially lit aisles of over-packaged and under-nourishing comestibles to the bakery in the far corner. "Sale—Day Old Fresh Donuts." Like a Whitman Sampler under glass, glazed, powdered, and jelly-filled vied for my attention. Along with a dozen discount pastries, I picked up my staples of bread and bananas and threw in a pound of pistachio nuts for variety.

On my way to the exit, I was confronted suddenly by an odor worse than my own. A trio of young men in spray skirts and Teva sport sandals were placing orders for double-shot espressos. The smell of lived-in polypropylene battled that of rich coffee. I caught alternating whiffs of each.

"How's the paddling around here?"

"It's great now," said the first one to get his coffee. He took a cautious sip. "But it might not last."

"How's that?"

"A.L.P."

"Alp?"

"The Animas-La Plata water project," said the second kayaker into the conversation. "It's the last big Bureau of Reclamation projects—been on the drawing board for twenty-five years. It's a whole series of dams, pipelines and pumping stations that'll draw about 200,000 acre-feet from the river every year. That's about what the entire city of Denver uses.

"Most of the water would be pumped a couple hundred feet uphill to irrigate hay and alfalfa at a cost of thousands of dollars per acre. But the farmers on the receiving end would only pay a couple hundred. The rest of the water is slated for municipal and industrial use. Up to sixty percent of the river could be siphoned off by the ALP."

"Not only that," added the third and final kayaker, "but it's been shown it would violate the Endangered Species Act, the National Environmental Protection Act, the Clean Water Act, and the Native American Grave Protection Act."

"Yeah," concluded the original speaker, "and all at a cost to tax payers of seven hundred million. The predicted yield is below forty cents on the dollar."

I was dumbfounded. Not just a group of river rats eager to shoot the next rapids, they were as passionate about protecting the river as they were about paddling it. One look at the river would explain why.

Free-flowing from its roots in the San Juan Mountains above the town of Silverton to its confluence with the San Juan River near Farmington, New Mexico, the Animas is one of only a handful of waterways in the West that have remained uninterrupted by dams. Whether thundering down narrow gorges in the highlands or meandering through the level glacial valleys below, the river and its associated wetlands provide important habitat to a surprising diversity of species. Occurring in the midst of a primarily arid desert ecosystem, the watercourse serves as an oasis for both native and migratory wildlife.

Like any wetlands, those along the Animas not only provide essential riparian habitat and nesting grounds, but also help filter pollutants and store excess water during times of flood. In this way, they become valuable not only to the organisms that live in and around them, but also to the human populations that live nearby. Early archeological evidence suggests a long standing and varied relationship between people and the river which continues to this day. Home to a thriving commercial rafting industry and a whitewater kayak course used by top international competitors, the Animas has been ranked as the state's fourth most economically valuable river. All without a single dam.

The significance is that along with being the largest free-flowing waterway in the Colorado Plateau region, the Animas has also been designated as one of the top ten endangered rivers in America.

Route 160 runs alongside the river for about four miles south of town before crossing it and heading east to Pagosa Springs. I turned south onto U.S. Highway 550 and began to climb as the Animas dropped out of sight, but not of mind. I would carry its burden of concern to the New Mexico border.

Within a mile I was hundreds of feet above the river on a plateau that angled imperceptibly to the south. Caused by an ancient geologic uplift, this flat tableland is an anomaly among the mountains of southern Colorado and plays host to hundreds of small farms as a result. But they ran together in a blur as a strong tail wind propelled me toward the state line fifteen miles away. Mejico Nuevo, it had been called by the Spaniards, Dine'tah, by the Navajo before them.

"Welcome to New Mexico—America's Land of Enchantment." If only it were true of the road surface. Cracked and pitted, the shoulder consisted of three inches of ragged macadam between a faded white line and four feet of loose sand and gravel. Riding the narrow strip was difficult enough without eighteen wheels of death passing within inches. After a particularly close call with a Peterbuilt, I deferred to the gravel at the first low growls of an approaching diesel engine. Assisted suicide may be fine for Dr. Kevorkian's terminally ill patients, but I had other plans.

The highway took me through Cedar Hill and across the Animas River where stout clumps of prairie spiderwort grew at roadside. Delicate, blue flowers bloomed among the long, narrow leaves—reflecting a perfect sky.

Not much had changed in Aztec, New Mexico since it was named "All America City" in 1963. The price of gas had reached a dollar a gallon at the Stop 'n Go, but Elvis was still on the radio. The King's soulful voice greeted me as I stepped into the convenience store. The girl behind the counter probably wasn't even born the year he died, yet she sang quietly along to "Love Me Tender." I smiled at her on my way to the bathroom.

By the time I'd filled my bottles, the improbable duet was mid-way through a trans-generational version of "Heartbreak Hotel." I bought a pair of granola bars before returning to Betsy for one last push before noon.

As the temperature approached 100, I climbed along Route 544 south of town. A parched wind blew beneath a molten sky. Loose sand blew across the road. The lush mountains of southern Colorado had given way to the withered plains of New Mexico. Simply looking out over it became a chore.

Topping the rise, a sign warned of road construction as miles of orange D.O.T. barrels became the dominant feature of the ashen landscape. Weaving in and out of them to avoid cars, I lost track of time and distance. My goal became simply to make it to the next town alive. As much as I'd come to respect Native American wisdom over the last two weeks, I had to disagree with Crazy Horse on this one. It was *not* a good day to die.

Bloomfield, New Mexico was a town of pawn shops and mobile homes. Blocks of single and double-wides branched off a lifeless Main Street. Roof lines were as flat as the landscape, and the pilot flame at the refinery burned as relentlessly as the scorching mid-day sun. There was nary a motel pool in sight.

The national chains—as well as the tourist dollars—had bypassed Bloomfield for Farmington, twelve miles to the west. A meager sign at the edge of town touted Bloomfield as the "Home of Jake Barnes, World Team Roping Champion in 1985"—little consolation even in a region where the five most popular sports are rodeo, rodeo, rodeo, rodeo and basketball, in that order.

At noon on a Sunday, it was a veritable ghost town, and even the ghosts were taking a siesta. At the Maverick Quick Mart, a chubby-cheeked girl filled my water bottles and gave me directions to the park where I'd spend the afternoon.

Like the petals of a posy, four baseball fields flowered from a common center. Backing up to one another, they formed concentric circles of chainlink backstops, rolled clay infields and grassy outfields. With wide bleachers and plenty of artificial lighting, a quadruple header could probably accommodate the entire town. But the stands were empty, and no Casey stood at bat. The sound of a metal ring clanging idly against a naked flagpole carried across the empty diamonds. There was no joy in Dustville.

Seeking shelter from the sun under a covered picnic area which contained no tables, I pulled out my Crazy Creek chair and lunch. Munching on pistachios and reading a paper I'd picked up in Aztec, the afternoon rolled slowly by. After poking feebly at the crossword puzzle, I turned to the comics and then the classifieds. "USED CARS," headlined one doubled-sized entry. "Why go somewhere else to be cheated? Come to Larry's first!"

By late afternoon, storm clouds gathered on the western horizon.

Thunderheads streamed skyward, boiling over, and spreading across the stove top that was New Mexico. Intense fields of electricity built up in the womb of clouds until suddenly, and without warning, a thunderbolt ripped earthward in a jagged projection. Displaced by time and muffled by distance, the sound of the report seemed unrelated when it finally arrived. Growing ever taller, the thunderheads would soon block out the afternoon sun.

Unable to resist the combination of cloud cover and tail wind, I decided to roll out early. "The rain is blind," say the Akimel O'odham people of the Sonoran Desert. "It must be led by the wind."

To a backdrop of cumulonimbus clouds, the smooth, wide shoulder of New Mexico Route 44 became the stage upon which I made my grand exit from Bloomfield. Between earthen berms, the road climbed gradually out of town. Traffic was surprisingly heavy for a Sunday evening, but riding well to the right of the white line made me feel safe enough to remove both my shirt and helmet. Lost in the ecstasy of a strong tail wind, I paid little attention to the pickups, campers and big rigs that sped by at an unthreatening distance. The best part of Bloomfield turned out to be the road out of town.

And it only got better. Leveling out and swinging eastward, the road allowed me to take full advantage of the northwest wind. Click. Click. Click. With Betsy in her highest gear, water pumps and walking sprinklers became a blur of spokes, rods and pipe. Yet still the wind implored me to go faster. It propelled me, embraced me, filled my heaving lungs. I skimmed over the rolling hills like a swallow in flight.

More than simply air in motion, it was a Holy Wind—what the Navajo call *nilch'i*. Central to their belief system, *nilch'i* includes the entire atmosphere as well as the air that swirls within each of us. Its presence allows movement, speech and even awareness. The Holy Wind serves as a messenger, communicating between the living and nonliving beings of the world. As such, it links us to the limitless powers of the universe. "Go faster," came a mysterious voice to my ear. "Go faster."

Angel Peak appeared to the north, shrouded by sinister clouds. The towering mesa dominated an otherwise horizontal landscape. Firebolts taunted the lonely monolith as the legendary thunderbird took flight, causing lightning with the blink of an eye and thunder by flapping its wings.

As a kid I was deathly afraid of thunderstorms. To reassure me, my mother said they couldn't hurt me if I always ate my vegetables, sat up straight, and said my prayers. Having taken the first bit of advice to the extreme, I shunned the second and proceeded directly to the third. Leaning into the aerobars, I prayed to heaven and pedaled like hell.

Twenty-six miles south of Bloomfield, the El Huerfano Trading Post came at a time when I was too geared up to stop. I flew by as the sky turned gun metal gray and the storm barreled down. The sound of cannons got closer and closer. Lightning split the sky to the north and west.

By the time the Blanco Trading Post came into sight, the wind within me waned. Although the storm continued to gain strength, I had spent mine. My heart rate slowed and my breathing returned to normal as I braked to a stop in the nearly empty lot.

Approaching the weathered, gray building, I noticed a pair of shadowy figures standing at one end of the covered porch. The low, guttural sounds of the Navajo language carried ever so slightly on the electric air.

As I approached, I could make out the form of an elderly couple. Facing the pay phone mounted on the wall, the man held the receiver carefully in his right hand. He spoke slowly, forming each word deep within his chest. A short, gray-haired woman stood beside him, listening intently to his words and straining to hear the responses from the other end of the line. Her head was cocked slightly toward the ear piece and her expression was one of intense concentration.

They glanced briefly in my direction as I clambered up the rickety wooden steps in my cleated shoes. Showing little interest, they returned their attention to the telephone as I fixed mine on the "CLOSED" sign hanging on the door. I cupped my hands and leaned into the window, hoping to see someone inside who could just open up long enough for me to buy a drink. There was no one, and I was left like a kid in a candy shop to gaze longingly at the stocked cooler on the far wall.

Click. My yearning was interrupted by the sound of the receiver returning to its cradle. I looked to my left as the man's weathered hand released its grip. He turned slowly toward the rusty blue pickup parked next to the stairs.

"Excuse me," I called after him, "do you know where I could get some water around here?"

He looked at me for a moment, then up at the approaching storm clouds, and then back at me. "The store at Nageezi might be open. It's eight miles."

Thanking him, I gave the sky a quick glance. The thunderbird was still behind me, but the ghost riders were gaining fast. With twenty minutes of daylight remaining and eight miles to go, I crunched the numbers in my head. Although the calculation came up in the red, I threw caution (and myself) to the wind, and made a run for it anyway.

Common to western folklore is the tale of a rider racing a fast-approaching storm. With spurs and slurs, he urges his horse forward at breakneck speed and arrives at his destination with dry head and shoulders, but waterlogged rear end. In the case of snow storms, his horse may arrive foaming at the mouth while its tail is frozen stiff. A

199

minute ahead of the storm, I coasted into the parking lot of the Nageezi Trading Post ready to add my tale to the list.

Weathered vertical pine planking, a long wooden porch, and a pair of pay phones made it look remarkably like the arrangement at Blanco. Unfortunately, a "CLOSED" sign on the door completed the ensemble.

Both phones were in use when I arrived. An old woman spoke softly in Navajo into one while a younger woman argued loudly in English over the other. A man, also Navajo, stood at a respectful distance, waiting for his turn. Wearing a denim jacket, blue jeans and a faded red cap, he looked to be in his early thirties. Watching as I scrambled up the steps and stood motionless before the sign hanging on the locked door, he confirmed the message, "Closed on Sundays."

"Yeah," I replied turning to him. "I noticed that back in Blanco too. Do you know where I can get some water around here?"

"Check around the back. There might be a spigot."

"Thanks," I responded heading off around the low wooden building only to find a locked bathroom, a ramshackle fence, and a vicious dog. Lips curled and baring a full set of canines, it let out a low, purposeful growl—the sound of pure hatred.

Without hesitation, I returned to the front porch as the curtain of night was drawn. The younger woman had gone and the man in the red cap took her place. He glanced at me as I rounded the corner, then turned his back in an attempt at privacy. I kept my distance.

Digging into my panniers, I pulled out the remains of a loaf of bread and nibbled as raindrops tapped the sheet metal roof. The Hopis—among other pueblo tribes—believe that their dead ancestors are the bringers of rain. Grandparents, great grandparents and those long forgotten fertilize the clouds for those who walk the Earth in flesh. In a necessary balance between life and death, moisture from the skies nourishes the crops that feed the current generations. In the eternal cycle, death feeds life. I watched as the thirsty land began its feast of water.

Click. I turned to my right.

"Any luck?" asked the man from under his cap.

"No water, just an angry dog."

"Where you comin' from?"

"Today it's Mancos, Colorado. But I started in North Dakota."

"Where you stayin' tonight?"

A bolt of lightning slashed the night sky before I had a chance to reply. We stood silently waiting for the report. It shook the porch and rattled my confidence. His question hung in the electically-charged air unanswered.

"Throw your bike in my truck," he said extending a hand. "Name's Jim."

Part 4
Indians

Chapter 32

You have noticed that everything an Indian does is in a circle, and that is because the Power of the World always works in circles, and everything tries to be round. In the old days when we were a strong and happy people, all our power came to us from the sacred hoop of the nation and so long as the hoop was unbroken the people flourished. The flowering tree was the living center of the hoop, and the circle of the four corners nourished it.
—Black Elk, 1930

Do not misunderstand me, but understand me fully [and] my affection for the land. I never said the land was mine to do with as I chose. The one who has the right to dispose of it is the one who has created it. I claim a right to live on my land, and accord you the privilege to live on yours.
—Chief Joseph

A nation is not conquered
Until the hearts of its women are on the ground.
Then it is finished,
No matter how brave its warriors
Or how strong their weapons.
—Cheyenne proverb

Raindrops hit the windshield with increasing frequency and intensity as we drove south along a rutted dirt road. Cats, dogs, javalinas and coyotes poured from the heavens. The Navajo call it a "Male Rain." Bucket after bucket, the world seemed to change from terrestrial to marine before our eyes. Surrounded by darkness, it was as if we were bumping along the ocean floor. Only the narrow beam of a single headlight pierced the blackness. Inside the four-wheeled Cyclops, we passed through a tunnel of light.

Sinking into darkness, the sides of the road remained a mystery as the rattling lamp provided only a view of the world ahead—an abbreviated, linear landscape of gravel, ruts and rain. Shutting out all else, the tunnel vision focused our eyes on progress alone. Limited in scope and goal oriented, it is a view distinctive of Western industrial society—one of short-term profits and the bottom line. Grounded in a mechanistic universe where inanimate objects fall into a fixed order, it is economically corporate and scientifically reductionist. It sees nature as the opponent—an object to be conquered, not a subject to be embraced.

Nothing could be further from the traditional Navajo view of a circular world—one of beauty and, despite the storm, one of harmony. Theirs is a way of living life with a natural sense of perpetuity which keeps the past fresh while fully absorbing the present and future in an endless flow of energy and spirit. Like that of Native tribes across Turtle Island, their belief system is based on the whole—a circle in which everything comes around, everything is connected. The days, the nights, and even our lives follow the sacred pattern. Locked in a timeless embrace, all beings feel the sacred nature of their connections through the Holy Wind. From its hallowed home in the four directions, *nilch'i* pervades all of nature, bringing life, movement, speech and thought to plants and animals, including the people themselves. The Lakota would call it the "Sacred Hoop," but in the Four Corners region it's known as the "Navajo Way."

Just as occasional flashes of lightening revealed a greater world beyond our limited vision, people like Jim were opening my mind to a broader perspective. There is no tunnel vision when you focus on the whole. There is no need for hindsight when you realize that the end is just the beginning again. A quarterly profit is meaningless when you look seven generations ahead.

"I was taught that it's wrong to have more than you need," he said in a calm, low voice. "Amassing personal wealth means you're not taking care of others. If you win a couple races in a row, you slow down a bit to give someone else a turn.

"A friend of mine quit the rodeo circuit because he was getting too successful, making too much money. The money changed him. He was losing his roots, his sense of being Navajo, so he just quit. But that kind of thinking is getting rare around here."

He explained how more and more Navajo are losing their traditional sense and going through life like a one-eyed pickup truck: following someone else's trail; seeing only so far ahead; blind to the world around them.

As the raindrops grew in size and frequency, the road responded with deeper ruts and larger rocks. When it seemed neither could get any worse, Jim swung the truck hard left and gunned the engine over a small rise. The sudden turn threw me against the door.

"Reservation roads are like government promises," Jim quipped. "Full of holes."

By the time I recovered, the truck had come to a rest with its lone beam shining through sheets of rain on a small cabin about fifty feet away. Jim left the headlight on and the motor running until the front door opened and the tiny figure of a *shimishani*, a Navajo grandmother, appeared.

As quickly as a wind-aided 100 meter dash, we crossed the drenching void between truck and cabin, but found ourselves soaked through none the less. By the dim light of a single candle Jim introduced me to Grandma Emily. Her hair was bound up in the traditional style, and she wore a capacious long skirt exhibiting classic Navajo modesty.

She welcomed me as one of her own and lit a second candle to honor the occasion. While volts, amps and ohms coursed through homes across America, electricity had not yet reached Grandma Emily.

"No electricity. No phone," said Jim after we had been seated at a raw plank table beside an ancient enamel cook stove. Grandma Emily slowly stirred the contents of a battered pot with a wooden spoon. Her bony hand disappeared in the steam.

Jim continued. "But the Department of Energy still has an interest in the reservations. You see, next to the federal government, tribes are the largest land holders in the country. We've got large deposits of coal, oil, natural gas and even uranium. We also have lots of open space. 'Wastelands,' they call it. Just right for nuclear waste.

"The DOE wants to store nuclear waste on tribal land?"

"Sure, the Apache down in Mescalero have been paid a quarter million just to consider building a storage facility for spent nuclear fuel in the Sacramento Mountains."

"Where's that?"

"Southern New Mexico. But the power companies are from New England."

I took a moment to consider the risks and morals of shipping radioactive waste thousands of miles from one of the wealthiest regions in the country to one of the poorest. Maine Yankee, Vermont Yankee and Connecticut Yankee, I'd later learn, were key players in the Mescalero deal. At least New Hampshire's Seabrook had kept it's nose clean. (After billions of dollars in construction overruns, it better.)

"They say the Indian wars ended in 1886 when Geronimo surrendered, but they're still going on. There's no longer a ten dollar bounty on Navajo scalps, but they're scalping us all the same. This energy imperialism is just another form of oppression and deception. Our land is being spoiled forever for the short term energy needs of cities like Phoenix and Las Vegas. After the coal and uranium run out, we're left with tons and tons of toxic waste, poverty and further loss of our identity and self-sufficiency.

"For most of this century my people were encouraged to raise sheep, but when coal was discovered over on Black Mesa, the government pulled a U-turn and initiated a stock reduction program to clear the land for strip mining.

"How can they do that." I asked. "Don't you have sovereignty on the reservations?"

"It's like this," explained Jim. "The land is held in trust for the tribes by the Department on the Interior, which also happens to contain the Bureau of Reclamation and BIA."

"BIA?"

"Indian Affairs."

"Gotcha."

"The result is an endless stream of sweet deals that make rich white men even richer and leave most Navajo out in the cold. Did you see the coal plants over in Page?"

"Only the dirty air."

Jim shook his head knowingly. "Most of the power generated over there is owned by Reclamation. So they nudge their little brother Indian Affairs to encourage the tribal councils to allow more mining. The deals they strike for leases are criminal. The council gets a token kickback, but the big money is made by the mining companies off the reservation. The BIA is supposed to look out for our well being, but it's just another tool for depriving us of what is rightly ours.

"The federal government signed 400 treaties with tribes across the country and broke every one. When my Grandmother was born she wasn't even a U.S. citizen. That didn't happen until 1924. Look at the privileges of citizenship." He extended an arm in a sweeping motion of the dimly lit room.

"The older generation doesn't understand laws that are written down. They only understand what has been passed down to them through their culture. For them, the mere idea of contaminating the land with tailings or nuclear waste runs contrary to their belief system. They simply can't understand. There are no words in Navajo for 'radioactive' or 'hazardous waste.' 'Scary' is about as close as we get."

In a gentler language, Grandma Emily said a short prayer as she set three bowls of mutton stew and a basket of fry bread onto the raw, plank table. Onions, potatoes and tomatoes floated among cubes of fibrous meat. Not wanting to appear ungracious, I weighed the options of upsetting my hosts versus upsetting my stomach. I chose the latter—it was outnumbered. I was willing to make a dietary compromise for the sake of manners.

Corralling the first piece of mutton with my spoon, I lifted it slowly to my lips. Hesitating for a moment, I looked up at my smiling hosts. Their spoons remained on the table. All eyes were on me.

I smiled back and gave a slight nod before taking the first bite. The meat was as unyielding as one would expect from an old ewe. Chewing became a battle between tooth and gristle. It was unclear which would emerge victorious.

We ate by candlelight and talked until the flame drowned in a puddle of wax. Lighting another, Grandma Emily led me to the room where I would sleep. She held the candle in the doorway while I crawled under the wool blankets and settled into the sagging mattress unaware, at the moment, that it was the only bed in the house.

I opened my eyes but saw nothing. Like a blind man, my other senses blossomed in the darkness. I heard the whisper of wind—Dawn Woman—gently rattling a loose pane of glass. I felt the stiff wool fibers against my bare skin. I smelled the pleasant aroma of baking bread.

The dim light of my wristwatch broke the darkness before the first rays of the sunlight appeared in the tiny window on the eastern wall. Five-thirty.

I followed my nose into the kitchen where Grandma Emily was standing beside the cook stove. "Good morning," I said. "You're up early."

"The morning needs to be honored," she spoke softly, but her words held the weight of a people. "The sun is our father. Each morning he makes a count of his children. The people awake and standing are counted as alive. The people asleep are counted as dead."

I sat quietly at the wooden table, anxiously watching her lift the first pillow-shaped loaf out of the oven and place it on a small towel. With the care a mother shows a new born, she cradled the bundle and placed it gently on the table before me. After weeks of store-bought bread, my mouth watered in anticipation. Her thin, brown hand picked up a long bread knife and sliced a piece off the end. A breath of white steam issued forth, doubling my anticipation. Grandma Emily set the first slice before me. With the slightest nod and a girlish smile, she set my spirit free.

Moments before sunrise, Jim entered the kitchen rubbing his eyes and yawning immensely.

"Up before sunrise?" I joked.

"I wouldn't want to be counted as dead with just two payments left on my truck." He grinned and shook his head ever so slightly. "With discrimination, unemployment and alcoholism, I still think the hardest part of being an Indian is having to get up so damn early."

We laughed as he sat down across from me and reached for the bread knife. "Don't worry," he assured me, "I'm not going to scalp you."

After our serious discussion the night before, I was surprised by his easy sense of humor. He was anything but the tearful Iron Eyes Cody I had known in childhood from the commercials which interrupted Saturday morning cartoons. Along with a generation of Americans, I grew up with the image of a noble savage crying at the site of roadside litter.

With a broad smile and hearty laugh, Jim shattered the stereotype of the stoic red man. Hopi jokes rolled off his tongue like water across a dry wash. He called them "cliff shitters" and "hopeless." He found humor where others wouldn't dare look. Confident in his identity, he had the rare capacity to poke fun at himself, at what it means to be an American Indian.

"Indian, shmindian. I don't care what they call us," he quipped. "I got more important things to worry about than what some lost Portuguese sailor named us 500 years ago. I'm just glad he wasn't looking for Turkey.

"That Columbus was quite a deal maker. He left Europe not knowing where he was going, and upon arriving, not knowing where he was. He returned not knowing where he had been, and did it all on borrowed money."

"What's in a name?" I asked, more statement than question.

"That's right. 'Navajo' isn't even our proper name. It's what the Spanish called us. We've always referred to ourselves as *Dine*—'the people.' But I guess I can forgive the misunderstanding. I grew up thinking white people were called 'Goddammies' because that's all I ever heard them say."

Smiling broadly, I leaned forward and placed my elbows on the table and chin in my hands. My entire body was saying more. Jim obliged.

"When you've been through as much as my people have, a sense of humor is essential to carry on. If you lose it, you've lost your spirit.

"It would be easy to dwell on the past and harbor deep resentments. Indeed, many of us do. But the past is the past—we can't change it. We need to learn from it and carrying on with a process of healing—healing the relationships we have with ourselves, with others and especially with the Earth.

"Building relationships is about spending time together. You have to discipline yourself to connect. If we don't believe that the winged ones, the water ones, and the four-leggeds are our brothers and sisters, then we'll never be able to make that relationship develop. We need to start supporting each other. If we don't, we're going to lose out on our future.

"The land is a very real being. It needs that time—that quality time—to be with it, to thank it, to thank her. Everything about us, the land itself is our definer. It tells us what our path is—our purpose. When I think of my personal relationship, I don't think that there really is a past or future—there just is. I think our relatives are all around us all the time.

He looked straight into my eyes. "We are all flowers in the same meadow. We need the same things to thrive: good soil, clean water, sunshine. Our fate is connected. In order for my people to be healthy, your people need to be healthy. We need to be healthy together. We are all children of the Earth and there are a lot of responsibilities that come with that."

Jim was silent for a moment. He turned his head toward Grandma Emily who stood quietly by the stove. Her face beamed with pride. Returning his eyes to me, he nodded once. "We should get you on the road. Can I carry anything out for you?"

We stepped outside as the first rays of sunlight spilled over the San Pedro Mountains, revealing a sea of rolling foothills stretching to the distant peaks. A light breeze—what the Navajo call a female wind—blew out of the west, carrying with it the sweet scent of sage.

"When I'm away from here for a long time," Jim said, "I miss it. All I want to see is dirt and sky."

"Thanks," I said, extending my hand. "Thanks for everything."

As we shook, Grandma Emily stepped forward and put a hand gently on my shoulder. "*Nihzhonigo,*" she told me. "Go in beauty."

Chapter 33

I rose and across the bare spaces did go walking,
Did peep through the openings in the scrub,
Looking about me, seeking something.
—Tohono O'odham salt gathering song

The rocks, ruts and washboard that had been a mild challenge to the four wheels of Jim's Chevy proved nearly impossible for Betsy's two. The adobe earth turned to grease. Milky puddles lay like thin sheets of lead. Only with the patience and perseverance of Grandma Emily did I make my way back to the uniform surface of Route 44.

Gradual climbs and short descents alternated over the first seventeen miles to Counselor where I stopped at the Bywood Mercantile for water. Not wanting to deplete Grandma Emily's precious supply, I had left with the same amount with which I had arrived—none. By the time I reached the Merc, my tongue was swollen and pasty. I didn't mind the warmth of the liquid that fell from the rusty tap, so long as it was wet.

"Which direction ya headed?" asked the woman behind the counter. She took a sip of her coffee. Steam fogged her glasses.

"East over the divide and then down to San Ysidro."

"Up the divide, huh?"

"Yeah, but it doesn't look too steep. Is there something I should know?"

"You're right it ain't that steep," she paused and took another sip. "It's just that the truckers that come through here say it's the only road in the country that's uphill both ways."

Passing it off with a chuckle, I had no idea that her statement would become a metaphor of the day. The first incident occurred about five miles east of Counselor when Betsy's left crank arm started to come loose. At first I pretended not to notice, then I tried to ignore it. But like a hungry cat, its whines persisted. As the play in the crank worsened and the creaking got louder, it became impossible to ignore. Reluctantly, I pulled over to examine the problem.

Although I did not know why it had happened, the bolt holding the crank to the bottom bracket had loosened, causing the soft aluminum arm to be worn by the hard steel. It was an easy fix with the right tool, but that tool was large, heavy, and tucked safely in my toolbox back in New Hampshire. Searching for a substitute among the hex wrenches and tire irons I carried would be futile. The answer would have to come from somewhere else. I looked up from Betsy's injured flank to see it staring down at me from the side of the road: "Rest Area - 3 Miles." There were bound to be truckers who were bound to have tools.

Trying unsuccessfully to smooth out my pedal stroke to cut down on the amount of gnashing, I soon learned it was no use. Unable to bear the feeling of the slipping crank any longer, I withdrew my left foot and was reduced to one-legging it the full three miles. I arrived at the rest area thirty minutes later, feeling as off-centered as Betsy.

Blood coursed through my right leg. Taught and sinewy, the muscle fibers twitched with every contraction. Meanwhile my left leg hung dormant, unused. Like a man long at sea, it took time to regain my balance after dismounting. I stumbled like a drunk past a dozen rusty barrels overflowing with the weekend's trash. A loose Budweiser can skittered across the parking lot in the light morning breeze. Coors, Hams, and Busch littered the ground around the the barrels.

The rest area consisted of little more than a pair of Clivus Multrum composting toilets and a half dozen picnic tables shaded by large teepee-shaped canvas awnings. There was no running water, but for once that wasn't my reason for stopping.

Despite any indication beyond his mere presence, a red-haired D.O.T. worker seemed to have been assigned to haul the trash. In no apparent hurry, he sat at a nearby picnic table contemplating the act of loading the trash into his bright orange truck. With the right strategy, he could milk it into a full day's job...maybe two.

"You got any tools?" I asked.

He looked at me quizzically. "Tools?"

Perhaps he was unfamiliar with the term. "I'm having a little trouble with my bike. I need a socket wrench for just a few minutes."

"They don't give me tools."

"You don't have any in your truck?"

"We can take a look."

The side panels creaked open to reveal nothing more than a rusty shovel and a set of jumper cables. "Guess not," he said, shrugging his shoulders.

Of the few other vehicles in the parking lot, none could help. But before I gave up hope, I noticed a trio of utility trucks not far up the road. A half-dozen electricians in yellow hardhats were dealing with a power line that had been damaged by the storm.

They eyed me suspiciously as I approached, but warmed up when I started talking tools. These guys knew their way around a hardware store.

"Socket wrench?" repeated a short, moustached man to my request. "No problem. Standard or metric?"

"Metric. And could I also borrow a hammer?"

"Sure," he said retrieving a giant Estwing from his toolbox. "The bigger the hammer, the better the mechanic."

Using a piece of wood as a buffer, I tapped the crank arm gently onto the axle. Although the blows were soft, striking Betsy felt awkward. But as with shoeing a horse, a moment of pain can prevent a lifetime of agony. With the crank arm wedged snugly against the axle, I tightened the bolt and returned the tools to the electricians.

"Good luck," he offered, unwrapping a thick cable from a monstrous spool.

"You too," I replied, resisting the temptation to direct them to Grandma Emily's when they had a chance.

The final three miles to the 7275 foot pass were gradual. Shadscale and black greasewood grew alongside the scattered sage. Isolated stands of junipers dotted the higher reaches of the climb, but it was not until I had crossed the Divide that they were joined by low growing pinyon and mountain mahogany. Pine, spruce and fir carpeted the rolling hills of the Santa Fe National Forest which stretched to the north and east.

Upon descent, I verified the trucker's contention. The gentle slope and deceptive surroundings made it seem as if I were still climbing. Although pedaling was noticeably easier, the grade would not allow coasting.

Leaving the Divide behind, Route 44 turned abruptly south and descended into the Rio Puerco valley. Cabezon Peak rose in the distance as I skirted the edge of the San Pedro Mountains.

Joining the Rio Puerco near its source, Route 44 parallels the river for the first part of a 1,000 mile journey to the Rio Grande and eventually the Gulf of Mexico. Shallow, brown and stinking, the river exuded those qualities of the rotund barnyard animal for which it is named. Discarded tires and trash bags spanned its meager width, awaiting the next flood to carry them away.

In response to the monthly boom that government checks bring to the local economy, every Tomas, Ricardo and Enrique in Cuba, New Mexico was having a tag sale. Yards, driveways and even the backs of pickup trucks were filled with second-hand items. Main Street was crowded with people buying and selling. The line at New Mexico Federal Savings ran out the door.

Ones, fives, tens and twentys circulated quickly, but would anyone come out ahead? My brother believes that tag sale "bargains" never really get put to use, they just move from one garage to another. No matter where you go, it's always the same stuff.

Stories of a son or daughter coming home with the very bowling shirt their father sold for a quarter seven years ago circulate as freely as the items themselves. Had Einstein been more alert, he may have found his perpetual motion machine in the form of a juicer/slicer that's been revolving for fifty years.

Even the sign on the local convenience store seemed to be a misprint made available at a bargain price. I stepped into the 7-2-11 to fill my bottles before catching a tail wind south of town. The temperature flashed ninety-five in front of the bank, and a highway sign noted forty miles to San Ysidro. If only they were misprints as well.

The numbers were against me, but at least I had the wind and a tight crank arm. Or so I thought.

Chapter 34

*[It is] our manifest destiny to overspread the continent allotted by
Providence for the free development of our yearly multiplying millions.*
—John O'Sullivan, 1845

*The time is coming, and fast, too, when, in the sense it is now
understood, THERE WILL BE NO WEST.*
—Unknown Union Pacific engineer's journal entry, late 1860's

Continuing along the Rio Puerco south of town, a flat road and
generous tail wind allowed me to ride Betsy's big chain ring well beyond
the border of the Jemez Indian Reservation. We covered the first twenty
miles in under an hour. It was not until we reached the neighboring Zia
Reservation, that a series of low hills called for easier gears. Route 44
turned east as the river swung southwest and disappeared behind the
legendary Cabezon Peak. According to Navajo mythology, it was formed
when the heroic twins, Monster Slayer and Child-of-the-Waters,
decapitated Big Monster and threw his massive cranium from far in the
west to where it now stands.

But it was a new and different legend that intrigued me about the
area surrounding the peak. No more desolate than the typical semi-
desert, this one captured my attention because of what it had once been.
Not long ago this region was so fertile that it earned distinction as "The
Breadbasket on New Mexico." Lush grasslands once flourished under
the moderate hoof action of small populations of deer, elk and antelope.

Years of intensive grazing by imported cattle thinned the vegetation
and compressed the ground surface sufficiently that water no longer
filters through the top layers. Instead it runs off, taking with it the soil—
the very cornerstone of the ecosystem. Massive erosion sends tons of
silt into waterways and reservoirs, spreading the impact of overgrazing
even further.

Any suggestion that a grassland ecosystem once flourished here has
been completely erased—washed downstream by the dirty waters of
the Rio Puerco. No amount of management can bring it back. The native
grasses have been eradicated, leaving invader species like broom
snakeweed and cheatgrass—both unpalatable to cattle—to spread across
the mesa tops and throughout the lowlands. A popular regional saying
notes that, "The best friend a weed ever had is a rancher who runs too
many cows."

But running more cows was exactly what Elmer told me Allan Savory
has proposed to restore degraded rangelands. He's chosen the once grass-
rich state of New Mexico as the home for his non-profit institute which
promotes his theory of Holistic Resource Management. While

conventional wisdom blames the devastation of Earth's once vast grasslands on cattle, sheep, and goats, Savory claims that overgrazed areas can only be restored by dramatically *increasing* herds of domestic livestock. His ideas have jolted ranchers, environmentalists, and government scientists alike.

Noting that conventional herding methods have failed miserably in the U.S. West as well as his native Rhodesia (now Zimbabwe), Savory has spent much of his life searching for workable solutions in a world where nearly 15 million acres of grassland turn into desert each year. While potential grassland accounts for about two-fifths of the Earth's land area, most of it has either been turned to desert already or is well on its way. Savory claims that "We keep making mistakes, because we have never learned to ask the right questions."

Savory challenges the tradition of scientific specialization, pointing out how consistently it runs afoul of nature. "Landscapes are dynamic. They are a function of four basic processes. To understand an existing landscape or set a landscape goal, you have to assess the cycling of minerals, the cycling of water, the flow of energy through the food chain, and the status of succession. Then you can consider tools and policies. This is where we make our big mistake. We always think backwards from symptoms."

Years of careful observation on the east African plain left a young Savory with more questions than answers: Why did the same land that thrived under the hooves of a great wild herd turn to desert once thinly stocked with cattle? Was overgrazing simply a function of numbers as popularly believed or was there something else? Could herd behavior and timing be critical factors? It was this unorthodox line of questioning that ultimately lead Savory to a coherent set of principles.

As with most counter-intuitive theories, his requires a broader understanding of the complex relationships that exist in nature. "My theories grew out of a long process of observation and deduction...I could look at a piece of land and predict with a high degree of accuracy what would happen to it and prescribe a proper response, but I couldn't explain how I did it. It was rather like tracking where signs that are insignificant alone combine in the mind of the experienced tracker to form a crystal clear picture that the layman cannot see. I finally realized that I was in fact basing my judgments on a deeper level of evidence than the surface description that we normally respond to."

Savory combined his insights regarding time, grazing intensity, and the relationship between grazers and grass into his theory of Holistic Resource Management. His goal was to come up with techniques for using natural resources without using them up. Central to his belief system is that grasslands should be periodically trampled and fertilized by large herds of hoofed animals—as they are by the great herds of the

213

African savanah and as they once were by buffalo and elk in the U.S. West. He believes that the grasses evolved *with* these thundering herds, and that the dynamic relationship between them must be restored. Intense hoof action breaks up hard surfaces, keeps the soil porous, helps decompose dead plant material, and works important minerals into the soil.

His ideas were widely rejected at first, but ultimately he convinced some open-minded ranchers to test them. According to his instructions, they moved their cattle in dense groups and carefully controlled the amount of time spent in each area according to the growth rate of the plants. Each area received a sharp dose of grazing and hoof action followed by time to recover.

To nearly everyone's surprise but his own, Savory's method worked almost immediately. Previously degraded rangelands came back to life, blooming for the first time in decades. Successful test projects in New Mexico, Montana, Namibia and Zimbabwe attracted the attention of many former skeptics. Results ranged from greater diversity of grass species, increased beef production per acre, and the control of noxious weed infestations.

"It is necessary to seek production, but that by itself tends to be an excuse for exploitation and thus in the long run is almost always self-defeating. To drive policy, a goal must include as well a vision of a quality of life for the people who actually depend on the land and a landscape that will sustain it."

With data supporting him, Savory has his points, but opponents ask why the "heavy, herding animals" he deams essential have to be cattle and sheep? "I love wilderness," claims Debbie Sease, a Sierra Club lobbyist and Savory skeptic, "and he loves productive feedlots." Why should domesticated animals graze these lands instead of wild bison, deer, elk and antelope?

Nothing remains of the town of Cabezon that had been a center of trade and commerce in the 1800's. At the site where it once stood, Route 44 veers east and begins to climb. The once thriving community was abandoned during the Dust Bowl of the 1930's when it lost its self-sufficiency. Overuse and failure to recognize the warning signs resulted in disaster. Why is it that until tragedy strikes close to home, we refuse to take it seriously? Once again, the road would provide an answer.

Downshifting on the climb, I decreased my speed while still enjoying the benefits of a tail wind. Although the push was helpful, its cooling effects were negligible under the mid-day sun. I took a swig of water and continued to grind out the climb. That's when I decided there is no God. In the middle of the sauna that is New Mexico in July, under the relentless southwestern sun, I felt the first signs of slippage in Betsy's drivetrain. No. It can't happen again. Not today.

I focused my attention on the left crank arm that had given me trouble earlier, but it was fine—not the slightest wobble. Yet the slipping persisted. With the next pedal stroke it became painfully clear that it wasn't the left crank arm at all, but the right. I wanted nothing more than to ride on and ignore it, but I'd be a fool not to take a lesson from the overuse surrounding me. Downshifting further, I spun lightly to the crest of the hill and dismounted with no utility trucks in sight. I looked among the roadside debris for something with which to pound. Alongside beer cans, cigarette butts and dirty diapers, I found a large piece of metal that looked like it had once been part of an engine. About the size of a football, it had grooves, holes and mounting pins on each corner. Rusty bolts stuck out here and there.

Bending down to pick it up, I recoiled the instant my fingertips touched its searing, black surface. Having baked in the sun for hours, it was impossible to handle bare-handed. I took off my already filthy shirt and used it to insulate my hands.

Equally important, I needed to find a piece of wood to buffer the blows. The few pieces of brittle sage available disintegrated upon contact. I searched in vain for something more solid, but found nothing. Ultimately, I was forced to strike the aluminum directly. "This is going to hurt me more than it hurts you."

Teeth clenched, I carefully swung the mass of steel into the crank arm. The sound of a bicycle screaming filled the air as the steel mass slipped to the ground, leaving me holding the t-shirt and my breath. Did it work? Exhaling, I bent down to examine my (not so) handy work. The crank arm had not budged, but came through the encounter suffering only a minor scratch. Four swings, drops and scratches later, it was still no tighter.

The map indicated another twenty miles to San Ysidro, my watch read one o'clock, and a lone vulture circled above. The symptoms of a terminal condition abounded, yet the shoulder ahead offered a sign of hope. Black on yellow, the silhouette of a truck nosing down a triangle suggested I just may survive this Jornado del Muerto.

Although coasting was intolerably slow, I had little choice. Testing my patience, my will and my faith, perhaps there was a God after all—a cruel and vengeful one.

At the run-out of the hill, my speed dipped below five miles per hour and I one-legged it along the ensuing flat section. After about a mile, I was faced with a long, gradual incline and a difficult decision. Regrettably, I slipped my right foot into its toe clip, down-shifted as far as possible, and tip-toed up the slope.

Although the wobble remained, I was able to minimize it by

concentrating on a smooth pedal stroke—the kind you're theoretically supposed to use all the time. Maintaining constant pressure throughout the rotation, I was able to reduce the amount of play to a minimum. Alternating periods of coasting with careful pedaling, I covered the next eighteen miles in just over an hour and a half. Fortunately, the road was mostly downhill.

I was two miles from an afternoon of couch surfing in San Ysidro when the problem outgrew my temporary solution. Glancing down, I noticed the entire right crank arm—chainrings included—swinging from side to side with each rotation. The chain itself grated against the front derailleur every time my right foot pushed forward, and against the frame with each left. Reluctant but resigned, I pulled onto the shoulder to have a closer look.

The crank arm bolt turned easily between my thumb and forefinger. It threaded smoothly for almost three turns before it became too stiff for hand-tightening. A pair of pliers from the tool pouch added another two turns, but they lost purchase as the bolt sank deeper into its recessed housing. At least another 720 degrees shy of the ideal, it offered enough stability to complete the fateful ride.

Limping into San Ysidro, I took a left onto Route 4 and proceeded for a mile northeast toward the far edge of town. It was nearly three o'clock when I reached the small white church where I'd been instructed to turn left. The single-lane dirt road led me away from the House of God and past a row of somewhat lesser dwellings. Ruts and potholes were filled with broken bricks and chunks of mortar, while a pair of once-red carpets laid across the road—not as a regal welcome, but in an attempt to reduce further deterioration. Rusty barbed wire fences lined the avenue, and a chorus of barks announced my arrival long before I reached the flat-roofed hacienda at the end of the lane.

As promised, the back door was unlocked, and a friendly note sat on the kitchen table. "Welcome! Eat. Sleep. Shower. Back 7 or 7:30." The cryptic message, a bottle of Jose Cuervo on the counter, and a sink full of dirty dishes told me Anna hadn't changed much since the last I'd seen her.

Despite a lack of air conditioning, the house remained surprisingly cool. Wooden shutters kept out both the afternoon heat and light, while a concrete slab radiated last night's coolness from underfoot. Exposed wooden beams ran the length of the ceiling. Brightly painted murals adorned the adobe walls. Zigzags, spirals and an assortment of geometric shapes framed a window here, a doorway there. Cabinets, mirrors and bookshelves were similarly painted in the uniquely festive southwestern style that so easily stimulates the senses. In contrast, the plain, brown couch helped dull them. It welcomed my weary bones and I slept.

The door creaked open and in stepped a piece of history, my history.

Anna chuckled as she hung up her keys beside the door. "You look comfortable."

"Can I take it with me?"

"Only if you promise to make the rest of the payments."

I stood and welcomed her into my arms. Our bodies fit like pieces in a puzzle.

"How was your ride today?"

"Don't ask."

"That bad? Well, at least you made it."

"Barely."

"You hungry?"

"Does a coyote shit in the desert?"

Waiting for the spaghetti water to boil, we exchanged rough summaries of the last six years. I sat on a counter as Anna scurried around the kitchen.

"I'm on a road crew for the summer," she said, opening a jar of Ragu. "I had been working at the elementary school up in the Pueblo, but I couldn't take it anymore. It was real hard—lots of distrust toward outsiders even when we're there to help. It's like that all around here. The Indians hate the Chicanos. The Chicanos hate the Indians. And both of 'em hate 'Whitey.'"

"Reverse racism."

"To them it's not reverse. It just makes you and I uncomfortable because we're not use to being on the receiving end."

"You're right."

"It's like that joke where the Lone Ranger says to Tonto, 'We're surrounded by Indians. What do we do?' And Tonto replies, 'What do you mean *we*, White Man?'"

I smiled and shook my head. "Guilty as charged."

"People don't like to talk about racism, but it's out there. It's everywhere. And you never really understand it until you are a victim. That's when it comes home."

I knew she was right but there was nothing I could say. I had never felt the sharp claws of hatred tearing at my soul. My upbringing had been progressive and liberal. I was taught early on that the words "Nigger," "Chink," and "Jap" were never to be used. "Wetback" and "White Trash" weren't even in the vocabulary of southeastern Michigan. I went to school with Jewish kids, Koreans, African-Americans, and even a boy whose parents came from Chile, but I never thought about what it was like for them to live in an upper middle class Christian neighborhood.

"We always hear how America is this great melting pot, but the reality is more like Chunky Soup. Once a neighborhood gets too dark, the light-skinned folks who can afford it head for the outskirts of town."

"And from what I hear, those outskirts are reaching further and further out."

"You heard right."

"My friends in Bicknell were telling me about that the other day. They said the sprawl was getting pretty bad around the Salt Lake-Provo area."

"It's the same here in Albuquerque. And over in Phoenix, and Tucson, and Jackson Hole and Denver. But please don't get me wrong. It's not all about racism. There are lots of factors."

"Such as?"

"It used to be that people followed jobs. That's the way an industrial economy works. Look at the Mid-West. Can you think of any other reason someone would live in Gary, Indiana? But economic patterns have changed. Some people move out here with jobs, some create them, and some don't even need 'em. Only in America could you get people from the country moving to the city to earn enough money to move back to the country!

"It's natural that people want to live in beautiful places. The need for open space is as American as apple pie, but with everyone wanting a piece, the slices get smaller and smaller. I'm on a job right now where we're widening a two-lane dirt road to four lanes paved. It's ten miles north of Albuquerque, an area that used to be all horse farms. Everything between it and the city has already been developed. One side of the road we're widening already has housing units and a golf course. The property owners on the other side are just waiting for real estate prices to rise a little more before they sell."

"Can you blame them?"

"No, but it's painful to watch."

"Then why are you part of it? Doesn't building roads just feed the process?"

I could see the tension in her eyes. "I'm well aware of that. It may not be as noble as teaching, but it's the highest paying job I could find for the summer. I'll make more money holding a stop sign than I did teaching Indian kids to read."

"Sorry, I just..."

"Don't worry about it. This whole issue has been on my mind a lot lately. I've got a friend who works for a local conservation trust and he's been on my case. He likes to point out that taxpayers subsidize roads and utilities that promote sprawl, and then pay to mitigate the results. Meanwhile his group of mostly volunteers are working on a shoestring budget to avoid that situation. He can't stand the fact that public funds are used to finance highway extensions, new interchanges, and roads that provide access to private developments."

"Subsidized sprawl?"

"You got it. And this is what really pisses me off. Since gasoline taxes aren't enough to cover the cost of road work, tens of billions of dollars have to come from other sources like property and income taxes—money that could be used for other things like education.

"But the highway lobby argues that more roads will lead to less traffic. That's bullshit. I have to leave here by quarter of six in the morning to beat the traffic heading into Albuquerque. I couldn't imagine having to commute all the way to center city."

"If you build it, they will come."

"But this ain't no 'Field of Dreams.'"

She told me of a people that lived in the Sonoran Desert for much of this millennium. At their peak around five hundred years ago, they cultivated hundreds of thousands of acres using a vast and carefully managed system of irrigation canals. Their culture thrived for a time. They traded with other peoples throughout the region. Expeditions were sent as far as the Gulf of California to collect resources not available locally. Artists experimented with new techniques while athletes played pelota—a Mesoamerican ball game—in courts 200 feet long.

But by the end of the seventeenth century, all that remained of this once rich culture were crumbling pueblos and sand-choked canals. The people had disappeared as mysteriously as the Anasazi, prompting the Pima Indians who subsequently moved into the area to call their predecessors *Hohokam*, meaning "Not There Anymore," or "All Used Up."

Anna poured me the last half glass from a bottle of merlot. As the final crimson droplets fell from the green bottle, she turned her head toward me. "All used up."

Chapter 35

They came with the Bible in one hand and the gun in the other. First they stole gold. Then they stole the land. Then they stole souls.
—Ginger Hillis, Navajo

The white man does not understand the Indian for the reason that he does not understand America. He is too far removed from its formative processes. The roots of the tree of his life have not yet grasped the rock and soil. The white man is still troubled with primitive fears; he still has in his consciousness the perils of this frontier continent, some of its vastness not yet having yielded to his questing footsteps and inquiring eyes. He shudders still with the memory of the loss of his forefathers upon its scorching deserts and forbidding mountain-tops. The man from Europe is still a foreigner and an alien. And he still hates the man who questioned his path across the continent. But in the Indian the spirit of the land is still vested; it will be until other men are able to divine and meet its rhythm. Men must be born and reborn to belong. Their bodies must be formed of the dust of their forefather's bones."
—Chief Luther Standing Bear, 1933

A chorus of barking dogs followed the rooster's wake up call. A Tabernacle Choir of the four-legged variety, they howled with the equal enthusiasm of Southern Baptists. What could possibly be more exciting at six in the morning than a dark room and a soft couch? I pulled a pillow over my head and went back to sleep.

Anna had left for work by the time I got off of the couch at eight. A pot of coffee and the *Albuquerque Journal* provided the perfect conditions for a lazy morning. It didn't matter that the paper was a week old, the coffee was fresh. Scanning the headlines, reading the comics, and flailing about the crossword puzzle filled most of the morning. By ten o'clock I was far too caffeinated to sit still, and turned my attention to Betsy. Anna's toolbox contained all I needed to put the wobbly crank problem to rest. Beyond that all the bike needed was a thorough cleaning and a few minor adjustments. By noon her chain, rims, head set, free wheel, and derailleurs were begging to be shown off. I consented to a short spin, believing it would do my stiff legs a bit of good.

Heading North on Route 4, I entered the Pueblo of Jemez where late model sedans and pickup trucks lined both sides of the road. Hand-painted signs offered salted pinon, pistachios, peanuts, beef jerky and cold Pepsi.

"What's going on?" I asked a white-haired woman beside an ancient Buick.

"Feast Day," she replied from behind a rickety card table covered with Ziploc bags full of pinon nuts.

"What's it for?"

"Oh, many things." She smiled at my ignorance. "The feast is for Saint Persingula, but there is also the Old Pecos Bull Ceremony, and, of course, the Corn Dances."

"All that today?"

"Yes. The dancing is beautiful. It's held in the plaza. You should stay and watch."

"Would I be welcome?"

"All are welcome."

"Sounds great," I replied, handing her two dollars for a small bag of nuts. "Thank you."

I headed for the plaza with high hopes. But on the way I encountered a large sign that nearly changed my mind. "No Photography, No Video taping, No Sketching, No Tape Recording, No Alcoholic Beverages. Objects Will Be Confiscated/Fined. By Governor's Order."

At first it seemed like a fascist decree, but I soon learned the reasons for the sign. Of course I already understood the issue with alcohol, but it took a short stop at the Visitor's Center to learn that the ban on photography stemmed from problems cropping up as far back as the turn of the century. Around 1900, picture-taking (referred to as "Kodakery" in a pueblo publication) in the United States had reached a fever pitch. Tourist were replacing the here-to-for written diaries of their trips with visual ones. Photography was becoming big business and travelers just had to get the best shots of everything along the way. On the pueblos, hordes of curious shutterbugs began to intrude on the every day lives of residents. The impact on Native Americans was humiliating and degrading, as simple courtesies were all but forgotten by tourists looking for the right shot. The conduct of some was particularly disgraceful as they openly invaded living quarters and sacred kivas without regard to privacy, pride or dignity.

While this phenomenon occurred all over the country, the Southwest Indians were particularly sensitive to it. Early suppression by the Spanish had forced them to carry on much of their religious ceremonies in secret. It's hard to believe, but this oppression was continued by the U.S. government into the 1900's. The Bureau of Indian Affairs punished disobedience, and the pueblo peoples quickly learned to be suspicious of whites, particularly those with cameras. Fearful of Bureau reprisals, most tribes ultimately forbade photographers from entering certain ceremonies, kivas, councils and sacred areas.

While the religious suppression of Native Americans is no longer practiced by our government, Indians have grown wary of any type of unauthorized reproduction of their religious affairs. Addressing a continuing sensitivity to the exploitation of their cultures for monetary profits by others, the bans remain. It is for these reasons that I cannot describe my incredible day among the gracious people of Jemez.

The feast was one not only for the lips, but for the eyes and ears as well. I savored the delicate flavors of drumming, singing and dance. The costumes. The art work. The smiles. In their traditional language, tribal members call this village *Walatowa*—"This is THE place."

Chapter 36

It is a soul-shattering silence. You hold your breath and hear absolutely nothing. No rustling of leaves in the wind, no rumbling of distant traffic, no chatter of birds or insects or children. You are alone with God in that silence. There in the white flat silence I began for the first time to feel a slight sense of shame for what we were proposing to do. Did we really intend to invade this silence with our trucks and bulldozers and after a few years leave it a radioactive junkyard?
—Freeman Dyson

Anna was home by the time I returned. She opened a bottle of wine as I began to describe my day in Walatowa. Nodding and smiling, she said she had gone last year and loved it.

"You should have come with me today."

"I forgot all about it."

We carried our conversation and wine glasses onto the patio. The air was comfortably cool, the companionship warm. Anna represented the last thing that could be considered a goal of my trip. There had been Michelle, Sean and Sharon, and now her. Seeing old friends in new places was important in connecting my present to my past, my East to my West.

I cherished the time with Anna, but as Orion revealed itself on the southern horizon, my thoughts turned to the future. The blinking red lights of an eastbound jet split the second and third stars of the hunter's sword.

A winter constellation for us in the Northern Hemisphere, Orion signals the coming of shorter days and longer nights. Perhaps not as grandly as the maples of New England, but its message was the same. As summer drew to a close, I was drawn home.

During the late 1800's, the highlight of a cowboy's year was the cattle drive. It marked the end of a long, hard season, but involved some of the longest, hardest, and dustiest days on the calender. Whether the drive took three months or just one, there wasn't a man who didn't look forward to the end once in sight.

One hundred years later, and riding a horse of a decidedly different color, I felt the same lure. Having made the third and final visit with transplanted friends, I sensed the beginnings of closure as I pedaled up the shadowed valley. Unlike the old time cattle drives—which started with long days and eased up toward the end as the animals tired—I would end mine with the longest rides of all. A reserved bus ticket waited in Denver, five days and 400 miles away.

The sun had not yet breached the head wall of the canyon as I passed the sleeping village. The echoes of celebration had long since faded from the plaza. A scrawny dog offered a half-hearted bark, but then fell hush. Even he knew it was to be a day of rest. But not for me.

North of *Walatowa* I passed the small town of Canon and the Jemez Valley Transfer and Recycling Facility: "No Burning, No Dead Animals, No Sewage." Beyond them lay the Santa Fe National Forest. Steep cliffs—some of red rock and others white—closed in from the sides. Aprons of talus stretched nearly to the banks of the Jemez River where tall cottonwoods and bushy tamarisks thrived. In just five miles, the landscape had evolved from desert to forest. Sparse junipers and gnarled sage gave way to an increasing abundance and variety of vegetation— at first mountain mahogany, gambel oak, and scrub maple, but then ponderosa pine, Engleman spruce and big-toothed aspen. Linked to elevation, the diversity increased as Route 4 climbed higher up the Canon de San Diego.

The butchered front end of a Volkswagen bus stood mid-way up a hillside at the edge of Jemez Springs. Mounted on an I-bean planted vertically in the ground, the former party mobile had been transformed into a work of art. With a ragged peace sign burned into the hood where the VW symbol would normally be, the sculpture said more about the town than the welcome sign along the road. A little rough around the edges, nothing could have summed up the funky little village any better.

Although quiet at seven in the morning, the signs I passed implied it was anything but a bedroom community: Leaping Lizard Cafe; Bodhi Mandala Zen Center; The Bath House (complete with massage parlor); Handmaids of the Precious Blood; and The Servants of the Paraclete. In what other town of 400 could one sip cappuccino, meditate, pray and get a rub down all in one afternoon?

Above town, the canyon rounds out into a stately basin walled by steep cliffs, eternally green with pine, spruce and fir. The increasing gradient necessitated a downshift as I reached Battleship Rock. The slow-down gave me time to savor the magnificent geologic outcrop. Like the bow of a naval vessel cutting through the waves, the solid, gray granite parted a sea of evergreens. I passed to starboard like a ship in the night, steaming toward a distant port. The sound of my breathing was the rhythmic puffing of smoke from the stacks.

At its junction with New Mexico 126, Route 4 makes a wide about-face in the shadow of Redondo Peak. Heading southeast, it crosses briefly out of the National Forest and then back in, only to leave once again at the mercy of topological whim. With similarly fickle intent, I abandoned Route 4 at Valle Grande and headed north toward Los Alamos on 502.

In the 1540's, Spanish explorers had come looking for the Seven Cities of Cibola and the legendary wealth they contained. Doors were rumored to be studded with turquoise, while roofs were solid gold. In his quest for wealth, Coronado left a trail of blood and misery, but never found what he was looking for. Four hundred years later, an explorer of a different kind did.

Once active volcanoes, the Jemez Mountains were born of fire, and in late 1942, that legacy would return. Chosen by nuclear physicist J. Robert Oppenheimer and approved by Colonel Leslie R. Groves, the secluded site on the Pajarito Plateau soon thereafter became the United State's most secret research laboratory. Hidden from the world, the purpose, and even name, of the Los Alamos Laboratory was initially known only by a few dozen military men, President Harry S. Truman and a select group of scientists at universities around the country. Charged with designing and producing atomic weapons, the lab was among the great secrets of World War II. Most of the participants in the Manhattan Engineering Project—of which the facilities at Los Alamos were critical—referred to the laboratory only by its code name, Project Y.

Selected over a number of proposed sites including Oak Ridge, Tennessee, Hanford, Washington and even Chicago, northern New Mexico would become known as the birthplace of the A-Bomb, and Los Alamos as the "City of Fire." As I'd come to learn, Jemez Springs narrowly escaped this dubious distinction. Because of its location in a deep canyon, and the corollary restrictions on space and security issues, it was bypassed as an workable site. How different a fate that crazy little town—with its Zen Center and bath house—would have seen if not for those steep canyon walls.

And so it was a fateful day in late November, 1942, that Oppenheimer and Groves turned their backs on the Canon de San Diego and drove thirty miles northeast to the secluded campus of the Los Alamos Ranch School. One can imagine them standing among the scattered wooden buildings high on the Pajarito Plateau on a blustery afternoon. As the sun sinks toward Cabezon Peak and golden aspen leaves shimmer in the breeze, Oppenheimer turns to Groves, nods his head, and speaks. "This is THE place." By mid-February of the following year, the students and teachers had been forced to split and the atoms were beginning to do so.

Oppenheimer's staff rose from the initial 100 to over 1,500 in just two months. Physicists, engineers and technicians were recruited from around the country. They descended on Los Alamos like the Four Horsemen of the Apocalypse: Conquest, War, Famine and Death. Hans Bethe, Enrico Fermi, Edward Teller and Victor Weisskopf left their personal research behind to join the project.

As the pace quickened, hundreds of additional staff were added, reaching a total of 3,000 by 1945. Racing against the clock, the military laid claim to an area south of Albuquerque that summer—forcing the expulsion of local ranchers, and code naming the site "Trinity." Early on the morning of July 16, 1945, Oppenheimer and his team witnessed a successful test of the implosion weapon. On the eve of the test, Fermi was brash and confident. "Don't bother me with your conscientious scruples," he told a skeptic, "after all, it's superb physics." Similarly proud, Oppenheimer quoted from the *Bhagavad-Gita*: "I am become death, the shatterer of worlds." Less than a month later, two bombs—nicknamed Fat Man and Little Boy—were dropped on Hiroshima and Nagasaki, killing 150,000 Japanese.

Within a year Oppenheimer was speaking differently about his accomplishment. Addressing journalists after receiving the Presidential Medal of Honor, he admitted, "I'm a little scared of what we built."

With the surrender of Japan and the end of World War II, the mission of Los Alamos was fulfilled. But five decades and four trillion dollars later, the Los Alamos National Laboratory remains. The original school buildings and wooden army barracks are gone. In their place stand concrete structures and a sprawling city of nearly 20,000 which boasts the highest concentration of Ph.D.s in the nation along with the lowest unemployment rate, and highest per capita income. An eighteen hole golf course, ski mountain, and forty-nine churches serve as weekend diversions for the "Cones"—as the scientists are called—and their families.

Although the gates were removed in 1957, and legislation signed by John Kennedy in 1962 returned to private hands much of the land on the Pajarito Plateau, there remains an aura of secrecy about the place. One can never be sure which areas are truly safe and which are still "hot." Housing developments, businesses, motels and restaurants now stand on what had once been Technical Areas. Despite the stamp of approval for such development, highly contaminated plutonium residue was unearthed while digging the foundation for a new hotel in 1976. As the excavators discovered to their shock and surprise, Oppenheimer's legacy lives on. With a half-life of 24,100 years, radioactive echoes will be heard for millennia.

Fifteen miles east of Los Alamos, the San Ildefonso Pueblo is a world away. It is one of eight northern pueblos consisting of both Tewa- and Tiwa- speaking peoples. While some are steeped in tradition, others support a more modern lifestyle while trying to revive a cultural heritage severely compromised by centuries of European influence. The history of San Ildefonso after European contact is typical of its neighbors. By 1793, smallpox had reduced the population to half that of pre-contact, while a flu epidemic in 1918 dealt the recovering pueblo another harsh blow.

Yet somehow, San Ildefonso has been able to retain their cultural identity with greater success than most New Mexican pueblos. Its members have worked diligently to preserve traditional customs, dances and artwork. Master potter Maria Martinez is credited with having put San Ildefonso on the map in the 1920's with her famed black pottery which can be found in museums across the country and around the world. San Ildefonso found an identity in her style, and generations of potters since Martinez have ensured that her techniques and style will never be lost.

Rising near the junction of 502 and U.S. 285, the Pojoaque Casino told of a pueblo along a different path. The smallest of the Tewa-speaking tribes, Pojoaque has exercised its sovereign right to make an easy buck. The pueblo's location along Route 285—the only major road north of Santa Fe—makes it ideal for attracting travelers en route to or from central Colorado. Only the Camel Rock Gaming Center—located on the Tesuque Pueblo six miles to the south—stands in the way of a direct link to Santa Fe's population of 70,000.

Gambling has become a top source of income for Native American tribes across the country as they tap into the $330 billion a year industry. From the Pequots in Connecticut to the Seminoles in Florida, and the Cabazons in California, casinos and high stakes bingo parlors gross more than $8 billion a year for seventy-one tribes. It is seen as one of the only ways to combat unemployment rates that often run forty to eighty percent (compared to a national average of seven).

As fast as a slot machine gobbles up quarters, I sailed through Nambre, Santa Clara, and San Juan. A strong tail wind propelled me north on 285 through the remaining pueblos like a bat out of Hell. But from the look of the storm clouds gathering on the horizon, there was also a distinct possibility that I could be heading there in a hand basket.

Billowing cumulonimbus flanked the highway ahead, but left a seemingly safe passage in between. Reminiscent of Moses, the clouds parted, leaving a thin strip of clear sky above Route 68 northeast of Espanola. The message was as clear as an eleventh commandment: Thou shalt ride!

But as with any Biblical tale, this one included a test of faith. It came north of Alcalde as the wind shifted and sprinkles began to fall. Lightening flashed to the east, but the way remained clear. I continued to ride in the gathering gloom, and although the wind and rain picked up, I persisted like a faithful disciple. Three miles out of Alcalde, however, I was forced to seek refuge under the awning of J.P.'s Bar and Drive-Thru Liquor Mart. My watch read 7:15 but is was darker than that.

A black El Camino pulled up to the drive-thru and a hairy arm emerged from the passenger side window. A dark hand exchanged a five dollar bill for a six pack of Coors and the car pulled away. Moments later, a light brown Buick pulled into the lot and parked about twenty feet away. The windshield wipers stopped, but the engine continued running. I paid it little mind as my attention focused on the weather.

The rain seemed to be letting up, but the wind had shifted once again—coming out of the northeast with the storm. I slipped my raincoat on for warmth and began to stretch my legs to keep them loose. I decided to make one final push before finding a place to spend the night.

The brown Buick continued humming as I finished my stretching. Combined with the darkness, a screen of water on the windshield made it difficult to see inside. A lone figure shifted periodically in the drivers seat. The shadowy presence made me nervous—thinking about moving on. One more stretch and then...

The driver's door swung open and a short, gray-haired man stepped into the rain. The bushy mustache across his upper lip was matched by a single eyebrow that stretched across his brow. Reaching back into the car, he pulled out a small box, and swung the door closed. Holding it carefully with both hands, he walked toward me. I grabbed Betsy's handlebars, ready to make a break when he spoke. "Thought you might like a biscuit and some 'slaw."

The familiar goateed portrait on the red and white striped box cleared up a moment of confusion. "Got some mashed potatoes and gravy too." He smiled. "Ate the chicken myself."

"Thank you." I said, accepting the gift.

"Saw you stretchin' there. I slipped a disk a couple years ago. Pain was terrible. Doc told me to stretch every day, and after a couple of months it was gone. Of course that was before my wife left me. She took off with a younger man."

Potent fumes of alcohol accompanied each sorrowful word. "The last I heard—a rumor now—they got married in Las Vegas. But she never got an official divorce!" A far-away look gathered in his eyes, though he insisted not to care.

There was a moment of silence. "Thanks for the food."

"Of course. I'm on more or less of a liquid diet these days." He turned and walked into J.P.'s ready to fulfill his daily allowances of malt, barley and juniper berry extract.

I slung a bungee cord over the KFC box, and headed into the light but persistent rain. Jagged streaks of lightening ripped the sky over the Sangre De Christo Mountains to the east—a safe distance...for now.

After ten minutes the puddles on the road had worked their way through my leather shoes and cotton socks. I could stand the wind's constant pummeling, but nothing is quite as discouraging as soggy feet. I pulled into the Cerca del Rio Cafe for another break.

The large awning and an exterior wall offered excellent protection from both the wind and rain. The large front window was an Edward Hopper painting come to life. Lonely diners sat at a long, white counter while a middle-aged man in a grease-stained apron worked at a wide, black grill. A bored waitress smoked a cigarette beside him.

The decision to get back on the road was forced upon me by the fading light. I needed to find a place to stay and I wasn't going to be picky. The small town of Velarde offered some interesting options, but the vacant lot was posted, an abandoned gas station was fenced off, and the church yard was too well lit. Before I knew it, I was out of town and options.

As the road swung left and headed downhill toward the Rio Grande, the spray coming off Betsy's front tire increased proportionately to her speed. Braking carefully on the slick pavement, I reached the bottom of the hill cold, wet, and tired.

This sucks. This really sucks. And then it appeared. Just as I had lost faith once again in the powers that be, she delivered. At first it didn't look like much—a rickety fruit stand on the side of the road. But closer examination revealed solid cinder block walls and a galvanized steel roof. It wasn't lit. It wasn't fenced. It wasn't posted.

Rolling Betsy through the side door, I was even more impressed by the interior. The poured concrete floor measured eight by eight—plenty of room to keep both of us dry for the night. The abundance of spider webs suggested the stand was not in regular use. A low counter provided a place to set my gear and a wobbly chair allowed me to take off my waterlogged shoes and socks with relative ease and comfort. As pink and wrinkled as newborn piglets, my feet greeted the world with squeals of delight.

Considerably less delightful were the swarms of mosquitoes that granted me instant popularity. Small but persistent, they tormented me mercilessly from the moment I began to unpack. Swatting between bites of the Colonel's finest side dishes, I kept them at bay until I had finished the coleslaw. It was during the mashed potatoes that I felt the acute pain radiating from inside my right thigh. I dropped the spuds immediately and slapped the affected area. That was no mosquito! Frantically, I unzipped my bag and fumbled for a flashlight convinced I'd been bitten by something much more horrid.

A Black Widow perhaps—an arachnid named for the female's dubious practice of devouring her lover moments after mating. The spider's venom is fifteen times more potent than that of a rattlesnake.

I waited for the symptoms to develop, starting with intense pain building rapidly for the first thirty minutes as the powerful neurotoxin takes hold. Next, an assault on the central nervous system resulting in nausea, dizziness, salivation, watering eyes and profuse sweating. Speech fails and breathing becomes difficult as muscle spasms in the jaw distort the face into a pain-wracked grimace. Other muscles follow suit with those of the abdomen affected most.

After five minutes of tense anticipation, only a slight stinging sensation remained. If not a black widow bite, it must have been a brown recluse. Known locally as "fiddlebacks," *Loxosceles reclusa* release an insidious toxin that kills the cells around the bite as a black gangrenous spot quickly develops. Previously unaffected skin around the wound peels away exposing underlying tissue. Like an unstoppable acid, the toxin continues to dissolve the surrounding epidermal layers leaving a gaping hole up to six inches across. Breathless, I awaited my fate.

Whatever the culprit, no amount of searching with the flashlight could expose it. After more than ten anxious minutes, I was neither locked in spasm nor dissolving into a puddle like the Wicked Witch of the West. I could, however, have used a field of poppies to help me sleep.

Shake—wind driven rain rocking the steel roof. Rattle—the sound of mosquitoes in my ears. Roll—wave after wave of thunder across the valley. The spirit of Jerry Lee Lewis was alive and well that night. Goodness, gracious, great balls of fire!

Chapter 37

*We are a people who live on the roof of the world; we are the sons of
Father sun, and with our religion we daily help our father to go across
the sky. We do this not only for ourselves, but for the whole world. If we
were to cease practicing our religion, in ten years the sun would no
longer rise.*
—Chief Ochwiay Biano, Taos

*Ours is the northernmost pueblo. We were a meeting place where the
white mountain men, the Spaniards, the Pueblos, and the Plains Indians
met to trade.*
—Rosarita Romero, Taos, 1975

*Taos is a magnet for modern fugitives. The Athens of the Southwest, it
was where the cultures of the Plains Indians and the Pueblos, and later
Eastern and Amerindian mysticism, met and cross-fertilized.*
—Alex Shoumatoff

Among the Rio Grande Pueblos, tradition dictates that there be a sun-
watcher whose special task is to observe the exact point on the horizon
of the sun's emergence. Each morning, the sun-watcher looks to the
farthest eastern mesa, "the sun's house," and feels the life within it. In a
profound unity, it is believed that the sun and earth are indivisible—a
sacred bond which gives life to plants, animals, and the wind.

But it wasn't until the sun had cleared the eastern ridge line that I felt
its power. Reveling in the first warm rays, I made my way north along
the Rio Grande through Embudo and the junction with State Route 75—
the only road leading into the "Hidden Valley" of the Picuris Pueblo. So
isolated was this tribe in the early days of European exploration that it
remained a mystery until being "discovered" by Spanish Conquistadors
in 1591. To this day, the Picuris, or San Lorenzo, Pueblo has signed no
treaty, and remains a self-ruled nation tribe of 300.

I remained on Route 68 as it struggled up a massive rock-ribbed gorge,
sometimes skirting the river, sometimes hanging high against to the
glowing cliffs. The town of Rinconada passed in a blink, and the village
of Pilar in half that. Higher up, a broad plateau stretched to the north
and west—a nearly perfect plane save for the massive invagination
carved by the Rio Grande. Over the last million years, the river has etched
a colossal trench through hundreds of feet of sedimentary rock.

The shadowed slopes of the Sangre De Christo Mountains rose along
the eastern edge of the plateau. Early conquistadors called them "Blood
of Christ" in reference to the reddish glow along the ridge caused by the
setting winter sun. In the heart of summer, and with the sun behind

them, the peaks—Truchas, Cerro Vista, Wheeler, and Latir—were an enchanted emerald green. I skirted the edge of Cerro Vista for the next eleven miles of rolling table land through Ranchos De Taos and then into Taos proper. "All-American City -1994."

As the sign implied, I found a melting pot rich in history, culture and the arts. Where the Great Plains meet the Southwest, Taos has been a crossroads for generations of mountain men, trappers and explorers. During the early days of European settlement, it served as a center of trade as well as communication. News of changing times almost always funneled through Taos on its way both east and west. So great was this intersection that legendary explorer, scout, and Indian agent Kit Carson settled here in 1843 after a life on the go. The home he shared with his wife Josefa is now a museum. Frontier tools, furnishings and firearms can be viewed throughout the twelve room adobe.

Not far away stands another museum which houses a much older collection. It recalls a time long before Carson, when the plateau above the Rio Grande was home to a very different culture. Dwelling in pit houses at the edge of the Sangre De Christos, native peoples lived in harmony with their surroundings. Their lives were governed by a cycle of rituals that defined their role in the world—a cycle which, remaining unbroken, would ensure harmony. "All is God," wrote D.H. Lawrence about the Taos Pueblo. "The whole life effort of man is to get his life into direct contact with the elemental life of the cosmos."

In the mid-1500's the sacred cycle was first threatened by outsiders. It's been under pressure ever since. Spanish explorers and missionaries saw native ceremonies as nothing more than pagan rituals. As their colonies spread throughout the region, the self-righteous Spaniards increased pressure on the pueblos, converting their inhabitants to Catholicism and stifling traditional religious practices. While resentment grew throughout the region, it was the Taos Pueblo in 1680 that successfully revolted against the constant persecution. Although there had been resistance before the Taos revolt and has been since, it was the only case in which the pueblo Indians could claim total victory.

Returning to traditional ways, however, proved impossible. Like those of all eighteen New Mexican pueblos, residents of Taos have struggled to retain their traditional culture and ancient rituals. Fortunately, its long history of independence and tenacity, has enabled the Taos Pueblo to strike a balance between the world of ancestors and that of neighbors.

Standing literally on the border of the reservation, the rambling adobe home of Mabel Dodge Luhan has played host to the likes of Georgia O'Keefe, D.H. Lawrence and Carl Jung along with a full palette of other colorful artists and writers. Ernest Blumenschein, Bert Phillips, Ansel Adams, Andrew Dasburg, Nicolai Fechin and Emil Bisttram all spent time working and living in and around Taos.

The area remains an artist colony. Nearly a hundred galleries exhibit the work of local photographers, sculptors, weavers, and painters. Ranging from traditional native arts and crafts to the cutting edge of contemporary work, Taos offers something for any art lover.

But it was not art that filled my thoughts as I rolled into town. The tantalizing smell of fresh bread lured me to the Taos Bakery where I purchased two loaves of cracked wheat. Still warm from the oven, I ate one on the spot. Art appreciation is always enhanced by a full stomach.

In the Tewa language, they are called *kosa*. To the Zuni, they are known as *koyemshi*. But in Taos the sacred clowns, the "delight makers," are called *chiffonetti*. Known to many whites as "mudheads," these cosmic comedians, these tricksters, are as unpredictable as they are outrageous.

He appeared out of nowhere, the bearded man in raggy jeans and torn flannel shirt. I had just passed through an opening in the low, brick wall that surrounds the central plaza when he met me eye to bleary eye. In the shade of a towering oak, he blocked my way, placing a dirty hand on Betsy's handlebars. "I know you," he said in a voice as wiry as his shock of white hair. Dozens of tourists milled around us, but the old man's gaze remained fixed on me.

"If you don't mind," I said, trying to free the bike from his grip.

He clenched his fingers tighter and grinned. "I know you," he repeated. "You're the one looking for answers."

I stopped pulling and relaxed my arms. He nodded approval, and continued to smile a knowing smile. "I'm right, aren't I?"

Of course he was, but I did not want to admit it. I felt uncomfortable, as if he were peering straight into my soul. I felt exposed, naked. And he knew that too.

Sensing my distress, he relaxed his gaze and lightened his grin. "Don't worry," he said in a voice just over a whisper. "It's all a facade—the Emperor's New Clothes."

I looked around the plaza at store windows filled with t-shirts, postcards, jewelry and pottery. "Genuine Native American Made Crafts." "Best Selection in Town." "1/2 OFF EVERYTHING AT CHARLIE'S CORNER."

"You know what I mean, don't you."

"I think so."

He removed his hand from the handlebars. "I could tell. You've got that look in your eyes."

"What look?"

"Questioning."

"I'm just curious."

"Don't defend yourself. The world has always needed those unafraid to question the dominant paradigm, now more than ever."

"I don't know that I'm going that far. I'm just trying to figure out...the truth."

"Like I said."

"What do you mean?"

"The Emperor's New Clothes." He made a sweeping gesture with his arms. "When's the last time you saw a sign advertising 'Genuine Mass-Produced Made in Taiwan Artificial Indian Crafts?'"

I smiled.

"But that's just a symptom," he continued. "The disease goes much deeper. At this point it's systemic."

"Systemic?"

"Economic system, political system, social system—all rotten to the core. The 'American Dream' is a fairy tale of wealth, power and mobility. 'Image is everything.' 'Any press is good press.' Shove it down their throats long enough and they're bound to believe it. Or at least be scared to death about questioning it."

"The Emperor's New Clothes."

He smiled broadly and slapped my shoulder. "American's use more resources and create more pollution than anyone else on the planet. We've got more toys than any of the other kids, yet depression, alcoholism and drug use are rampant. With all the finery money can buy, our souls remain naked to the world.

"Our society is losing something profound—its relationship to the natural world. Yet it is this very relationship that is at the core of any culture. It is this relationship that underlies who we are, what we believe, and how we act. You don't have to go to the mountaintop to find the truth, but it's as good a place as any. You heard of Summitville?"

"No."

He pointed north. "It's just over the border in Colorado. They say it's gonna cost a hundred and twenty million to clean up the site."

"A hundred and twenty million dollars! What happened?"

"Greed."

"That's always a good start."

"They used to mine up there in the old days, but the site was closed after World War Two. It was considered too high, too wet, and too damn cold to operate efficiently. It remained closed for decades until a Canadian company came down and reopened it—guess they're used to the cold.

"They were in a hurry to turn a profit, so they laid their heap-leach pad in the dead of winter. Big mistake. The pad ripped and cyanide started leaking into the Alamosa River. When the fish started dying, someone tipped off the 'feds.'

"Well, it didn't take long for that company to declare bankruptcy and head back to the great white north—leaving the good old EPA to clean up the mess. Guess who's paying the bill? You and me. They got the gold and we got the shaft."

I was silent for a moment. "I'd like to say I'm surprised, but at this point I'd believe anything."

"And what was it all for? Gold—the ultimate symbol of wealth, power, superiority."

"Didn't the weavers order gold thread to sew the Emperor's clothes?"

He nodded. "The market price may be down, but the cost of gold is most definitely rising. There are hundreds of abandoned mines up there in the Rockies. It's not 'beaver fever' you need to worry about when drinking the water, it's the aftermath of 'gold fever.'

"Makes me think twice about heading that way."

"When's that?"

"Probably this afternoon."

"Make sure you check out the flea market before you leave. It's a good place to look for truth."

"I will, thanks."

He nodded, offering his right hand. "Good luck. And remember—don't take any wooden nickels or gold-plated lies."

The slightest hint of cannabis wafted through the parking lot where people of all shapes and sizes had come to hock their wares. From teenage hippie wanna bees to old Mexican women, everyone had something to sell. Rusty tailgates and rickety card tables supported bizarre collections of yesterday, today and tomorrow. Along with the requisite supply of jewelry and hardware, there were old clothes, guns, knives, rugs, handbags, purses, beads, books and coins. It was Haight-Asbury and Greenwich Village rolled into one.

A new age couple sold crystals out of the back of their pickup truck, while the next booth offered sharks teeth, turtle shells, and dried alligator heads. Further down the line, a shaky card table supported an ample collection of water pipes—"For Tobacco Use Only."

Amid the rows of random miscellany, my eyes let upon a second-hand Stetson. Sun-bleached and water-stained, it couldn't replace the one I'd lost in Mancos, but it was as close as I'd ever come. Fifteen dollars was all it took for the look of a weathered buckaroo.

At the end of the last row of booths—off by herself in the corner of the parking lot—a petite woman sat behind an equally scaled card table. She wore a sleeveless cotton dress that looked more like a night gown. Long blond hair fell freely about her face and shoulders. Slightly darker tufts sprouted from under each arm. Bundles of sage tied with red yarn were neatly stacked in three piles with an index card next to each: $1,

$2, $3. Hanging behind her on the low branches of a gambel oak were a half dozen dream catchers. They were not priced.

"Hi," she said, looking up from a pink paperback. Although I couldn't see the title, the color and sprouting wrench were unmistakable—*Zen and the Art of Motorcycle Maintenance*.

"Good book."

"So I've been told," she replied, motioning with her arm. "Picked it up over there for a quarter."

"Can't beat that," I said, leaning forward to admire the dream catchers. "These are quite nice."

"Thanks," she smiled. "And I'm not half, quarter, eighth, or even a sixteenth Indian. I'm not gonna pull that. Who'd believe it anyway? I'm just an artist trying to make enough to get by. Barely enough at that."

I liked her no-nonsense style. "You're an artist?"

"More than anything else."

"You picked a hell of a town to try."

We fell easily into a conversation that ranged from Taos and the local art scene, to civil unrest in Nicaragua, to clearcutting in the Northwest.

"As a matter of fact," she said, "my boyfriend, Bobby, just got back from Oregon and we're having a party tonight out at our place. Do you want to come?"

"I don't want to crash anything."

"Don't worry. It's nothing fancy—just a few friends from around here. Consider yourself formally invited."

"Where do you live?"

"Out in the desert northwest of here. It's on the other side of the river— about six miles past the bridge."

"Sounds good. That's the direction I'm headed. By the way, I'm Nelson."

"Mercy."

"Is something wrong?"

"No, my *name* is Mercy."

With size and weight in mind, I limited my purchases to items that would fit easily inside my panniers. Earrings not only suited this requirement, but would also make nice souvenirs for mom, grandma, and, of course, my brother. I struck a deal on two and a half pairs and returned to the plaza for a lazy afternoon in the shade.

When the town clock rang five, I packed my journal, strapped my sombrero to the bike, and hit the road. The crowded Paseo del Pueblo Norte lead me out of town. I followed it to the junction of state Route 64 where I turned left, and into a headwind. Combined with the low, western sun, the persistent breeze turned the relatively flat section of highway into an uphill battle.

My intention had been to get to Mercy's place in one push, but the Rio Grande Gorge demanded a stop. Dozens of cars were parked at both ends of the broad concrete bridge. I coasted to a stop among a gaggle of gawkers. Cameras hung from every neck.

Leaning Betsy against an abutment, I walked onto the span and peered over the railing at the river 688 feet below. At this height the Rio Grande was barely discernible—a testament to the powers of water and time. Sheer, gray cliffs stretched up from the river, interrupted periodically by stepped terraces. A crumpled white automobile rested on the highest eastern shelf—still 100 feet below the bridge. A man beside me on the rail nudged my elbow. "That's a hell of a wrong turn."

Part 5
Peacemakers

Chapter 38

We reached the old wolf in time to watch the fierce green fire dying in her eyes. I realized then, and have known ever since, that there was something new to me in those eyes—something only known to her and the mountain.
—Aldo Leopold

I took one last look at the Sangre De Christos behind me and headed into the high New Mexican desert. The broad plateau before me ran to the foot of Canjilon Mountain, blanketed with the colors of late summer sage. The angled rays of a setting sun brought out the silver down of the tri-tipped leaves and the plum-colored hue of shaggy bark. Kangaroo rats emerged from their dens. Lizards retired for the night.

I pushed on as sand blew freely across the road. I lowered my head to the wind, looking up occasionally in an attempt to match the landscape with Mercy's oral directions. "Six miles past the bridge; turn right at the break in the fence; follow the tire tracks to where they split; take the left fork for a quarter mile. The place is on the left."

The double track ended beneath the wheels of a rusty blue Datsun but there was little other evidence that this was "the place." I dismounted behind the Japanese hatchback and proceeded on foot toward a trio of small structures reminiscent of the tar paper shacks that once covered the Great Plains or, more recently, the shanty towns of South Africa. A pair of thread-bare sofas and a torn car seat formed a semi-circle around a fire pit filled with scrap wood.

A stocky, dark-haired man emerged from the left-hand shack accompanied by a pair of cats. He wore cut-off blue jeans and nothing else. His sinewy muscles were highlighted by the shadows of the setting sun. He extended a calloused hand. "I'm Bobby."

"Nelson."

"From the flea market?"

I nodded.

"Mercy told me you'd be on a bike. No wonder I didn't hear you coming."

"Is she around?"

"No right now. She went over to the neighbors for a minute."

"Neighbors?" I looked out across the sage.

"It's got different meaning out here."

"I'd say."

"Hey, could you give me a hand?" Bobby asked, turning toward the building on the far right.

"Sure."

I followed him inside the darkened structure, examining its construction as best I could. The lower part of the walls consisted of red clay and straw within a framework of chicken wire while odd bits of plywood stretched above to a sheet metal roof. Strips of corrugated cardboard had been tucked here and there to keep out drafts. A white sheet hung over the back wall. "This is where we sleep," Bobby said, placing his hands on one end of a table opposite the door. "I want to move this into the kitchen for the party."

I grabbed the other end, but upon lifting two of the legs fell to the floor with a synchronous thud. I remained holding my end, while Bobby set his down and retrieved the castoffs. He placed them on the table top and we continued without difficulty until we reached another building of similar construction. Bobby placed his end down and set to work guiding the long nails which stuck down from the corners I held into the tops of the legs. Years of wiggling had widened the holes, but Bobby was confident the table would hold together at least through the party.

"Set it down lightly," he told me. "As long as we have a little weight on top, it won't come apart." He bent down to pick up a brick in the corner.

"Hey," he said when we were back outside. "You know what would be really helpful? Could you dig a new shitter."

He led me into the third building—by far the sturdiest. Consisting of similar materials but reinforced with two by fours and angle braces, the fact that it was the tool shed said a lot about Bobby. Hand tools, hardware and painting supplies were neatly arranged atop wide shelves running the length of the back wall. A portable generator sat in a corner alongside a collection of long-handled tools. Bobby grabbed a shovel from among them.

"This is quite a workshop," I remarked as we stepped outside.

"I suppose," he paused. "But I'm still sore about having to sell my welder to get to Oregon." He took a moment to scan the vicinity. "How about putting the shitter over behind that tall sage—in case the women want some privacy."

We walked over to take a closer look. "This is a good spot," Bobby said. "A foot wide, a foot deep, and three feet long. You can bring the chair over when you're done." He pointed to the naked frame of an aluminum lawn chair. "I don't think the Green Stamp people ever expected this."

By the time I finished, Bobby had started the fire and put a large pot of soup on to warm and Mercy had returned from the neighbors. "Welcome," she smiled.

239

The first guests arrived as the sun began setting behind Canjilon Peak. The closest neighbors to the south—Martha and her son David—walked through the sage accompanied by their large, black dog, Roscoe. I shook hands with all three.

Fleeing an abusive husband, Martha brought David here a little over a year ago. They lived under a tarp for five months before getting their first small building up—a rickety shack that collapsed during a November gale. Fortunately they were not home at the time. But it was enough to convince Martha to build with cinder blocks. Mid-way through the construction, they were back to living under a tarp but hoping they'd be done by *this* November. Martha had recently found work in Taos and David was ready to start at the local high school. He mentioned saving money from a summer job so he could join the hockey team. Upbeat and positive, they were optimistic about making it on their own.

The sun had set by the time Dan arrived. He parked his red pickup truck behind Mercy's Datsun and walked slowly toward us. He was dressed all in brown—the color of the desert he loved. Long, curly blond hair hung below a wide-brimmed Peruvian hat. He carried a long, wooden drum under one arm.

"You're a sight for sore eyes," Mercy said, throwing her arms around him.

"Been a while," he said in a voice as soft as a desert breeze.

Bobby invited him over for a bowl of soup—a simple yet hearty broth of potatoes and greens. I contributed a loaf of fresh bread, and Mercy added three melons she'd bartered at the flea market.

"I don't think I caught you're name," said Dan, extending a hand.

"Nelson Lebo."

"Lobo?"

"No, Lebo."

"One letter shy of being mighty unpopular around here."

"Why's that?"

"Fish and Wildlife is planning to reintroduce Mexican wolves to the southern part of the state and over in Arizona. Big controversy."

The return of los lobos? It's been sixty years since the scruffy carnivores roamed the Southwest. Could it be true? Dan nodded.

Driven from U.S. soil by the late 1930's and nearly extinct in Mexico soon there after, the lobo is stepping out of its own grave. Shot, trapped and poisoned for decades, the wolf's return, if realized, will be remarkable. Despite recent polls that suggest most residents of Arizona and New Mexico support reintroduction, los lobos still give some folks the "shakin' shakin' shakes."

"Cattlemen are up in arms," Dan continued. "They've convinced both

240

governors to oppose the plan. The Arizona House has even proposed legislation that would put a bounty on the lobo even before the first one has set foot in the state. It'd be easier to introduce a nuclear bomb to Arizona than a wolf."

For good or bad, the Mexican wolf has always had an extreme effect on people. It has changed lives. Aldo Leopold is a case in point. Sixty-five years ago, the young ecologist was involved in an effort to increase the number of deer in the Southwest by exterminating their chief predators—wolves and mountain lions. Years later he received reports of skyrocketing deer populations and the resulting damage to vegetation. Without predators to keep their numbers in check, the deer population exceeded the carrying capacity of the land. Starvation followed and the population crashed.

Regretting the misguided policy that lead to this disaster, an older, wiser Leopold put pen to paper, describing the "fierce green fire" in his famous essay, *Thinking Like a Mountain.* After shooting a she wolf from a ridge top, he descended to reach the animal as the last flicker of life left her body. The experience with a common lobo became a turning point in the naturalist's life. Perhaps it could do the same for others. Are we willing to let that fierce green fire die again?

"Predators are an essential part of the ecosystem," said Dan. "They are as much a part of it as the native grazers and the plants they graze on. They all evolved in a balance together. We ought to leave natural systems to function without human interference. Without wolves, mountain lions and coyotes, the land is out of equilibrium—*koyaanisqatsi.*"

"Like that tripped-out movie," a voice called out from across the fire. "The one with the soundtrack by Philip Glass."

"That's the one," said Dan. "It's a Hopi term that describes life out of balance, when the world has gone crazy. It's an entire social, political, ecological commentary in five syllables. It's a warning.

"We need to find ways to return the land—our world—to harmony. Without high-end predators, this ecosystem has been out of balance for over half a century. We'll soon have Canadian gray wolves coming down from the north and hopefully Mexican lobos from the south. But too many simply refuse to see where we need to stand—the middle ground.

"The Navajo call it *hozho,* 'walking in beauty.' It's about being in harmony with everything on Earth: the human world, the animal world, the sky, the land, the soil, the water...everything. Most importantly we have to be in harmony with ourselves. That's where we need to begin to build a world that is balanced and whole."

Moonrise found us sitting on second-hand furniture around a first-rate bonfire. Flames leaped high into the air, offering not only light, but also warmth against the descending cold. Although the wind had died, a falling temperature became the latest challenge offered by the desert.

Burning in the darkness, the fire became a beacon in a sea of sage, offering direction to those adrift. They came like moths to a candle: Janet and Arthur. Gabriel, J.R. and Russ. Susan and Susanne. Paul, Manuel, Simon and Jem. With drums in hand and songs in heart, the quiet desert came alive with rhythm. Palms on leather—tapping, patting, thumping.

A marijuana cigarette made its way around the circle. The tiny orange ember at its tip grew bright with each inhale.

"You want to know the truth," came a passionate voice from across the fire, "go to the ancients. Ask the Mayans, the Aztecs—they know the truth, they know what's real. They are the *In Dios*, 'the people of God.' Now you can't believe what's real because now they're feeding you all this crap on television. That's not reality. They give us this MTV, this Nintendo—it's not real."

The bearded man grabbed a handful of soil and stood. "What's real is this dirt, this fire, this sky. That's what we're made of—dirt and sky. We come from the Earth to experience living and to learn from those before us. I am my grandfather, and his grandfather and his grandfather. It's just one continuous loop. Scientists call it DNA...shit. It's pure energy, man. It's the Mobius band between the Yin and the Yang—the continuous cycle and flow.

"The Yin and the Yang are the balance of everything. It's all around us. We just need to feel it. We just need to listen—not with our ears, but with our hearts. There is something in everyone that speaks the truth of life, but some people don't listen to it, don't respect it, don't hear. Instead they accept what society claims as right and wrong—government-approved bullshit. It's all a lie.

"Right now there's an Indian in the rainforest with the cure for cancer in his left pocket. But he won't tell us where he found it because it's a secret. Secrets are the truth, and people can't handle the truth. He's seen our bombers.

"So do we judge this man, this Indian from the Amazon? Jesus said, 'Don't judge others lest you be judged yourself.' Jesus Christ and Buddha taught the same thing. I think maybe they were the same person. There ain't no color, no prejudice, in the eyes of the almighty. We're all the same. We're all just people."

Just people.

The drumming grew louder and was spontaneously joined by a rhythmic chanting that started off low and grew as more and more people joined in. The words were of no language, but at the same time of all languages. They had never been written down, yet we all knew them as if deep in our collective memory we had sung them before. They came easily, effortlessly, naturally. They came from deep inside.

As the flames danced across the faces of strangers, I caught glimpses of familiarity. Smiling, winking, nodding, they had gathered to see me off. I was overcome by a sense of well-being as each one flashed to life— if only for a moment—reflecting the golden flames. Tom Kemp was there, grinning as if he had just told a whopper of a tale. Hank and Martha took a break from bickering, Dave Baum with his cheap stogie, and all three Highfeathers glistening in sweat. Billy Weirs beamed with pride at his coma record, while my "adopted" family from Green River spoke feverishly in Spanish. These were the faces of kindness—the faces of the American West beyond conflict and controversy. Among them I felt safe.

I glanced at Mercy and Bobby across the circle. Their faces faded in and out with the flickering flames. As Bobby leaned forward to place another log on the fire, his short, dark beard grew long and white. His smooth forehead became furrowed, and a far away look crept into his eyes. Sensing my stare, he looked up and winked, just like the old man outside the bus station in Dickinson, North Dakota. In the time it took my jaw to drop, the flames pulsed and the old-timer was gone. Bobby withdrew from the fire and reclaimed his seat on the tattered sofa.

Energized by this humanity, I could have stayed up all night. But it was already well past midnight and a long day lay ahead. Thanking my hosts, and saying good night to the others, I grabbed my sleeping bag and headed into the sage.

Away from the comfort of the firelight, darkness engulfed my body but not my spirit. The warmth was gone from my skin but not my heart. I laid my bag within ear-shot and crawled inside. The rhythmic beating became a lullaby, the dancing flames a night light. The big questions plaguing my mind faded into darkness. I slept at peace with the world. They had sung me back to *hozho.*

Chapter 39

The history of the West is a study of a place undergoing conquest and never fully escaping its consequences. Conquest basically involved the drawing of lines on a map, the definition and allocation of ownership, and the evolution of land from matter to history.
—Patricia Nelson Limerick

With a logic that cannot rest we are forced to this conclusion, that the agencies of civilization now in action are such as will secure a complete victory over wilderness and waste places of western territory. The plow will go forward. God speed the plow. By this wonderful provision, which is only man's mastery over nature, the clouds are dispensing copious rains... To be more concise, Rain follows the plow.
—Charles Dana Wilber, 1879

Silence. Pure and utter silence. The sun was up, the fire was down, but what I first noticed was the deafening silence. I listened from the warmth of my sleeping bag for echoes of midnight drums. Nothing. Nothing hung in the still morning air but a biting cold that gnawed its way through my insulated nylon cocoon and into my bones. Shivers came in waves, gripping my shoulders and tingling down my arms. For all the misery they provided, the involuntary convulsions did make it easier to get up since any level of physical activity would be an improvement.

I dressed quickly and loaded the bike. A small, black cat brushed up against my leg as I wheeled Betsy past the fire pit. The slightest puff of smoke rose from the smoldering embers. Four cars were lined up behind Mercy's Datsun, but there was no one in sight. The cat continued its plea for attention as I leaned the bike against a tattered, blue sofa. I scribbled a quick thank note for Mercy and Bobby on a half-priced post card from Charlie's Corner, and anchored it with a screw driver in the loose sand beside the fire pit. One of a growing collection of tools I'd picked up along the road, it was a sturdy Sears Craftsman—far too good to leave on the shoulder, but now too heavy to take back into the mountains. I knew it would find a good home with Bobby.

Kneeling beside the fire, I took a moment to warm my hands above the coals. The cat rubbed against my thigh and let out a needful meow. I scratched his head and stroked his spine. He arched as my fingers ran over each vertebrae. He purred his thanks.

Now it was my turn to stretch. I stood, reached my arms to the sky, and let out a immense yawn. Tired but anxious, I could feel the end approaching. Two hundred and ninety miles to Denver. Two and a half days to make it. Pacing would be the key. Having learned this lesson many times, I walked Betsy the half mile of double-track back to the highway where there were more prairie dogs on the Tarmac than cars.

A light wind out of the north offered a slight challenge, but I was more concerned about the creaking that came once again from my cranks. Pedaling softly, I reached Tres Piedras—about twelve miles—in just under an hour. Slow, but safe.

As luck would have it, the gas station/general store/garage was open...sort of. As I stepped through the door, a plump, middle-aged woman looked up from her paper. "Outta gas," she said. "Delivery ain't 'til tomorrow."

"Don't need gas," I replied, "just a drink and maybe to borrow a socket wrench."

"I can take care of the drink, but you'll have to see Neil about the wrench. He's out in the garage.."

The Gatorade cost a dollar, but Neil lent me the wrench for free. It did the trick and I reached the Colorado border—twenty-two miles later— squeak-free. "Leaving New Mexico - Hasta La Vista," read one sign. "Entering Colorado - Mountains and Much More," read another. Other than the signs, there was little indication that I'd entered the Centennial State. No ridge line, no river, not even a low mesa marked the transition. The southern border of Colorado is no more than an east-west trending line 390 miles long.

Although Colorado and Wyoming are the only purely rectangular states in the Union, all but three states west of the Mississippi River have at least two straight (or nearly so) borders. The Rocky Mountains offer the most rugged terrain in the lower forty-eight, yet the states that contain them appear on maps to be little more than tidy boxes, as if a giant hopscotch court runs from the Mexican border to Canada. It is this abundance of linearity and right angles that causes Colorado and Wyoming along with Nebraska, Kansas, Utah, New Mexico and the the Dakotas to be the last pieces added by children to jigsaw puzzles of the United States.

But the use of rulers and t-squares by pioneering cartographers was not limited to the delineation of state boundaries alone. Within most western states, land is divided into 640 acre sections (one square mile). Sections were originally divided into sixteen forty-acre squares, or combined into groups of six to form townships. Although seemingly neat and orderly, this simple method does not do justice to a land as varied and complex as the American West. Thousands of visible and invisible lines cut across what was once simply wide open space: state lines, county lines, town lines and telephone lines; rail road tracks, roads and fences. Never before in the history of the world has there been such a profusion of perpendicularity and parallelism.

But despite their best efforts, map makers cannot overcome the fact that a spherical planet does not conform itself to right angles. Traveling from the equator poleward, lines of longitude grow closer and closer together. Examining the Colorado road map I picked up a week earlier in Cortez, I discovered that the state is noticeably narrower at its northern border as if Nebraska and northern Utah were squeezing harder than Kansas and southern Utah.

As this seeming anomaly indicates, nature abhors the straight line. She loathes parallelism. Look for her ruler and you'll be wasting your time. Try to find her T-square and she'll slap you in the face. Who else could etch the rugged coast of Maine? Trace the Connecticut River? Sketch an Appalachian ridge line? There simply is no logical transition across a linear state boundary. Had congress taken John Wesley Powell's advice a century ago and laid out borders along watershed boundaries, the continental divide would have split Colorado into two states.

Defying the map makers, a rolling sage desert spread for miles on both sides of the border. It didn't care whether it was in the Centennial or Sunshine state. Only the distant Rockies to the north gave an inkling of what lay ahead.

Six miles beyond the border, Antonito lived up to its diminutive moniker. Not much more than a whistle stop on the Denver & Rio Grande Western Rail Road, its offerings were meager. Indoor plumbing, however, was a step up from where I had spent the night. I stopped at Gary's Gulf with the intention of nothing more than a porcelain encounter. Paying little attention to the sign on the rest room door—"Customers Only"—it was not until after I had taken care of business and was scrubbing my fingers at the small sink that guilt settled into my conscience. Unlike Hamlet's dark spot, my culpability was erased easily with a pair of granola bars, and I was soon on my way to Alamosa.

Crossing its namesake river, I was reminded of the cyanide contamination from the Summitville mine thirty miles upstream. As I'd been told in Taos, work at the abandoned site continues as sixty full-time EPA workers carry out the process of "reverse mining"—trucking the contaminated waste back to the pit from which it had come at an expense of $33,000 a day. The projected total cost, I'd been told, would reach $120 million.

Running parallel to the railroad tracks, the next twenty-nine miles of U.S. 285 felt more like the plains of Kansas than the Rocky Mountains. Straight and flat, the road forced me out of the saddle for both physical and mental relief. Cumulative fatigue rose from my hands, through my shoulders, and settled at the base of my skull. My gluteus maximus had been whittled to a minimus—pelvic bones dug into the bicycle seat producing numbness in the paper-thin layer of soft tissue and skin that held them in. If those who are bed-ridden can suffer from bed sores, what happens to those who are bicycle ridden?

A half mile up, a half mile down—the pattern repeated itself under the late morning sun. Mile markers became tick marks on the number line that was Route 285. The strain on my mind became as challenging as that on my body, and I welcomed the sticky link in Betsy's chain that forced me out of the saddle and into my panniers for the small can of WD-40. A few squirts and a little manipulation between my fingers did the trick. With Betsy running smoothly we reached Alamosa just after noon.

Founded in 1878 as the latest terminus to the Denver and Rio Grande Western Railroad, most of the buildings had come by rail from Garland City—the previous end of the line. Houses, businesses, and even churches were loaded onto flat cars and hauled to Alamosa. With a railhead at its southern end, the San Luis Valley became a viable food producer for the first time.

The largest of five mountain-rimmed plateaus, or "parks," in Colorado, the agricultural potential of the valley was immense. Carefully engineered irrigation projects were organized and a land boom resulted. Land speculation skyrocketed as pioneers poured in by the thousands. Naturally, the best sections were taken first and late-comers had no choice but to accept what was left. After the initial excitement of striking out on ones own, many found that—like anywhere else in the West—there just was not enough water to go around. Faced with the arid truth, hundreds abandoned their homes, their land, and their dreams—moving on to new promises further west.

Alamosa still offers promise for those who know where to look. I found mine at the neighborhood IGA. Stepping through the automatic door, I discovered a boatload of bargain-priced brown bananas and a special on six count bags of bagels. Sorting through the stack for cinnamon-raisin, I ran across a bag of egg bagels that contained one extra. In the blink of an eye "The Magnificent Seven" took on a whole new meaning. Without hesitation, I grabbed the baker's half-dozen and headed for the checkout.

Although peanut butter and bananas were a far cry from lox and cream cheese, the way I devoured those bagels would have made any Jewish mother proud. Had a rabbi witnessed the event, he probably would have converted me on the spot. But with no synagogue in site, I settled for a long nap in a shady park on the west side of town.

By the time I awoke late in the afternoon, the motel parking lot across the street had filled with out-of state plates. The Mid-West was strongly represented by the Big Ten states: Michigan, Illinois, Indiana, and Ohio. New York and Pennsylvania held there own while a smattering of New Englanders had also made the long journey—hardy pilgrims from Rhode Island and Massachusetts. So many travelers, so far from home.

Heading north out of Alamosa on Colorado 17, I was faced with a fifty mile stretch of road even straighter and flatter than the one that had carried me into the city from the south. Not a bend. Not a dip. Not a rise. Route 17 splits the wide valley like a knife would cut the last tortilla between two hungry friends—right down the middle. The San Juan Mountains rise twenty miles to the west while the northern Sangre De Christos lay an equal distance to the east. Although numerous creeks flow into the northern half of the valley, not a drop flows out. Only by evaporation and freight car does water leave the enormous trough.

A highway map of the valley looks more like the plan for a circuit board. Color-coded federal, state, and county roads run parallel and perpendicular like the inner workings of a computer. No twists. No turns. No curves. Although the San Luis Valley is known for its agricultural production, on paper it could pass for Silicon Valley.

Despite a light head wind, I made good time through Mosca and Hooper. Physically easy, the long, flat section became more and more of a mental challenge. To break up the monotony, I tuned my senses into the changes taking place as day turned into night. According to the Navajo, Changing Woman—wife of the Sun—lives far to the west and waits there each day for his return. Nature owes its fertility to her. I smiled at the setting sun and asked him to convey my best wishes.

A flock of yellow-throated warblers glimmered in the angled rays of evening. Swooping and turning in a sympathy of motion—like a single great bird—the flock sailed effortlessly over the undulating waves of grass. Killdeers flitted erratically along the edges of Saguache Creek. A night hawk called nearby.

I looked up, searching the sky for the small bird, but failed to see it. When my eyes returned to Earth, I noticed him there beside me, his tawny fur blending into the dull grasses of late summer. On the other side of a barbed wire fence not ten feet away, the coyote matched my pitifully slow pace without effort. A model of efficiency, he cut into the wind with his long, narrow muzzle. His ears were pressed flat, his mouth slightly open, exposing teeth and a lolling tongue. Short, white fur trailed down his chin, blending into the longer brown and gray hairs of his chest. He bounced along in an easy rhythm.

I downshifted, sat up and smiled. There he was—the sly one, the trickster, the survivor. Independent, resourceful, free—he is everything we hold dear in this country, yet we hunt him mercilessly. As I'd learned, coyotes—along with bobcats, mountain lions and wolves—have been ruthlessly pursued, often with both the government's approval and funding. Under the official authorization of the Animal Damage Control Act, millions of taxpayer dollars have been spent on a wide range of lethal measures against the coyote: aerial hunting, trapping, snaring, and denning (killing pups in their dens). After poisoning prairie dogs, mice and other rodents, coyotes were forced to eat dogs, chickens, calves and lambs, generating more outrage and increased pressure to get rid of them.

The average cost of killing a coyote over the last decade has been slightly over $100 per animal, with some particularly elusive individuals requiring up to $2,000. With so much money and so many options available, bounty hunters working for the federal government push the death toll of the coyote ever higher. Simultaneously that same government spends millions of dollars to reintroduce Wolves in Idaho, Montana, New Mexico and Arizona.

The coyote disappeared at the next crossroad, fading into the grass, fading into the night. Crickets chirped as a broad shadow spread across the valley, leaving only Great Sand Dunes National Monument glowing on the eastern slope. Winds sweeping into the valley from the southwest over thousands of years have deposited hundreds of feet of sand at the foot of the Sangre De Christos between Blanca and Crestone peaks. Reaching up to 700 feet above the valley floor, they are the highest inland dunes in America.

But like the sands of an hourglass, they disappeared through a hole of time as the spreading cloak of night enveloped them. The shadow climbed slowly up the golden dunes and onto the mountain slopes above where a curious band of green marks a double tree line. While the cold and wind that accompany altitude serve as the upper limit of woody growth along the massive eastern slope, it is aridity that marks the lower boundary. Only within a thin strip along the mountainside are the conditions right for arboreal growth.

Thirty-seven miles north of Alamosa I passed up a night in Moffat for the slightest hint of a bend in the road ahead. I'd already ridden 100 miles, it would be dark in an hour and the next town, Villa Grove, stood eighteen miles away, but I just had to make that curve. Needless to say, it came and went without fanfare, and I was faced with another ten miles of one dimensional riding. Acres of golden grasses bent under the north wind, offering a constant reminder that I was fighting the tide.

Like small towns everywhere, Villa Grove possessed the standard elements: post office, gas station, general store, restaurant. But here they were nearly all rolled into one: Food - Gas - Groceries - Beer - Cafe - Automotive - Hunting and Fishing Licenses. The entire commercial district under one roof, Noreen's Villa Grove Trade promised everything short of internet access and tax services.

A string of bells tied to the inside knob rang as I swung the door open. An antique cash register sat atop a burnished wooden counter to the right of the door. Three long sets of shelves stretched lengthwise nearly to the back wall where a small sign for the cafe hung above a single doorway. Through it came the sounds of dining.

I took the middle isle, strolling past neatly stocked rows of canned goods. The worn wooden floor creaked beneath my feet, and the smell of frying beef greeted me as I passed through the doorway. A woman worked the grill behind a tall counter. Her long, blond ponytail stuck through the gap above the adjustable plastic band of a blue baseball cap. She turned and smiled. "Groceries or dinner?"

"Dinner."

"Grab a menu and give me a shout when you're ready to order."

Three long, wooden tables ran parallel to the counter, each with a pair of matching benches. The first was filled with a half dozen husky young men with thick necks and crew cuts. They ate burgers and shared a pitcher of beer, joking in between the action of the baseball game on a television mounted in the corner.

The second table was empty, and a lone, gray-bearded man bent over a bowl of chili at the third. He lifted his head and smiled as I approached. His round cheeks were red from too much sun.

"Mind if I join you?"

"Not at all. Have a seat."

We exchanged names and hometowns. "Sam Harris," he told me, "and right now I guess I'm from Villa Grove."

"What do you do here?"

"As little as possible." He smiled broadly. "Actually I'm a musician, or at least I used to be."

"Used to be?"

"Never was that good. Got sick of playin' smoky bars and honky tonks, so when my folks died a couple years ago, I came into some money and bought a little place up the valley. I still play my guitar from time to time and write a song or two, but I've given up tryin' to make it professionally. Nowadays I spend a lot of time reading, napping, taking walks up in the National Forest. I do a little volunteer work with some land management agencies, but mostly I'm just trying to find balance in my life."

I nodded in agreement.

"It's not easy."

"Tell me about it." I agreed. "I started this trip thinking I was going to see the Wild West. It's been wild all right, but not the way I expected. Instead of a land united in identity I've found one divided by controversy. Everyone seems to have an opinion on how the land should be used.

Logging, mining, ranching, water rights, energy development...and then there's the whole reservation system."

"Sometimes it's not so easy to tell who's wearing the white hat and who's wearing the black."

"Or the headdress."

"True. The folks who's great grandparents took the land from the Indians are seeing the same thing happen to them. They're concerned about how fast the West is changing, but don't realize that's the way it's been ever since their ancestors arrived. The ax, the plow, the cow, and barbed wire transformed this entire region in less than a century."

"The latest agent of change is development. Some folks call it 'Californication,' but it's more than just disenchanted L.A. suburbanites. The wealth that's pumping into some areas has caused property values to as much as triple. Local folks suddenly find themselves unable to afford to live in their own homes anymore.

"But the new wave of settlers are not just rich people leaving crowded cities, they're also Mexican and Asian immigrants. At the core, they're after the same things as the original pioneers—sanctuary and opportunity. They're coming in record numbers and the locals can't stand it.

"The West is in a process of reinventing itself and a lot of the long-time residents feel as helpless as the Indians did. They think the land belongs to them because their ancestors fought for it, suffered for it. They feel it's being taken away. They feel they're being crowded out. They feel they're losing their inheritance and that nobody really cares—not the newcomers, not the tourists, and certainly not the government. Unless they step up with creative and realistic strategies, they will lose their voice to outsiders making the decisions for them.

"When a town like Durango down here starts to go the way of cappuccino and gourmet pizza, a lot of the real locals simply move further into the mountains to get away from it. Ironically, it's often the neo-locals—those who were attracted early on to the quirky character of a town and decided to make it home—that are the ones who put up the biggest fight when development doesn't stop at their backyards. After they get their piece of the mountain, they want it to be over. But who's to say who gets to be the last house on the road?

"And so the valleys fill and the mountainsides become dotted with million dollar homes. I've heard folks say developers are to Colorado as Serbs are to Kosovo. In a lot of cases, they destroy the very thing people seek in coming here."

"Wide open spaces."

"Exactly. And a lot of those wide open spaces belong to private ranchers who operate on thin profit margins. Most grazing land has an agricultural value of about two hundred dollars an acre. The real estate value of that same land can reach upwards of five thousand! A lot of ranchers are cash poor but land rich, so when a developer comes along offering millions, they're faced with a tough decision. Sell out or hang on."

I thought back to the sign I'd seen outside Durango a week ago. "Better cows than condos."

He nodded and took a spoonful of chili.

"So what's the solution?"

"Cooperation from both sides."

"Ranchers and environmentalists working together?"

"It's already happening up in Gunnison with the Legacy Project. And that's just one example of cooperation between the cattleman's association and conservation groups. They've come to the understanding that people are a part of the land they're preserving. Consensus builds trust and strengthens community. Reaching an agreement brings former adversaries together. Both sides want to retain open lands and the quality of life they represent. It's all about finding balance between ecology, economy and community."

"How do they do it?"

"Land trusts are one way. They use conservation easements to preserve open space and enhance wildlife habitat."

"How does it work?"

"An easement is an agreement written into the property rights. The power company, for example, holds easements on almost everyone's land to access meters and do electrical work. I bet most folks don't even know it.

"What makes conservation easements special is that they limit or prevent certain types of development not only for the current resident but for all time. It's a way to know that future generations will have open space."

"So it's basically a ban on new construction."

"It's not that simple. Since every land owner has different wants and needs, a cookie cutter approach won't work. In this area, the Continental Divide Land Trust works with people on a case by case basis. Their role is simply to help each person or family meet their individual conservation needs—whether it be a property-wide ban on new construction or simply protecting certain parts of it. A lot of older folks like to set aside house sites for their children, and that's ok—at least they're protecting the rest.

"It's important to remember that there is no change in ownership. It does not belong to the land trust. It's not open to public access, but the public still benefits from the views. So in a sense, it is for the public, but also for wildlife and, most importantly, future generations."

"Sounds like a great system, but you need to have willing landowners."

"Of course. I was an easy sell, but a lot of people are skeptical. It'll take a while for them to come around. In the meantime, there are a number of other techniques being used. I've heard that the Grand Canyon Trust has a Grazing Retirement Fund which they use to negotiate buy-outs of grazing rights on certain sensitive public lands. From what I understand, it's a complicated process involving public agencies—BLM or the Forest Service—to rewrite management plans and cancel the grazing permits. It's surprising how many ranchers will take the cash and move their cows. Those who are less willing can be further enticed by access to 'grass banks' in less sensitive areas that can be opened for grazing during times of drought or other emergency."

"Creative problem-solving at its finest."

"Indeed, but there are still groups that hold fast to more traditional approaches like advocacy and litigation. I've even heard of proposals for bans on house lots under 160 acres."

"Those sound like eastern words."

"You're right. Zoning used to be a four letter word around here. If someone would've brought it up twenty years ago he'd been laughed out of town. Fifty years ago and he'd been shot. The old timers used to oppose land use planning, but now they see it as a solution. I think the alliances forming between environmentalists and traditionalists give a glimpse of the politics of the future."

The bean burritos I'd ordered arrived, but I hesitated.

"Go ahead," Sam told me. "Dig in.

I did, and with the kind of vengeance only a hundred mile ride can produce. I chewed happily as he continued. "But sometimes even old-timers who are willing to embrace new ways of thinking find the deck stacked against them. It's a clash of lifestyles further complicated by changing economics and misguided subsidies."

There it was again. "Subsidies?"

"Oh yeah, the kind that have a tendency of accumulating unintended costs. Quite often public funds that finance road building can be used to guarantee mortgages for single-family homes, but not for multi-family or mixed-use development. As housing prices rise in places like Telluride and Aspen, members of the non-leisure class are forced to live elsewhere and commute to service-based jobs. This results in a secondary sprawl of bedroom communities with the sole purpose of servicing their upscale neighbors. Each day, scenic vistas and vital wildlife habitat—the prime reasons many people moved here in the first place—are being despoiled by the sprawl of large-lot developments.

"Ultimately more tax dollars must be spent to deal with the consequences: chemical runoff increase in rivers and streams; destruction of wetlands; loss of productive farmland; and increased air pollution.

"Wildlife is hit hardest. Beyond habitat loss, there's often a diminished food supply and the introduction of chemical pollutants. Covering a broad area with concrete and asphalt channels toxic runoff into waterways already stressed by high levels of withdrawal. Sediment loads originating from sprawl have been measured at three times higher than those from more compact development patterns. With over 35,000 square miles of this country paved over, a raindrop has little choice of what to do once it reaches the Earth. The way I see it, asphalt is two words trying to assign blame."

Chapter 40

*The hardships I endured in this journeying business were long to tell—
peril and privation, storms and frost, which often overtook me when
alone in the wilderness. By the unfailing Grace of God our Lord I came
forth from all.*
—Alvar Nunez Cabeza de Vaca

*I told the officer that this was a very bad business; that it was very bad
for the commissioner to give such an order. I said it was very bad; that
we ought not to fight, because we were brothers, and the officer said
that that didn't make any difference; that Americans would fight even
though they were born of the same mother.*
—Nicaagat, of the White River Utes

According to Navajo mythology, the choice food of the gods is a
delicate medley of moistened pollen with game broth blended with the
dew of wildflowers. As the first light of predawn whispered the valley
awake, I would have settled for a donut and cup of coffee. A visit to
Noreen's ought to do the trick. Faster than she could say "Have a nice
day," I'd be sated and back on the road.

I'd spent the night hidden among Cottonwoods on the north bank of
Kerber Creek not a half mile from the center of town. Packing had become
second nature—done without thought: pannier, pannier, crazy creek,
sleeping bag, bungee cord, bungee cord, water bottles. Everything secure,
I wheeled Betsy onto U.S. 285 and rode the short distance to the store.

The creaky steps outside Noreen's broke the early morning silence,
but the sign on the door broke my heart. "Hours: Mon-Sat 8 A.M. - 11
P.M." I couldn't afford to wait an hour and a half. Denver and home
were calling, but so were hunger and thirst.

A pair of bananas left over from the day before put a dent in the former,
but three empty water bottles were as useful at soothing my parched
throat as teats on a bull. A nearby spigot offered momentary hope, but
nothing in the form of hydration. Desperate for liquid in any form, I
settled for a pair of Pepsi's out of a machine. "The choice of a new
generation" was the only choice I had. I swallowed one on the spot and
poured the other into a water bottle before heading north.

Still relatively straight, Route 285 begins to climb alongside San Luis
Creek at the north end of the valley. I started slowly, feeling the effects
of yesterday's 120 miles. Had this been the Tour De France, the European
papers would have reported I was suffering from *Le jour sans*, "The day
without." Without strength. Without energy. Without much food or water.
My legs were hollow, helpless, empty. My stomach moaned in protest.

I pulled over less than five miles up the climb to see what, if anything, my panniers could offer in terms of calories. With four mountain passes ahead, I'd need plenty of fuel, but the oatmeal, powdered milk and almonds I found qualified as somewhat less than a stocked pantry. Mixed together into a paste with a splash of Pepsi, the amalgam fell short of the food of gods, but I suppose it could have been worse—just ask the Donner Party.

Pasty enough to mortar bricks, the makeshift *dejeuner* kept my legs turning up the long, gradual climb out of Saguache County. Adapted from the Ute word, *sa-wa-ci*—meaning blue-green place—the name describes perfectly the stands of ponderosa pine and Colorado blue spruce through which the road ascends. Originally cut by the entrepreneurial Otto Mears in 1867, the first trail from the San Luis Valley into the Arkansas River basin was used to transport wheat to miners at California Gulch. Local Utes called the trail *poo-paca*—literally translated as "trail shoe"—or what we would call a footpath. But in a typical blunder of the time, the word was mispronounced by white settlers and subsequently misspelled when the time came to write it down. To all those who pass through it on U.S. Route 285, the 9,010 foot saddle which had once offered Mears the easiest access to hungry miners on the far side of the mountain is known as Poncha Pass.

Labeled as such by a large, green, highway sign, the low spot in the ridge line offered its congratulations with a clear northwest view of a cluster of snow-covered 14,000 foot peaks. From the pass, Mount Antero (14,269) rises slightly above Mount Shavano (14,229) to the south and Mount Princeton (14,197) to the north like the middle scoop of ice cream in a banana split. Barely visible over the western shoulder of Shavano, Tabeguache Mountain (14,155) draws as much attention in comparison as a single scoop of vanilla. Owing its name to the Ute tribe that populated these mountains for hundreds of years before the arrival of miners and mountain men, the peak's name literally translated means "sunny side," christened presumably by a northern band that wintered on Colorado's western slope—the side of the setting sun.

Despite an abundance of Ute place names in varying degrees of debacle, one would be hard pressed to find any tribal members living within the original 16 million acre reservation appointed the peaceful tribe in 1868. Carefully negotiated by Ouray, representing both the northern and southern bands, the document he finally signed stipulated that no unauthorized white men would "ever be permitted to pass over, settle upon, or reside in" the boundaries of the reservation.

Despite the restriction, miners continued to trespass, discovering great mineral wealth in the process. Over the next twelve years, the reservation was systematically carved up amid false rumors of savagery spread by Denver editor William B. Vickers and the state's first governor, Frederick Pitkin. The campaign to rid Colorado of Indians splashed across front pages from Fort Collins to Durango under the headline, "The Utes Must Go!" The lies had been so successful at convincing the fine citizens of Colorado that there was no room for red men, women or children, that a heart sick and terminally ill Ouray was brought to Washington in 1880 to sign away the last of his people's land, and agree to their relocation to a new reservation in Utah—on land the Mormons did not want. Except for a narrow strip of land in the southwestern corner of the state—set aside for a small band of southern Utes—Colorado had been cleared of Indians.

For all intents and purposes, the only Utes left in the central Rockies are "sport-utes." The one that flew by me at the pass was as big as Texas, as gadget-filled as the space shuttle, and as red as Santa's suit. With more cup holders than miles per gallon, the Ford Behemoth shot through the gap like a full back on a dive play. Colorado blue spruce closed in around the "light truck" as it crossed into Chaffee County and disappeared into the narrow canyon that leads down the northern slope to Poncha Springs and the rest of the Arkansas River Valley.

Still in morning shadow, bold smears of color filled the chasm—splashes of green among shades of crimson and carmine, as tenacious pinon grew where cracks in the red rock would allow. A fringe of darker spruce and ponderosa pine lined the higher ledges above browns, grays, and intermediate shades of granite. Deeper in the gorge, bluish limestone lurked in the shadows along side the growing creek. In a full tuck, I coasted all the way to Poncha Springs with hardly a pedal stroke.

A Texaco station stood on the far side of the bridge across the South Arkansas River. I stopped for water and something a bit more palatable to eat. A thin man with a crew cut stood behind the counter. He eyed my suspiciously as I walked up and down the isles searching for granola bars. Ultimately, he had to point them out.

North of Poncha Springs Route 285 flattens out as it makes its way through a wide valley carved by the Arkansas River. Legend has it the water is so cold that a rare breed of fur-bearing trout evolved in response. Of course when it came time to produce such a fish, explanations for its disappearance were similarly ludicrous. They ranged from interbreeding with the local fox population, to a leaky hot spring that changed the water temperature, to a bizarre life-or-death challenge race between the trout and a particularly competitive group of Mango-bats. Now *that* is one fish story.

Barbed wire crisscrosses the valley where bovines outnumber humans nine months of the year. It's only during June, July and August that the tables turn. As locals are apt to put it, "summer people, some are not."

With mine closings and a depressed beef market, tourism centered around commercial rafting has become the primary industry along the upper Arkansas. From Buena Vista to Canon City, over 120 outfitters share an eighty mile stretch of the river. Their operation brings millions of dollars into the region yearly.

Second-hand school buses hauling trailers stacked high with rafts labored by me on their way to one of dozens of put-in points. Boldly painted on the side of each bus, company names ranged from highly ambitious (Wild Water Runners) to relaxed (Lazy J Rafting). There were the politically correct (Wilderness Aware), the brash (Rif Raft), and even the biblical (Noah's Ark Rafting). Interspersed among the converted buses were roughly equal representatives of the trucking industry, retired mobile homers, and those young, attractive, outdoorsy SUV owners you see in all the ads. Fortunately, a wide shoulder turned the heavy traffic into more of a diversion than a threat.

Breezing over Brown Creek and through Nathrop on a tail wind, I was nearly tempted into an unplanned detour by a sign for the Mount Princeton Hot Springs. But the morning's ride had been kinder than I had expected. I felt loose and strong. My legs had limbered up to the point where they could make it without a warm soak.

All soreness was gone—or at least masked—by the time I reached the junction of U.S. 24 just outside Johnson Village. I turned right and rolled into a Mobil station where I filled my bottles and emptied my bowels. Before heading out, I opened the map and noticed "Antero Jct." lay just fourteen miles ahead on the other side of Trout Creek Pass (9,346). I felt it unnecessary to carry three full bottles up the 3,000 foot climb when I could refill just over the top. I drank most of one on the spot, dumped another, and slid the third into the cage on Betsy's down tube. After all, it was just fourteen miles to the next source. Or so I thought.

Blissfully ignorant, I took the bridge over the Arkansas River and began to climb in a low gear. A steady stream of cars, vans, campers and trucks—nearly bumper to bumper—passed inches to my left. The deadly combination of heavy traffic and a narrow shoulder had me on edge for the rest of the morning. Like drugs and alcohol, most people can handle them singly, but take their chances when mixing the two.

To stay out of the loose gravel, I had to ride directly on the white line—a technique that did not pose a problem to the majority of motorists courteous enough to pull over and give me room. But twice within a five minute span, monstrous RVs nearly knocked me off the road. "Peace on Earth," said the bumper sticker on the Ship Ahoy Land Lubber Limited Edition. But the message was lost on one trembling with fear and rage.

Despite sharing the same roads, I'd come to learn that I have almost nothing in common with those tourists who travel at five miles per gallon. Conversation after conversation made it clear that they are not, for the most part, seeking answers, but fleeing the truth of failing cities and the death of small-town America. The extent of their ornithological knowledge is represented by three descriptions: "little birds," "big birds," and "dead birds." Anything with needles over eight feet tall is identified as a "pine tree," while those under that height are called "Christmas trees," as if they constituted their own species—*Treeus chrismasius.*

While I sleep under the stars with nothing but sagebrush, snakes, and coyotes within miles, they crowd into RV parks—aluminum suburbs with steaks on the grill and beers in the ice box. Satellite dishes the size of a dinner plates complete the scene, and offer relief from the potential threat of boredom resulting from spending the night "in the middle of nowhere."

Protected from the sun, heat, and wind, these recreational nomads see America from the insides of Denny's and McDonald's restaurants. I've noticed they have trouble recalling the names of places they've been, as if checking them off a grand list is more important than building meaningful memories. Driving six figures on four wheels, it may appear to an accountant that their experience would naturally be twice as rich as mine. But life by the numbers cannot begin to approach the incalculable complexity and wonder of our interrelationships with the natural world.

I hit the pass with a holler and a fist raised in victory—one which proved bittersweet as I reached Antero Junction only to find a weathered cluster of abandoned buildings. A strong wind clawed at loose boards and rattled window panes. A rusty weather vane creaked from a rooftop. Antero Junction was a vacant as my water bottles—a sad testament to departed wealth.

I consulted the map and found Fairplay—twenty-one miles away across a broad plateau—to be my best bet. Even with a strong tail wind it would be at least an hour's ride.

Pushing a big gear, I made good time to Salt Creek and past the Antero Reservoir. I gazed longingly at millions of gallons of water through a chainlink fence. A thick, low ceiling of stratus clouds offered shelter from the mid-day sun. Combined with the elevation of the plateau, they kept the air comfortably cool. I hardly broke a sweat while turning a forty-six / fourteen mile after mile.

Fatigue began to set in near High Creek, and was fully present by the time I crossed the bridge over Fourmile. The flatness of the first ten miles out of Antero had given way to rolling hills, the last of which tested my will as well as my strength. I stood on the short climbs and coasted down the gradual descents—sure signs of muscle failure. The message was as clear as a telegram from the home office in Bonk City— forced retirement. At that point I would have traded the gold watch for a glass of water.

I could see the Texaco on the outskirts of town for what seemed an eternity. But like one of those brain teasers where you get halfway to your objective, and then half of that, and half of that, and so on, when do you finally reach it? My legs turned as they were trained to do but the gas station got no closer. Was it just a mirage?

The first thirty-two ounces may have been because they disappeared before I could even taste the lemon-lime flavor. Seven-up, Seven-down. A middle-aged woman behind the counter eyed me suspiciously as I refilled my largest bottle at the self-serve soda fountain. "Don't worry," I said. "I'll pay for all of it."

My assurance did nothing for the scowl on her face. Not even a joke at the register could budge a smile. Some folks are just as happy as they want to be.

I turned left onto Colorado Route 9 where a short, steep hill leads to downtown Fairplay—home of the World Championship Pack Burro Races. Each summer, men and beasts compete over a thirty mile course to Mosquito Pass and back, vying for the crown of world's swiftest jackass. A shorter course for female athletes was established a few years back as well as a llama division. Now women and guanacos have equal opportunity to compete for a crown.

The Fairplay Country Store was my finish line, and a jar of golden Skippy peanut butter my award. Along with a loaf of bread and a jar of jam, I headed across the street to where I shared a sandwich with an affectionate golden retriever in a wide, grassy park. Amazingly, he ate faster than I did.

Once the food was gone, he lost interest in me and tromped across the lawn to where a young couple had just laid out a blanket and opened an Igloo cooler. It looked liked the golden would have little time to charm them into a snack, however, as a bolt of lightening split the steel gray sky to the south. Moments later, a thunderous crash shook the electric air. An unbroken mass of violent clouds rolled into Fairplay like a locomotive. As the first drops fell, I scanned the area for options. The clearest also happened to be the closest.

A public library occupied the first floor of the old Park County Courthouse while the upstairs had been preserved as a museum. I tucked Betsy under the fire escape on the leeward side of the building and scrambled up the wide stone stairs to the front door. Driving rain assaulted the granite steps as I swung open the heavy, oak door and stepped inside. Dark. Quiet. Perfect.

The quintessential little old lady sat behind a desk to the right of the door. Stacks of books stood at each end of the desktop like paperback ramparts. Her sweet face peered out from between them. With short white hair, bifocals, and a warm smile, she was everyone's grandmother.

I suspected she had a tin of home-baked snickerdoodles tucked away somewhere within the fortress of her desk.

She remained seated and spoke through the twin parapets of literature. "Welcome to the old Park County Courthouse and library. If you're here for the museum, there is a self-guided tour available for the original courtroom upstairs. It's full of interesting history about law and order in the early days of the county. Would you like a copy?"

"No thanks. I'm not really here for the museum."

"All right then, to check books out you need to become a member. I've got the slips right here in my desk." She leaned to her left and disappeared behind a stack of books.

"Thanks, but I'm not here to take out books either."

She reappeared with an intensely worried look on her face. "We don't keep a cash drawer."

"No, no, no. I just wanted to get out of the rain."

"Oh, that's fine." She sighed with relief. "But as long as you're here, you might like to take a look around."

"Sure."

"Let me know if you have any questions."

"Thanks." I turned away and then back. "How did Fairplay get its name?"

"Well, it was originally called Park City, but that was changed when they put in the first post office. The name Fairplay came from the miners over in Jefferson. You know where that is?"

I nodded even though I didn't.

"Well, they staked all the claims over on Michigan Creek and Tarryell Creek too. After a while there was no room for any new prospectors. So they decided to come over here to the South Platte to get their "fair play" of the gold.

Chapter 41

Reading western history according to the frontier model was a bit like reading Shakespeare in an edited version allowing only one character per play.
—Patricia Nelson Limerick

Fair play is all they wanted. A square deal for straight-shooting men. We use less colorful terms today—like equity and justice—but their meanings are the same, and their attainability equally elusive. In a region that prides itself on independence, strength and honesty, it's impossible to ignore the hypocrisy inherent in a system of government handouts that weakens the land and perpetuates itself through a movement based on deception. Where is independence in government subsidies? Where is strength in lost fertility? Where is honesty in the Wise Use Movement? The West is where the past, present and future of America's frontier come together in a jumbled mass of myth and reality, straight talk and contradiction.

I climbed the creaky wooden stairs and entered the courtroom. From a chair behind the prosecutor's desk, I looked to the empty judge's bench, witness stand, and jury box. Placing my elbows lightly on the desk, I leaned forward, set my chin on my knuckles, and took a deep breath.

Independence

Despite the temptation to romanticize my journey, it would not have been possible without the efforts of others. Color me resourceful, hearty, optimistic and hopeful, but certainly not independent. Traveling on carbohydrates rather than gasoline does not isolate one from a fossil fuel economy. Oil built these roads, built my bicycle, grew my food, and delivered it. A bicycle tourist is as dependent on the American economic and political structures as surely as those structures rely on the greater ecological systems within which they exist. "Independence," wrote George Bernard Shaw. "That's middle class blasphemy! We are all dependent on one another, every soul of us on earth."

By most accounts America is a middle class nation infused with a resounding belief in independence. We hold tight to a history that recalls liberation from colonial oppression. Our forefathers cut the cord and freed a nation. Yet seven generations after Thomas Jefferson penned the Declaration of Independence, the time has come for a Declaration of Interdependence. We enjoy the protection of a Bill of Rights, but what about a Bill of Responsibilities? Debates have raged over the nature of rights, but little is mentioned about the rights of nature.

Economic systems in which natural resources are treated as essentially unlimited have become known as "cowboy economies." They exist primarily in nations settled by European emigrants—Australia, Canada and the U.S.—and are often supported by government subsidies, the oldest and most destructive of which cater to the mining, logging and livestock industries. Thanks to the General Mining Law of 1872, hardrock mining is essentially free on most public land in the West. Timber sales in National Forests regularly bring in less revenue than the Forest Service spends on administering the contracts. The federal government loses millions more dollars annually leasing public rangelands at roughly one third the going rate on privately-owned land. In effect, American taxpayers are paying private interests to fleece our public lands.

Of course the thought of abolishing resource-based industries is ludicrous. Ranching, logging and mining provide jobs as well as much-needed raw materials. Ranchers further benefit society by preserving much of the open space that gives the region it's identity. Walter Prescott Webb contends that the ranching system in the West is "perhaps the most unique and distinctive institution that America has produced." Be that as it may, there needs to be a greater balance between economics and ecology that the current system of cowboy economics does not allow. Of what value is a subsidy that leads to ecological degradation?

The Soil Conservation Service has determined that fully one half of irrigation water in the West never reaches the intended crops due to inefficient systems of dispersal. Twenty-three million acre-feet are lost annually to evaporation and non-crop vegetation. Almost all government subsidies like the one that allows this gross mismanagement of a precious resource are rank with similar flaws.

Most subsidies go to large corporations that do not generally provide a substantial number of jobs. Agriculture and other resource-based industries including logging and mining are only modest contributors to total personal income in the West compared with revenue generated by the service industry, retirement payments, and federal, state and local governments. Along with retirees and tourists, information-based entrepreneurs using global communications systems serve as the backbone of the new western economy.

With this in mind, many contend that the time has come to strip resource-based industries of out-dated subsidies and force them to shoulder the true costs of their activities. After all, a free market economy relies on a level playing field. If the subsidization of rural communities is indeed a goal that America wants to pursue, there are less environmentally damaging ways to go about it.

Taking the bull by the horns, it's time we dare the seemingly un-American act of reexamining the role of the cowboy. Any notion that remains of a lone man on horseback wrestling a noble living from an unforgiving land is purely romantic. Although this image embodies what it means to be an American, it should not, and cannot be preserved at the expense of the land and future generations. Where will they go to get their fair play?

The stakes are high for the American West, higher than we can understand. It would take someone fluent in double-talk, stock quotes and the call of the wild to make sense of it all. The problems we face are much more complex than those of the 1800's, and clinging to centuries-old laws is about as useful as fixing a flat tire with a horseshoe.

Strength

In theory, public lands are managed for the public. This is not always the case in practice. Government agencies such as the BLM, Forest Service, and Park Service are caught between two factions with vastly different views on how to use the land. While one maintains a strictly economic interest, the other urges conservation. As the political tide of our nation ebbs and flows, either one may find itself invited to the bargaining table at any given time. While neither side can ever claim complete domination in Washington, the decisions they influence seem always to be the same. Land that cannot support grass or timber and does not hold any valuable minerals is set aside for protection, while land with even a hint of economic value is adamantly contested. "Money makes the world go 'round," they say. But does it?

In many ways the pursuit of material wealth is gumming up the natural machinery that makes life possible on the planet. World wide, governments direct over $500 billion a year toward programs and activities that compromise ecological integrity. In the United States, seventy-two such programs—many of which operate primarily in the West—have been identified as costing taxpayers over $52 billion annually. And at what cost to the environment?

Subsidized grazing fees often lead to overstocking on marginal lands that have led to soil erosion, watershed disruption, and the loss of native habitats and the species that depend on them. The BLM reports that grazing on its lands causes twenty-five percent of all plant and fourteen percent of all animal endangered species listings. A 1992 report by the General Accounting Office estimates that fully one half of rangeland in the U.S. is severely degraded—its carrying capacity reduced by over fifty percent.

Below-cost timber sales result from the Forest Service doing much of the site work itself instead of passing the costs on to the timber companies that benefit. The work includes engineering and building roads, conducting environmental assessments, and cleaning up after a cut. Along with the loss of $400 million a year, national forests are also losing precious top soil, wildlife habitat, and migration routes. Soil erosion and water pollution have resulted in lower productivity in many areas, while pesticide use has increased due to a move toward carefully managed monoculture where only certain economically valuable species are encouraged to grow.

Development, both commercial and residential, is just the latest threat to rural America—most recently and rapidly in the West. A 1996 landscape survey indicates that open land is being developed at a rate of 1.2 acres per hour. Roughly 168,000 hectares, an area the size of two New York Cities, was paved over each year between 1982 and 1992. In the West, where growth rates are highest, thirty-nine counties in Arizona, Idaho, Montana, Nevada, New Mexico, Utah, Wyoming, and Colorado grew anywhere from twenty and sixty-five percent from 1990 to 1995. Of the 281 counties in those eight western states, it's estimated that fully one-third of the 2 million newcomers settled in just those thirty-nine. The cumulative effect of such rapid growth is becoming evident from space where satellite images show that the largest western cities—Denver, Albuquerque, Phoenix, Las Vegas and Salt Lake—are gradually spreading toward each other like ink blots across parchment.

In Colorado alone, 532,000 acres of rural land were developed between 1982 and 1992. With 3,500 acres of rural land bulldozed each day to make room for buildings, highways, and other developments, what is to become of the wide open spaces that define the West? Joni Mitchell warned us all about "paving paradise," but did we listen? How long will it be until that "Big Yellow Taxi" comes to take *us* away?

We can flex our mechanically enhanced muscle with the help of chainsaws and bulldozers, but for us to prove our strength in a zero-sum expression of power, there must be a weaker. More often than not, that role is played by nature. In a culture dominated by "male thinking," Father Time is given priority over Mother Nature. After all, time is money. And money makes the world go 'round.

But what good is a million dollars to someone who is spiritually bankrupt? Why does the United States—one of the wealthiest nations on Earth—also have the largest drug problem? Why do executives with six figure incomes, three cars, and two houses leap from their twenty-third floor office windows on random Tuesday afternoons? One hundred years ago, John C. Van Dyke recognized the intoxicating power of money; "The main affair of life is to get the dollar, and if there is any money in cutting the throat of Beauty, why, by all means cut her throat."

In the name of economic development, we've grown fat and happy by playing Jack the Ripper on this continent for centuries. Our so-called "cowboy economy"—where natural resources are treated as limitless—

has provided vast wealth and built the most powerful nation on the planet. When we finally wake up from this "American Dream," how will the hangover feel?

Public lands contain critical habitat for wildlife, provide clean drinking water for communities, store atmospheric carbon in their vegetation, absorb flood waters during storms, and are home to numerous archeological and cultural treasures. Can we put a price tag on these?

Do we really need more roads, more beef, more dams, more jewelry? What we need is an open and honest discussion about the future of our species—not to mention a quarter of a million others. We are performing a grand experiment on the planet with absolutely no idea how it will turn out. Instead of conducting it cautiously—using carefully reviewed scientific theories—the driving force is purely financial. We are headed into the twenty-first century at breakneck economic speed. When national policy around the world is set using the assumption of continued economic growth, one can't help but to ask how such growth can continue indefinitely on a planet with quite definite limits. Like hyper-competitive lemmings we are racing each other toward the brink of the great unknown.

Strength in a human form was first defined on this continent by native peoples. It was written into the bodies of Sioux braves during the Sun Dance ceremony. Offering up to one hundred pieces of flesh cut from his arms and shoulders, a warrior could sacrifice a "red blanket" to the Great Mystery. Often times, a first time participant offered himself to be strung up to a sacred pole by skewers pierced through the loose skin of his breast. Similar skewers thrust through his back were fastened by thongs to heavy buffalo skulls. As an ultimate show of sacrifice, he was raised into the air and left to dangle until the skulls pulled themselves free, and finally his own body weight tore the skewers from his breast.

This display of strength, faith and stamina is at once perhaps the best known of Indian festivals and the least understood. The severity of the self-torture shocked whites who failed to understand it's deeper meaning. According to tribal tradition, the offering of material possessions to the Great Mystery was simply an act of giving back what was originally his. The only true sacrifice a man could make was one of body and blood to the highest manifestation of the Great Mystery: the sun.

Beyond the Sioux, similar ceremonies performed by other tribes were called variously "Thirsting Dance," "Medicine Dance," "New Life Lodge," "Lodge of the Generator," and "Making a Home." Although the names may differ, at the heart of this ceremony practiced by nearly all Plains tribes is the respect and sacrifice offered to a greater power, the provider of light and life.

The beliefs of a people rooted to a place despite the efforts of others to uproot them come as precious gifts to their former oppressors. As industrialized western culture hurtles helter skelter toward the judgment of a new millennium, can their simple words of wisdom be heard? If America—as the most powerful and consumptive nation on the planet—is to survive the next century, it must take to heart the ideology of the first inhabitants of Turtle Island. Native Americans are the first to admit that their strength and perseverance come from a deep faith in the land, and that their "self-reliance" is due to its generosity.

As native peoples have recognized all along, ecological integrity—the level of stability or *strength* of an ecosystem—relies on the diversity of its inhabitants. Although biologists have also come to recognize the importance of a complex web of interrelationships, habitats across the country and around the world continue to lose species at alarming rates. Harvard entomologist E.O. Wilson urges us to bear in mind, "that the rest of life is the cradle in which the human species evolved, and all those millions of other species that surround us run the world the way we would wish it to run. They create an atmosphere, a soil, a total environment around us to which our genes—our biology—are beautifully adapted. It is very much to our advantage to maintain it."

Do we have the courage to do what it takes, or will we be remembered as the generation that impoverished the Earth more than any other in history? What else have we to offer our grandchildren but dirty air, fouled streams, and 40 million acres of cheat grass? In cowboy jargon, much of this great land has been "rode hard and hung up wet."

Honesty

Truth be told, the code of the West was not written on the American frontier. It was penned by eastern authors like Owen Wister (Philadelphia) and Zane Grey (New York). Neither man ever worked as a cow-boy (as Wister spelled it), or even spent much time in the West. But they didn't let those facts get in the way of a good story. Along with creating a genre and setting the standard, Wister accomplished the formidable feat of making the cow-boy a respectable—even honorable—character. Although the traits embodied by his nameless hero in *The Virginian*—courage, honor, chivalry and individualism—have little foundation in fact, Wister's book sold over 3 million copies through fifteen printings in just seven years. It later went on to become a hit play on Broadway and a series of films starring Gary Cooper (1929), Joel McCrea (1946), and Bill Pullman (2000).

With the coming of motion pictures in the late 1800's, Hollywood fueled the fantasy sparked by Wister and Grey. The terms "gunslinger," "bounty hunter," and "itchy trigger finger" were all coined by screenwriters who turned the Saturday matinee into a mainstay of American life. From the early days of William S. Hart and Will Rogers through John Wayne, Roy Rogers and Clint Eastwood the Western has endured as the most successful movie formula ever. These men came to exemplify the genre, achieving idol status among millions of boys yearning to prove they too had the stuff. The legend of these celluloid heroes spread across America and to unlikely places like India, Italy and Japan. The cowboy became our ambassador to the world and his message was the freedom of self-reliance.

In an attempt to keep audiences entertained from one generation to the next, the legends of Custer, Billy the Kid, and Wyatt Erp became adaptable, with Hollywood consistently changing and evolving the portrayal of these western icons. Legends were manipulated to suit the tastes of the day, and even the clear sense of right and wrong known as "Frontier Justice" has changed with the times. None the less, it remains at the heart of the genre. But what has that sense of justice come to mean at the brink of a new millennium? No longer simply a man who brings cattle to market, it's time we took a broader look at the *idea* of the American cowboy.

Over the last month, I'd come to learn that this image we hold as a culture has little to do with cows, or boys for that matter. The Colt 45 did not tame the West. Barbed wire, windmills and pickup trucks have long since put an end to the traditional role of the vaquero, just as skidders and chainsaws have done to the lumberjack, and drag lines and dump trucks to the prospector. Four-wheelers, snowmobiles and even helicopters have replaced the man in the saddle. No longer are the techniques of riding and rope handling a necessity. Like so many of our grandparent's skills, they have been bypassed in the name of progress— preserved only in a forum of entertainment and competition at the rodeo.

Over 40,000 men once worked as cowhands in the U.S. territories. Today, less than half that number remains. As Paula Cole's recent hit asks, "Where have all the cowboys gone?" According to history, most were replaced to barbed wire. Of those who survived the cut, many have replaced the wide-brimmed sombreros emblematic of the trade with baseball caps—it's easier when driving a pickup truck. Even a hundred years ago, you'd be hard pressed to find a cowboy riding around with a six-shooter dangling from his cartridge belt. Such accouterments only hampered work, and were generally stored out of sight in a chaps pocket or saddle bag. Sheep herders were far more likely to be toting lead since coyotes, wolves and mountain lions alike seemed to prefer raiding flocks to wrestling with an ornery steer.

The West as it was is gone: cattle can be trained to respond to a whistle; rustlers are no longer hanged; and the famous Boot Hill Cemetery now lies under a supermarket parking lot in Dodge City, Kansas. Of the thirty-four people buried there during the city's infamous decade of lawlessness, most died of natural causes. Davy Crockett never even wore a coonskin cap, and according to recent research, may have spent much of the battle of the Alamo hiding under a bed.

Running the risk of impaling myself on the horns of a sacred cow, I feel it's important to expand our understanding of the true history of the American West and its most beloved icon. We cannot wrap our mythologies around us like blankets to fend off the cold chill of truth. As Aldus Huxley has reminds us, "Facts do not cease to exist simply because they are ignored."

To find the earliest "American" cowboys, one must look beyond the mid-1800's—as popularly believed—and even beyond the Great American Dessert. At least thirty years before the mainland, Hawaiian cowboys known as *paniolos* were raising cattle. Although not yet a state, the island chain supplied much of the beef for California's Gold Rush prospectors.

What mythology survived the questioning of the Vietnam era and the Equal Rights Movement, Gary Snyder claims was rubbed out by the 1980 presidential election of Ronald Reagan. According to Snyder, it was on a Tuesday in November that the CEO replaced the cowboy as our nation's dominant archetype. Corinthian leather bucket seats replaced weather-buffed saddles, as it became a corporate buckaroo riding off into the sunset proudly displaying his brand—BMW.

Despite the Reagan years, however, the legend of the West lives on. The cowboy ethos in this country dies hard. Although it is undeniably a part of our American identity, does it really exist beyond our minds? In an age of automobiles, fast food, and home shopping, a vast majority of us are losing touch with those very ideals. With the world at our fingertips, most of us no longer work with our hands. In the land of the free and the home of the brave, we are slaves to the clock and afraid of...almost everything: losing our jobs, growing old, cancer, gaining weight, losing weight, public speaking, crime, the list goes on and on. Millions of Americans live lives in quiet desperation—alienated and alone, but not independent.

Putting an American icon on trial plum tuckered me out. I dozed in the darkened courtroom while a heavy gray sky let loose over Colorado's high country. Hours later, sunshine streaming through the west-facing windows woke me from a fitful sleep. I sat up and looked at the twelve empty seats to my right. The jury was still out.

"Did you have a nice visit?" the librarian asked when I reached the bottom of the stairs.

"Yes, thank you."

"That's nice. I'm glad you liked it. Now I just wanted to let you know that we close up at five o'clock."

I looked at the wall clock behind her and then at my watch. They both agreed it was 4:45. "I'm about to head out now."

"You take care of yourself."

"I will," I said, but I didn't.

Climbing to Red Hill Pass (9,993) was just the beginning. On cold legs, the relatively easy ascent became formidable. Turning the pedals was like pushing pistons in syrup. The pass came slowly and passed without ceremony. Simple relief marked the summit.

Spinning past the turn off for Como and into Jefferson offered relief to my awakening quadriceps, but it was just the eye of the storm, a sucker hole, the calm before the real squall. The day's last climb through Kenosha Pass (10,001) took a final toll. Arduous, onerous, irksome and more. Herculean. It was the Cretan Bull, the Nemean Lion, the Lernaean Hydra...all twelve labors rolled into one. Lactic acid burned like the fires of Hades. Digging deep and thinking Greek, somehow I managed to keep the pedals turning.

Cramping muscles forced me to stand on Betsy's lowest gear through the last two switchbacks. Little more than body weight made each half-revolution possible. The bike swung slowly from side to side as I shifted my entire torso over one leg and then the other. The slow, deliberate movement repeated itself like an exercise in Tai Chi. A simple mantra accompanied the rhythmic motion. I think I can. I think I can. I think...I think...I thunk...I thought. I did!

Standing where Sisyphus never had, I joined the immortals. I felt the strength of Atlas, the power of Zeus...the hubris of Odysseus. The gates of Heaven slammed shut as I glanced to my left and saw Mount Evans towering another 4,000 feet above me. Remembering that the map showed a road leading to its summit put my minor accomplishment in proper perspective. I pedaled on with humility, making a deal with myself that where ever Betsy stopped coasting, we would stay for the night. When her momentum ceased, so would mine.

But like many deals people make with themselves, it was soon broken. We often underestimate our abilities—both as individuals and collectively—when pushing our perceived limits, and come to realize we are capable of far more than we ever imagined. As a fellow cyclist once told me, "Sometimes your mind makes a decision but your legs don't agree."

Spinning lightly down the back side of the mountain, I found my legs again. They recovered more quickly than I had expected. After 100 miles and four mountain passes, they still held signs of life. This is not to say that the weary appendages would have consented to a fifth climb, but they were agreeable enough to spin alongside the North Fork of the Platte River through Grant and Shawnee.

At the far end of Bailey, while the river continues southeast to its confluence with Craig Creek, Route 285 swings northeast and up Crow Hill. Experience dictates that when a hill is large enough to deserve a name, it's for good reason. At the foot of the climb, I suddenly became enamored with the little town of Bailey. All at once, its charm was irresistible. I headed for the Country Store to pick up supplies for dinner.

I placed a dozen corn tortillas and a can of refried beans on the wooden counter where a hundred thousand transactions had worn away the varnish. An acoustic rhythm came from a portable radio beside the cash register. I'd heard the song a hundred times before, but found myself listening to it for the first. The lilting melody of a young songwriter from West Virginia drew my ear in a way like never before. His words touched my soul. They could have been my own. Suddenly I understood his Rocky Mountain High.

> He was born in the summer of his twenty-seventh year,
> coming home to a place he'd never been before.
> When he first came to the mountains, his life was far away-
> on the road, hanging by a song.

Epilogue
The Upshot

Traveling is largely a business of intentionally journeying into yourself and what you mean in relation to the rest of the world and all of history.
—Paul Fussell

The planes won't fly, the rockets won't go up. The bomb won't work. Somebody will turn off the electricity. The computers go crazy. The whole goddamn system, the wasichu system will break down. The commanders and generals, the senators and the millionaires, the president himself and all the scientists, won't know what to do. They'll wind up eating snakes, nothing but snakes.
—Henry Crow Dog, Rosebud, South Dakota, 1981

Our migratoriness has hindered us from becoming a people of communities and traditions, especially in the West. It has robbed us of the gods who make places holy. It has cut off individuals and families and communities from memory and the continuum of time. It has left at least some of us with a kind of spiritual pellagra, a deficiency disease, a hungering for the ties of a rich and stable social order.
—Wallace Stegner, 1987

Evening found me on a dirt road off 285 behind a housing development. Located an hour's drive from Denver, Bailey marks the cutoff for most of those who spend their days inside the city's glass towers. A few foolhardy commuters may live further up, but many thousands inhabit the hillsides below. Nestled among evergreens on the slopes of Crow Hill stood houses of every size, shape and color-big ones, small ones, white ones, brown ones. Park County is one of the fastest growing counties in Colorado-a real estate agent's dream, but a cyclist's nightmare.

I pushed Betsy further up the rutted jeep trail alongside a babbling brook until a locked gate blocked my way. "Keep Out - Abandoned Mine Site." Both warning and legacy, the message adorns gates and fence posts throughout the Rocky Mountain West. A sign of the times usually hangs from a rusty nail.

Standing before the iron-stained placard, the song I'd heard earlier echoed in my head.

His life was full of wonder but his heart still knows some fears
of the simple things he cannot comprehend.
Like why they tear the mountains down to bring a couple more
more people, more scars upon the land.

On my last night in the mountains, the anguished words of John Denver came home like they never had before-reminding me of the harsh reality which faces a land known to most American's only through myth.

I crossed my arms and leaned against a sturdy pine. Above the feathery canopy, a crescent moon glowed like a silver shaving on a velvet cloth. Two thousand, one hundred and sixty miles across, its diameter roughly equal to the distance I'd bicycled over the last four weeks-one lunar cycle. A depression on the near side-the Sea of Tranquility-stretches as far and wide as the Colorado Plateau.

I laid my head back against the scaly, golden bark. A faint smell of butterscotch wafted through the air. I knew without looking it was a ponderosa pine. In Latin, ponderosa describes something heavy, weighty, significant. In verb form, it means to mentally weigh or reflect upon. As the last rays of direct light slipped over the ridge behind me, I looked back upon the last month-my time to ponder.

Through the Dakotas, Wyoming, Utah, New Mexico and Colorado, I'd covered over 2,000 miles of heat, wind, sand and sage-garnering an appreciation for the West unmatched by a whirlwind tour of eight national parks in ten days.

The odyssey became one of deep knowledge, one of empathy for the land and its diverse inhabitants. The western landscape is defined by its size, climate and lack of water. I knew them all. My legs had propelled me over the vast expanses. My skin had burned like the desert sands under an unforgiving sun. My parched throat had yearned for moisture like a dry arroyo. I'd learned more from four weeks on the road than four years in college. Yet strangely, questions still outnumbered answers.

Not far from the Sea of Tranquility lies the Ocean of Storms. The Moon appeared as much a place of contrast as the American West. From burning droughts to freezing blizzards, from Pike's Peak to Death Valley, from the tiny prairie dog to the mighty bison, the West is a land of extremes-extremes that extend beyond the climate, topography and wildlife to include people, history and the law of the land.

1872 may not have seemed like a particularly significant year to those eking out a living on America's frontier, but back in Washington, decisions were being made that would effect forever the way people see the land. That otherwise indistinguishable year gave birth to two of the most significant programs the West would ever see. One marked the beginning of an era of land preservation, while the other encouraged exploitation.

On March 1st, President Ulysses S. Grant signed an act of Congress setting aside 2,142,720 acres of unblemished wilderness. "The tract of land in the Territories of Montana and Wyoming lying near the headwaters of the Yellowstone River...is hereby reserved and withdrawn from settlement, occupancy, or sale under the laws of the United States, and dedicated and set apart as a public park or pleasuring ground for the benefit and enjoyment of the people." With these words, Yellowstone became the nation's, the world's, first national park.

An American original, the conservation program has been adopted by over fifty countries. Central to the national park idea are two principles: that a nation should identify and preserve its finest natural areas; and that these areas should be maintained in accordance with the laws of nature for the benefit of present and future generations.

Later that same year, Grant signed the General Mining Law which permitted any citizen to explore for hardrock minerals on public land and to enter a claim. The new law was the latest in a series of attempts by Washington to settle the left-hand side of the continent. Like the Homestead Act signed by President Abraham Lincoln in 1862, an enticing array of incentives, discounts and rewards were offered for any young man or woman daring to "Go West."

Collectively, the incentive programs convinced scores of pilgrims to follow the setting sun in search of prosperity. With a jump start from the gold rush, settlement occurred more quickly than anyone had anticipated. Prospectors came from all walks of life and in every conceivable size, shape and personality. By 1893, blank spots on the map were sufficiently scarce for Frederick Jackson Turner to declare the frontier officially closed. The laws had served their purpose and it was time to move on.

Everything went according to plan until the time came-as originally intended-to phase out the subsidies. But it never happened. Ranching, mining and timber industries-as well as the railroads-had grown to enjoy the subsidies far too much to see them go. Silver-tongued lobbyists were dispatched to Washington and have kept a tight rein on western politics ever since. More than a century after the General Mining Law had run its course, it remains on the books. On the verge of a new millennium, the western economy refuses to loose its grip on a nineteenth century public lands policy designed to encourage settlement. As we enter the twenty-first century, it is time to break free from the 1800's.

Arches, Bryce, Zion, Canyonlands, Capitol Reef, Mesa Verde, Grand Canyon, Dinosaur, Natural Bridges. The Colorado Plateau is home to the nation's greatest concentration of National Parks and monuments-hundreds of thousands of acres set aside not only as "pleasuring ground(s) for the benefit and enjoyment of the people," but also as reservoirs of biological diversity. (The name Colorado Plateau is itself a fine example of diversity-a Spanish word coupled with a French word set in the middle of the American West.) Only recently have ecologists recognized what most native cultures have known all along-that all life is connected in a vast and intricate web. Everything effects everything. Nothing happens in isolation.

It is no coincidence that the latest discoveries in many disciplines of science echo what has been for thousands of years an integral part of indigenous philosophy: "All things are connected." Chief Seattle spoke the words in 1855. Aldo Leopold echoed them a century later in the final section of *A Sand County Almanac,* as did James Lovelock in another thirty years in his "Gaia Theory." Native peoples were "systems thinkers" long before the term was coined.

To understand the world systematically requires one to put its individual pieces together into a context of space and time, to establish the nature of their relationships. Contrary to what the Cartesian world view has drilled into western minds over the last three centuries, the properties of individual objects are not intrinsic properties. As physicist and philosopher Fritjof Capra contends, they "can be understood only within the context of the greater whole." The character of an individual plant cannot be discerned without reference to the soil in which it grows or the insects and animals that feed off it. Yet none of those creatures can be understood without looking at other plants and animals with which they interact up and down the food chain.

In the same way, each tract of preserved land cannot be understood without reference to the unprotected acreage surrounding it. Piecemeal conservation is no longer recognized as sufficient in what Paul Erlich calls "an increasingly polluted and overpopulated world." Without a coherent policy that addresses the issues of population growth and the pollution that accompanies it, the national parks will not survive despite our best efforts to save them. They cannot exist as islands of purity in a sea of sprawl and waste. The effects of pollution are already evident in even the most isolated parks.

"Do nothing to mar its grandeur," commanded President Teddy Roosevelt of the Grand Canyon in 1903. "Keep it for your children and your children's children, and all who come after you, as the one great sight which every American should see." But on many days the "one great sight" goes unseen by those very children's children. Air pollution from as far away as Phoenix, Los Angeles and Las Vegas often cuts visibility in half at the canyon's rim, draining the thick rock layers of their color and contrast. For an average of forty-two days each winter, canyon visitors must peer through a murky soup of tainted air. The culprits are primarily cars, power plants, and mining smelters.

During this century the 1872 Mining Law has primarily served large companies, allowing them to "patent," or buy, twenty-acre tracts of land often for less than five dollars an acre. Called by opponents a "license to steal" from the public trust, there are three main factors which contribute to billions of dollars in lost revenue and cleanup costs annually. First, the federal treasury receives no royalties from mining companies which extract close to $3 billion worth of hardrock minerals from public lands each year. Second, the patenting process allows corporations to pick up mineral rights for pennies on the dollar. And finally, the cleanup of abandoned sites is estimated to cost between $32 billion and $72 billion. With these factors in mind, it's not hard to see why the Law is known to those who oppose it as the "Grandaddy of All Subsidies."

Environmentally, the law has been the kiss of death for rivers throughout the West. When mines are abandoned and pumping stops, contaminated groundwater rises and seeps into free flowing creeks, streams and eventually public drinking water supplies. According to the Bureau of Mines, over 12,000 miles of riparian habitat have been polluted by mining activities. More than 550,000 abandoned hardrock mines riddle the country, leaving open pits, tailing piles, and an endless string of questions. (Like how can patenting under the General Mining Law turn public lands into golf courses, ski resorts, and condominiums?)

With a wave of political reform sweeping the nation, western extractionists are preparing for battle. After giving out more than 287 million acres to homesteaders, 61 million acres to veterans, 94 million acres to the railroads, and 328 million acres to states, the federal government is finding that many of those entities want more. Leading the way, the Wise Use Movement is pulling out all the punches in an attempt to force Washington to hand over much of the remaining 726 million acres of federal land-including that already protected-to states, counties and private interests. The General Mining Law of 1872 has become emblematic of the struggle.

Set against the National Park Act, it helps define a rift in land use policy as deep and wide as the Grand Canyon itself. Ironically enough, it was a small group of determined entrepreneurs with their hearts and wallets set on the mineral wealth of the Canyon that blocked its designation as a national park for thirty years. In this classic struggle over a massive hole in the ground lies the heart of our relationship to the land, and, in a very real way, to ourselves. Our understanding and treatment of the outer landscape, as Paul Rezendes believes, is inseparable from that of our inner landscape, a realm "as vast and deep, and wild as the outer" but whose path is one less traveled.

Ours is a culture drawn to the quick fix, medicated solutions, and looking outward for answers to life's deepest questions. Time and again, we turn to "the experts" for their "professional opinions." More and more often, those opinions suggest the regular use of prescription pills. From squelching toenail fungus to easing depressions, pharmaceutical companies promise better living through chemistry. Never mind that "side effects" may include headache, nausea, upset stomach, watery eyes, running nose, congestion, dizziness, diarrhea, constipation, and "liver and kidney problems." DDT and thinned egg shells, CFCs and the ozone hole, dioxin and cancer-isn't it clear to us by now that there are no "side effects?"

Word play. It's all in the spin. There may be desired effects and undesired effects, but they are both *effects*. Describing undesired effects as "side" may ease our minds, but it does nothing to the way the chemical behaves. Once again we're faced with the reality that everything truly is connected. Impossible to ever fully understand, yet comprehensible to a newborn, the web of life enfolds our every movement, thought, and breath.

It's easy to talk about interconnectedness and the web of life, but talk is cheap. How can we implement these beliefs into our lives? How can we act accordingly?

In the Navajo tradition, a life of harmony, or *hozho*, comes only to those who walk through this world of infinite temptations with great care, building strong bonds with the Good Winds by maintaining a great respect for the land. Far from a passive participant, the deeds and thoughts of an individual can affect the Air in myriad ways. *Nilch 'i*, the Holy Wind, embraces every man and woman-indeed, every being-filling their lungs, filling their lives. It is through this involvement with the invisible wind that the Navajo believe they can influence events in the landscape itself. From bringing rain to ensuring an abundant game supply, the emphasis on deep reflection and prayer is to ensure the yet to emerge will come when the time is right.

For the Navajo looking to renew his *hozho*, or anyone wishing to attain a condition of harmony and beauty, the journey lies within. For it is only by being at peace with oneself, can one project that peace to the universe. After the individual has released *hozho* to the cosmos through ritual, he breathes it back into himself, thus ensuring his place in the greater order he has helped to create.

Central to the Blessingway ceremony, this belief is one of a reciprocal relationship between the people and their animate surroundings. Both inhaling and exhaling the sacred winds, Navajos are sustained by the cosmos while simultaneously sustaining it. The air, therefore, has a particular capacity to allow cognition as well as intelligence. Living in a world where the air occupies every unfilled space within the body and without, traditional Navajos believe that our thoughts do not belong to us alone. Instead, the mind belongs to the greater world in which humans-along with all organisms-are but participants. Thus, one's sense of personal identity is merely a small part of the identity of the land itself, and any harm that may befall the land, in turn, befalls those who live there. In this way, the beauty and harmony of each individual becomes inseparable from that of the earth.

This way of seeing the world, however, is not limited to the shores of Turtle Island. Norwegian philosopher Arne Naess calls this way of thinking "Deep Ecology." Englishman James Lovelock, a former engineer, uses the term Gaia. Yet another European, Austrian physicist Fritjof Capra, in his aptly named *The Web of Life*, contends that the "connection between an ecological perception of the world and corresponding behavior is not a logical but a psychological connection." And that "if we have deep ecological awareness, or experience, of being part of the web of life, then we *will* (as opposed to *should*) be inclined to care for all living nature." In the words of Mahatma Gandhi, "Be the change you want to see in the world." Coming from an Indian who lived 3,000 miles from the American Southwest, the message is more or less the same.

Only by looking within and recognizing our connection with all of nature can human beings be at peace with themselves and the world. We realize our humanity only within the world that enfolds us. This is the most ancient of truths. It is the basis of religion, the allegory of faith, and the foundation for wonder. Each of us is the universe trying to express itself through us.

After years of living on the plains of South Dakota, Kathleen Norris believes that the longer Europeans remain in America, the more Indian we will become-a deep connection to Turtle Island built slowly over generations. She recognizes our longing for connection, but believes we will never find it by looking outward as we are apt to do. Instead we must look inward to find the deep-seeded tribal spirituality that lies within us all.

Much of the history of Europeans on this continent centers around some form of exploitation. First there were the eastern tribes, and then the African slaves. From beaver pelts to buffalo hides. From gold, and silver, and copper mining to lumber, and petroleum, and uranium. Every boom in the West has ended not only in bust, but in a busted landscape: abandoned mines, polluted watersheds, clearcuts, desertification. And if anything ever stood in the way of profit, we got rid of it: the Indian, the grizzly, the wolf. By now we ought to be familiar enough with the pattern to break it, to find balance, to live in harmony with the land.

Although this may seem like a radical brain shift for most Americans, closer examination reveals that much of the groundwork has been laid. It is a very real part of our paleo-history, the echoes of which reach us in the form of language. When we talk to each other, we can actually hear the past. In English, the word psyche-referring to soul, spirit and mind-comes originally from the Greek *psukhe*, meaning not only soul but also breath and life. Likewise, spirit-the vital principle or animating force within living beings-derives itself directly from the Latin *spiritus*, containing the Navajo-like dual definition of breath *and* wind. Indeed, the "Holy Spirit" refers to more than just the third person of the Christian Trinity, but to the ethereal realm to moving air-the whole of the winds. Jews, Arabs, Romans, as well as Aztecs have also taken their words for "spirit" from the word for wind.

Likewise, animal, animism and animation share a single root in the Latin term *anima*, whose principle definition is soul, but also includes breath and air. These linguistic connections not only reveal a deep connection in the way mainstream America speaks and writes, but also that our individual ancestry must have embraced a belief system much like that of the Navajo. With this in mind, the change that Norris predicts in Americans of European descent is not about learning something new, but rather remembering something very old.

The issue reaches far beyond subsidies and the use of public lands in the American West. The real question involves the course of Western civilization. History shows that unbalanced civilizations do not survive. Where are the Romans, Mayans, Easter Islanders? Those who do not learn from history are bound to repeat it.

This generation has a choice to make. On the verge of a new millennium and a population of six billion, the timing for great decisions could not be better. We must come together, all the nations of the world-rich and poor, north and south, light-skinned and dark-and literally *make* history. Carefully considered and cautiously developed, we can implement a plan for sustainability that remembers thousands of years of wisdom and sees seven generations into the future. How noble! How epic!

The Hopi believe in the existence of a number of worlds stacked one upon the other. We are currently living in the fourth world, the other three having been destroyed as a result of human evil. When their ancestors no longer took good care of the Earth, the world they inhabited disintegrated under neglect and abuse. Only a few survivors escaped the destruction by climbing a cornstalk or pine trunk through an opening in the sky called *sipapu*-the hole of emergence.

Traditional Hopis warn us that our world is facing just such a fate if we do not mend the damage we have done and adopt a more ecological world view. But perhaps the destruction of our current world would not be such a bad thing if it were done in a mindful way-more of a careful dismantling than an all-out Armageddon. Replacing our Industrial Growth Society-and all of its associated problems-with a Life-sustaining Society is a process that Joanna Macy calls the "Great Turning." By changing our *modus operandi* from "power over" to "power with," we can help all peoples of the world make the precarious climb up the corn stalk and through a much-needed cultural *sipapu*.

But the difficult ascent can only be made by those unburdened by the weight of outmoded thinking. "Dump excess baggage" was a popular saying among westering pioneers who meant it literally. Their trails were lined with heavy oak furniture, curios and knickknacks. A figurative interpretation applies well to the proposed transition into a sustainable world. We cannot make the journey burdened with the excesses that define our present culture. We need to dump old laws. We need to dump consumptive lifestyles. We need to dump wasteful practices. We need to dump exploitive attitudes and ideas. We need to travel light, content with the feelings of wind in our hair and sun on our faces.

Developing a sustainable economy will be, in the words of William Ruckelshaus, "a modification of society comparable in scale to the Industrial Revolution. The undertaking will be absolutely unique in humanity's stay on Earth." Yet if we act quickly, we can still find guides to help us along the path. Hopi farmers give us both example and inspiration of what can be accomplished. They have survived for centuries on the low rainfall and marginal soils of their central Arizona mesas. They have recognized all along that the hydrosphere and lithosphere cannot be understood without also considering the interrelationships between them, as well as those those with the biosphere.

On the moon, sunrise to sunset takes seven-and-a-half Earth days. Some of mine felt that long, but through them I developed a kinship with the land-a common bond, an understanding.

The stories of saints and prophets are often set deep in a desert or high on a mountain. It is under the burning sun of one, or against the blowing winds of the other that a vision comes or a challenge is met. Jesus, Buddha, Mohammed, Black Elk-each knew when to leave other men behind and seek the solitude of aridity or altitude. Loneliness is essential to the process-an extreme kind of loneliness offered only where the air is dry or thin.

Desert and mountain. Mountain and desert. I experienced both. Tested, tormented, tortured. I survived, even thrived. Sitting on top of the world and watching the moon glow in a flawless sky, if ever THE ANSWER were to be whispered in my waiting ear, this would be the time. Are you there God? It's me, Nelson.

But there was no voice from above, no sign to point the way, no vision of my future-just an intense feeling of belonging. Inhaling deeply the clean mountain air, I felt a presence greater than myself. I could not see it. I could not hear it. I could not touch it. But it was there.

Looking back over my personal journey, I saw with unusual clarity. The man in the mirror came into focus. He returned a knowing glance. Knowing his strengths, weaknesses and limits. Knowing how to push them. Knowing when not to. Setting out to discover the West, I found much more. The sun had tanned my hide, the miles had hardened my muscles, but my heart had grown the most.

Selected Bibliography

Abbey, E. Desert Solitaire: A Season in the Wilderness. Ballantine Books, New York, 1968.

Abbey, E. The Monkey Wrench Gang. Avon Books, 1975.

Abbey, E. A Voice Crying in the Wilderness: Notes from a Secret Journal. St. Martin's Press, New York, 1989.

Abrams, D. The Spell of the Sensuous. Vintage Books, New York, 1996.

Berry, T. The Dream of the Earth. Sierra Club Books, San Francisco, 1988.

Bishop, J. Epitaph for a Desert Anarchist: The Life and Legacy of Edward Abbey. Atheneum, New York, 1994.

Bowman, J. (ed). The World Almanac of the American West. Pharos Books, New York, 1986.

Brown, D. Bury My Heart at Wounded Knee: An Indian History of the American West. Washington Square Press, New York, 1970.

Brown, L., Flavin, C., French, H. et al. State of the World 1997. W.W. Norton and Company, New York, 1997.

Capra, F. The Web of Life: A New Understanding of Living Systems. Anchor Books, New York, 1997.

Erdoes, R. Crying for a Dream. Bear & Company Publishing, Santa Fe, 1990.

Gore, A. Earth in the Balance: Ecology and the Human Spirit. Houghton Mifflin, Boston, 1992.

Heat-Moon. W. L. Prairyerth. Houghton Mifflin, Boston, 1991.

Kline, B. First Along the River: A Brief History of the U.S. Environmental Movement. Acada Books, San Francisco, 1997.

Krutch, J. W. The Desert Year. The Viking Press, New York, 1951.

Lame Deer, J. and Erdoes, R. Lame Deer Seeker of Visions. Washington Square Press, New York, 1972.

Leopold, A. A Sand County Almanac. Oxford University Press, Oxford, 1949.

Macy, J. and Brown, M. Y. Coming Back to Life: Practices to Reconnect Our Lives, Our World. New Society Publishers, Gabriola Island, BC, Canada, 1998.

Matthiessen, P. Indian Country. The Viking Press, New York, 1979.

McLuhan, T.C. (ed). Touch the Earth: A Self-Portrait of Indian Existence. Promontory Press, New York, 1971.

Nabhan, G. P. The Desert Smells Like Rain: A Naturalist in Papago Indian Country. North Point Press, San Francisco, 1987.

Norris, K. Dakota: A Spiritual Geography. Houghton Mifflin, Boston, 1993.

Outwater, A. Water: A Natural History. Basic Books, New York, 1996.

Pirsig, R. Zen and the Art of Motorcycle Maintenance: An Inquiry into Values. Bantam Books, Toronto, 1974.

Reisner, M. Cadillac Desert: The American West and Its Disappearing Water. Viking, New York, 1986.

Rifkin, J. Beyond Beef: The Rise and Fall of the Cattle Culture. Dutton, New York, 1992.

Robbins, J. Diet for a New America. Stillpoint Publishing, Walpole, NH, 1987.

Russell, S. A. Kill the Cowboy: A Battle of Mythology in the New West.

Rezendes, P. The Wild Within: Adventures in Nature and Animal Teachings. Berkley Books, New York, 1998.

Shoumatoff, A. Legends of the American Desert: Sojourns in the Greater Southwest. Knopf, New York, 1997.

Shabecoff, P. A Fierce Green Fire: The American Environmental Movement. Hill and Wang, New York, 1993.

Strong, D.H. Dreamers and Defenders: American Conservationists. University of Nebraska Press, Lincoln, 1971.

Welsch, R. Shingling the Fog and Other Plains Lies. University of Nebraska Press, Lincoln, 1972.

Williams, T. T. Pieces of White Shell: A Journey to Navajoland. University of New Mexico Press, Albuquerque, 1983.

Zakin, S. Coyotes and Town Dogs: Earth First and the Environmental Movement. Viking, New York, 1993.